Scott Foresman - Addison Wesley
MATH

Practice Masters

Grade 1

S F
A W

Scott Foresman - Addison Wesley

Editorial Offices: Menlo Park, California • Glenview, Illinois
Sales Offices: Reading, Massachusetts • Atlanta, Georgia • Glenview, Illinois
Carrollton, Texas • Menlo Park, California

http://www.sf.aw.com

Overview

Practice Masters provide additional exercises for students who have not mastered key skills and concepts covered in the Student Edition. A Practice master is provided for each core lesson of the Student Edition. In addition, a Practice master is also provided for each Mixed Practice and Cumulative Review lesson.

Lesson masters provide exercises similar to those in the Practice and Explore lessons of the Student Edition.

Mixed Practice masters review skills and concepts covered in the Student Edition section and include application problems that review previous material.

Cumulative Review masters cover important skills and concepts from the current chapter and from previous chapters.

ISBN 0–201–50120–1

Copyright © Addison Wesley Longman, Inc.

Printed in the United States of America

6 7 8 9 10 – BW – 02 01

Contents

Chapter 9: Money

Chapter 10: Telling Time

Chapter 11: Measurement

Chapter 12: Facts and Strategies to 18

Chapter 13: Two-Digit Addition and Subtraction

Numbers 1, 2, 3

Write 1, 2, and 3.

1.

2.

3.

Write how many.

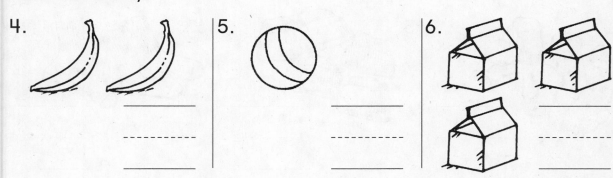

4.

5.

6.

Problem Solving Visual Thinking

Look for a group of 1, 2, or 3 in something you are wearing.

Draw what you see.

Notes for Home Your child wrote the numbers 1, 2, and 3. *Home Activity:* Ask your child to find a group of 1, 2, or 3 objects in the kitchen and write the number for how many.

Numbers 4, 5, 6

Write 4, 5, and 6.

1.

2.

3.

Write how many.

4.  _____
‑ ‑ ‑ ‑ ‑ ‑ ‑ ‑

5.  _____
‑ ‑ ‑ ‑ ‑ ‑ ‑ ‑

6. 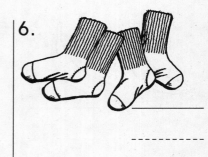 _____
‑ ‑ ‑ ‑ ‑ ‑ ‑ ‑

Mental Math

Write the next number.

7. 2, 3, _____

8. 4, 5, _____

9. 1, 2, _____

10. 3, 4, _____

Notes for Home Your child wrote the numbers 4, 5, and 6. *Home Activity:* Ask your child to draw groups of 4, 5, and 6 objects on a sheet of paper.

Numbers 7, 8, 9

Write 7, 8, and 9.

1. 7 7 7

2. 8 8 8

3. 9 9 9

Write how many.

4. _____

5. _____

6. _____

7. _____

8. _____

9. _____

Journal

10. Draw 8 things.   11. Draw 9 things.   12. Draw 7 things.

Notes for Home Your child wrote the numbers 7, 8, and 9. *Home Activity:* Have your child find a group of 7 objects and write the number for how many.

Zero

Write 0.

1.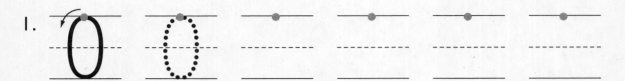

Write how many.

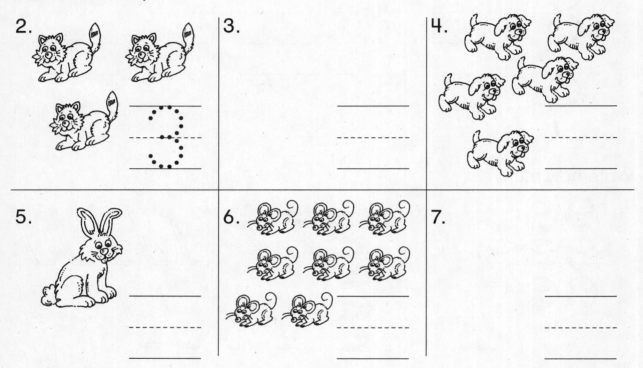

2.

3.

4.

5.

6.

7.

Tell a Math Story

Use numbers to tell a story about what you see.

Notes for Home Your child wrote the number 0. *Home Activity:* Ask your child to make up a math story using any numbers from 0 to 9.

Numbers to 10

Write 10.

1.

How many? Write the number or draw the picture.

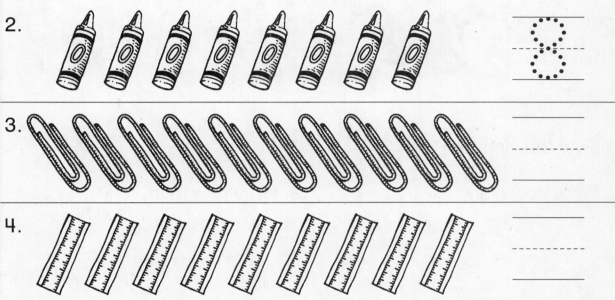

2.

3.

4.

5.

Problem Solving Visual Thinking

Circle the picture that shows 10.

Notes for Home Your child wrote the number 10 and counted and drew up to 10 objects. *Home Activity:* Ask your child to find 10 objects in his or her room and draw a picture of them.

Name _____

Problem Solving:
Use Data from a Picture

Look at the picture.

1. Write how many  .

<u>2</u>

2. Write how many 🐘 .

_____

3. Draw a ◯ for each child.

4. How many did you draw?

_____

Critical Thinking

Draw a bird in each tree.

How many birds are in the picture now? _____

Notes for Home Your child solved problems using pictures. *Home Activity:* Ask your child to explain how he or she found the answer for Exercise 3.

Name _____

Mixed Practice: Lessons 1–6

Write how many.

1.

_____

2.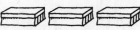

_____

3.

_____

4.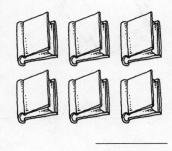

_____

5.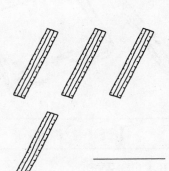

_____

6.

_____

Problem Solving

Look at the picture.

7. How many ?

_____

8. How many ?

_____

Journal

Draw one picture that has 7 trees, 9 flowers, 5 birds, and 1 rainbow.

Notes for Home Your child practiced counting and identifying groups of objects to 10. *Home Activity:* Set out 3 groups of objects containing from 1 to 10 objects each. Ask your child to count the number of objects in each group and to write the numbers.

Name _____

Cumulative Review

1. Circle the ones that are the same size.

2. Circle the ones that are the same shape.

Test Prep

Fill in the ○ for the correct answer.

3. How many 🌀 ?

○   ○   ○   ○
7   8   9   10

4. How many 🧍 ?

○   ○   ○   ○
2   3   4   5

5. How many 🔲 ?

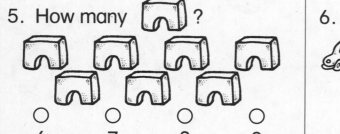

○   ○   ○   ○
6   7   8   9

6. How many 🚗 ?

○   ○   ○   ○
7   8   9   10

Notes for Home Your child reviewed sorting by size and shape, and counting from 1 to 10 objects. *Home Activity:* Ask your child to explain how he or she chose the correct answer in Exercise 6.

Explore More and Fewer

Write how many.
Circle the group that has more.

1.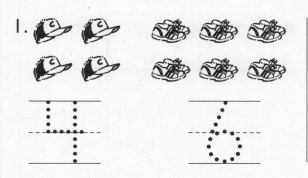

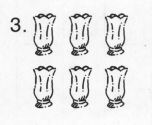   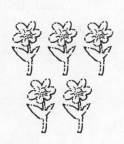

2. 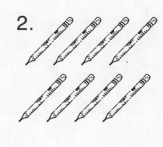   

_____   _____

Write how many.
Circle the group that has fewer.

3.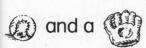

4.    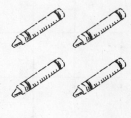

_____   _____   _____   _____

Problem Solving Critical Thinking

Draw a line to give each child a

 and a .

Do you need more or ?

Circle   .

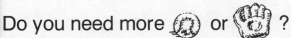

Notes for Home Your child practiced telling which group had more and which group had fewer.
Home Activity: Arrange two unequal groups of objects, each with 10 or fewer. Ask your child to tell
which group has fewer.

Order Numbers to 10

Draw the missing towers. Write how many.

1.

$$\underline{\textbf{4}} \qquad \underline{\textbf{5}} \qquad \underline{} \qquad \underline{\textbf{7}} \qquad \underline{\textbf{8}} \qquad \underline{} \qquad \underline{}$$

Problem Solving Critical Thinking

Connect the dots in order.

What do you see?

_____

- -

_____

Notes for Home Your child practiced ordering numbers from 1 through 10. *Home Activity:* Say a sequence of two numbers, such as "4, 5," and ask your child to say the number that comes next. (6)

10 Use with pages 21–22.

Understand 11 and 12

Write how many.

1.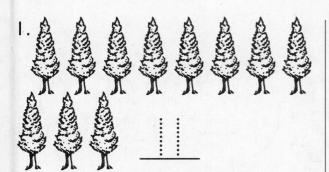
_____

2.
_____

3.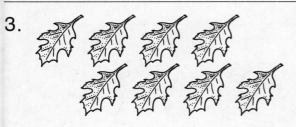
_____

4.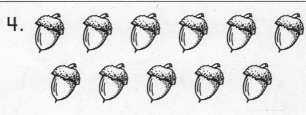
_____

5.
_____

6.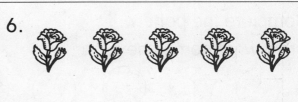
_____

Problem Solving

Solve.

Joshua has _____ .

Tanya has _____ .

How many are there? _____

Notes for Home Your child counted from 1 to 12 and recognized the symbols for 11 and 12. *Home Activity:* Make groups of 10, 11, and 12 objects, such as paper clips or rubber bands. Then ask your child to count the objects in each group and write the number.

Problem Solving: Look for a Pattern

Complete each pattern.

Color what comes next.

1.

2.

Complete the pattern.

Draw what comes next.

3.

Write your own pattern.

4. Make your own pattern. Draw it 3 times.

Journal

Find and draw 3 patterns you can see in your house.

Notes for Home Your child completed a pattern and made his or her own pattern. *Home Activity:* Ask your child to say the pattern in Problem 2 on this page aloud and then make up a new pattern.

Name _____

Mixed Practice: Lessons 7–10

Write how many.
Circle the group that has fewer.

1. ☆ ☆ ☆ ☆   🌙 🌙 🌙
   ☆ ☆ ☆ ☆   🌙 🌙
   ☆ ☆ ☆

   _____   _____

Write how many.

2. 📎 📎 📎
   📎 📎 📎
   📎 📎 📎

   _____

Draw the missing towers.
Write how many are in each.

3. _____

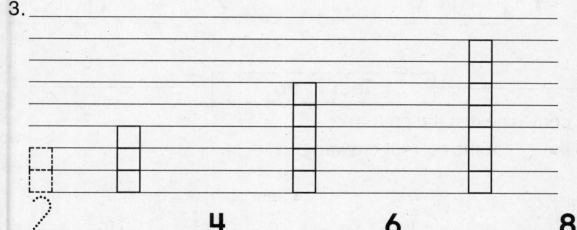

_____ 2 _____ 4 _____ 6 _____ 8

Problem Solving

Draw what comes next in the pattern.

△ ▢ ◯ △ ▢ ◯

Journal

Draw a pattern. Use colors and shapes in your pattern.

Notes for Home Your child reviewed sorting by size and shape, and counting from 1 to 10.
Home Activity: Ask your child to explain how he or she determined what to draw next in the Problem Solving
pattern.

Name _____

Cumulative Review

1. Draw 7 .

Write how many.

_____

2. Write how many .

_____

3. Write the missing numbers.

	4		6	

4. Write the missing numbers.

	9		11	

Test Prep

What comes next in the pattern?
Fill in the ○ for the correct answer.

5.

　　　　　　　　　　　　○　　　　○

6. 　　　　　　

　　　　　　　　　　　　○　　　　○

Notes for Home Your child reviewed counting and ordering numbers from 1 to 12, and continued a pattern.
Home Activity: Ask your child to continue the pattern in Exercise 6 by drawing the next three items. (sock, mitten, sock)

Explore Sorting and Classifying

Circle the shape that goes with the group.

1.

2.

3.

4.

Problem Solving Visual Thinking

Count the shapes above. Write how many.

_____   _____   _____   _____

Create a Graph

Use the graph.
Which has more?
Circle the answer.

Small Animals We Saw at the Aquarium

1.

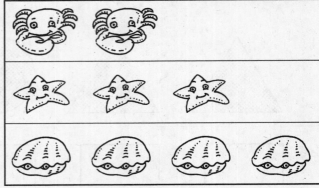

2.

3.

Use the graph.
Which has fewer?
Circle the answer.

Large Animals We Saw at the Aquarium

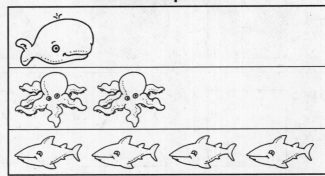

4.

5.

Write About It

Make your own graph.
Draw a picture to
complete the sentences.

My Graph

I have more ☐.

I have fewer ☐.

Notes for Home Your child used a graph to tell if there was more or fewer. *Home Activity:* Ask your child to make a graph of food or snack items at home.

Create a Pictograph

Make a pictograph to show how many of each.

Short Sleeves or Long Sleeves

Short									
Long									

1. How many ? _____

2. How many ? _____

Sort another way.

Count the and that are plain.

Count the and that have dots.

Make a pictograph to show how many of each.

plain									
dots									

3. How many more than ? _____

Problem Solving Critical Thinking

Does either graph show you more or fewer than ? _____

Do you have to count them? _____

Notes for Home Your child created and used a pictograph. *Home Activity:* Ask your child to make a pictograph of two types of objects at home.

Name _____

Problem Solving:
Make a Bar Graph

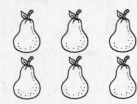  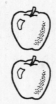 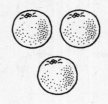

1. Make a bar graph. Color a box for each kind of fruit.

Favorite Fruit

🍐								
🍌								
🍎								
🍊								

Write the number.

2. How many more than ? _____ more

3. How many fewer than ? _____ fewer

4. How many more than ? _____ more

Tell a Math Story

Tell a friend a math story about the graph.

Notes for Home Your child made a bar graph and told a math story using the information on the graph.
Home Activity: Ask your child to tell you how many more pears there are than bananas. (2)

Mixed Practice: Lessons 11-14

1. Make a pictograph.

   Color a picture for each and .

Do You Like Corn or Carrots?

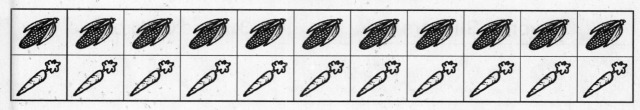

2. Are the more or ?

Problem Solving

Use the graph.

My Favorite Pet

3. How many ? _____

4. How many more than ? _____ more

Journal

Ask a question about the graph. Tell the answer.

Notes for Home Your child practiced using graphs to answer questions. *Home Activity:* Ask your child to make a bar graph of two types of things in his or her room at home.

Cumulative Review

Circle what comes next.

1.

2.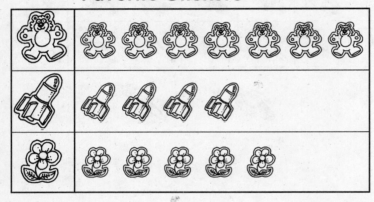

Problem Solving

Use the graph. Circle the answer.

Favorite Stickers

3. More Children like
 or .

4. Fewer children like
or .

Test Prep

Fill in the ○ for the correct answer.
What goes with the group?

5.

○   ○

6.

○   ○

Notes for Home Your child reviewed concepts taught in Chapter 1. *Home Activity:* Ask your child to explain how he or she determined what came next in the patterns.

Name _____

Explore Ways to Make 4 and 5

Show ways to make 5. Color the Snap Cubes.
Write the numbers.

1. ____3___ and ___2___ is ___5___.

2. _____ and _____ is _____.

3. _____ and _____ is _____.

4. _____ and _____ is _____.

5. _____ and _____ is _____.

6. _____ and _____ is _____.

Problem Solving Critical Thinking

7. How can you use to show that 4 and 1 is the same as 1 and 4?

Notes for Home Your child used Snap Cubes to find ways to make 5. *Home Activity:* Ask your child to find four different ways to make a group of 5 using household objects.

Ways to Make 6 and 7

Show ways to make 6. Color the Snap Cubes.
Write the numbers.

1. __4__ and __2__ is __6__ .

2. _____ and _____ is _____ .

3. _____ and _____ is _____ .

4. _____ and _____ is _____ .

5. _____ and _____ is _____ .

6. _____ and _____ is _____ .

Mental Math

Solve. You have 3.

7. Circle the card you need to make 6.

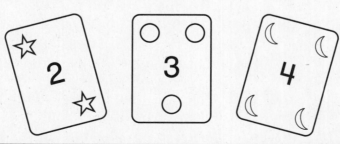

Notes for Home Your child used Snap Cubes to find different ways to make 6. *Home Activity:* Ask your child to draw groups of 6 and 7 objects.

Ways to Make 8 and 9

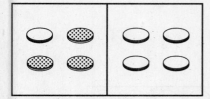

Spill 8 ⬭ ⬬ .

Show gray and white
on your ☐☐ .

Gray	White	In All
3	5	8

Use the table to
record.

Spill counters and show ways to make 8.
Record the ways.

	Gray	White	In All
1.	3	5	8
2.			
3.			
4.			

Problem Solving Visual Thinking

5. Match the groups with the same number.

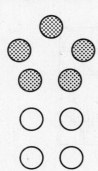 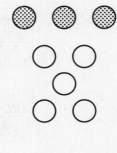 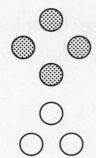

Notes for Home Your child used counters to find different ways to make 8. *Home Activity:* Ask your child to show
a way to make 8 using spoons or cups.

Ways to Make 10

Spill 10 ⬤ ◯ and show ways to make 10.

Record the ways.

1.

_9_ and _1_ is _10_.

2.

_____ and _____ is _____.

3.

_____ and _____ is _____.

4.

_____ and _____ is _____.

5.

_____ and _____ is _____.

6.

_____ and _____ is _____.

Journal

How are these the same?

How are they different?

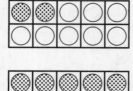

Notes for Home Your child looked for ways to make 10. *Home Activity:* Ask your child to use small objects, such as pennies or buttons, to make groups of ten.

Name _____

Problem Solving: Make a Table

1. How many ways can you put

   8 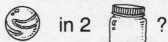 in 2 🛍 ?

🛍	🛍	In All
0	8	8
1	7	8

2. How many ways can you put

   10 🍈 in 2 🫙 ?

🫙	🫙	In All
0	10	10

Problem Solving Critical Thinking

3. How many ways are there to make 9? _____

4. How many ways are there to make 6? _____

   How do you know? _____

Notes for Home Your child made tables to find all the ways to make 8 and 10. *Home Activity:* Ask your child how many ways 9 pencils or pens can be placed in 2 glasses. (10 ways)

Name _____

Mixed Practice: Lessons 1–5

Use 1 or 2 colors to make 7 and 8.
Color. Write the numbers.

1.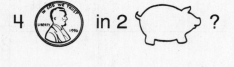

   _____ and _____ is _____.

2.

   _____ and _____ is _____.

Write the number sentence.

3.

   _____ and _____ is _____.

Problem Solving

4. How many ways can you put

   4  in 2  ?

🐷	🐷	In All

Journal

Write a math story about **6 and 4 is 10.**

Notes for Home Your child practiced finding ways to make numbers through 10. *Home Activity:* Ask your child to tell a story about 2 groups of 3 animals.

Name _____

Cumulative Review

Write how many.

1.

_____
- - - - - - - -
_____

2.

_____
- - - - - - - -
_____

Use the graph. Write the number.

Our Favorite Fruit

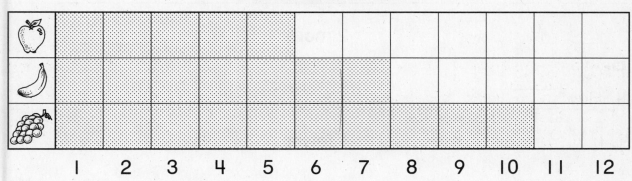

| | 1 | 2 | 3 | 4 | 5 | 6 | 7 | 8 | 9 | 10 | 11 | 12 |

3. How many more like than ? _____

4. How many fewer like than ? _____

Test Prep

Fill in the ○ for the correct answer.
5. What comes next?

○ 7
○ 1
○ 9
○ 6

Notes for Home Your child reviewed counting to 12 and reading a graph. *Home Activity:* Ask your child to make a graph of your family's favorite animals.

More and Fewer

Use ⬜.

Write how many.	Make a train with:	Write how many now.
1. ⬜⬜⬜ ___3___	1 more	4 ___
2. ⬜⬜⬜⬜⬜ ___	2 fewer	___
3. ⬜⬜ ___	2 more	___
4. ⬜⬜⬜⬜⬜ ___	1 fewer	___
5. ⬜⬜⬜⬜ ___	2 fewer	___

Mental Math

Circle the number that is 2 more than 3.

| 3 | 5 | 6 | 1 |

Notes for Home Your child showed more or fewer objects than a given amount. *Home Activity:* Ask your child to tell you the number that is 2 less than his or her age and the number that is 2 more than his or her age.

Name _____

Odd and Even Numbers

Make pairs. Draw what you make.

Circle odd or even.

1. Use 5 ◯ .

odd

even

_____

2. Use 10 ◯ .

odd

even

_____

3. Use ◯ . How many did you use?

odd

even

_____

Problem Solving Patterns

Color even numbers . Color odd numbers .

1	2	3	4	5	6	7	8	9	10

What color did you color the number 7? _____

What pattern do you see? _____

Notes for Home Your child used objects to decide whether a number is odd or even. *Home Activity:* Ask your child to draw groups of 3, 4, 5, and 6, and tell whether each group is odd (3, 5) or even (4, 6).

Name _____

Ways to Make 11 and 12

Use ⊛ ○ and ⬚⬚⬚⬚⬚ .

Spill and show ways to make 11.
Record the ways.

1. __7__ and __4__ is __11__.   2. _____ and _____ is _____.

3. _____ and _____ is _____.   4. _____ and _____ is _____.

5. _____ and _____ is _____.   6. _____ and _____ is _____.

7. _____ and _____ is _____.   8. _____ and _____ is _____.

9. _____ and _____ is _____.   10. _____ and _____ is _____.

Problem Solving Critical Thinking

Use , , Green to show 11.

Write the numbers.

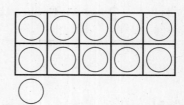

_____ and _____ and _____ is _____.

Notes for Home Your child used two-colored counters and a ten-frame to find ways to make 11.
Home Activity: Ask your child to use small objects, such as buttons or pennies, to make a group of 11
and a group of 12.

Find Missing Parts
Through 7

How many 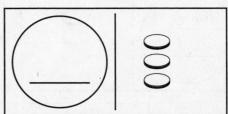 are under the ?

1. 5 in all

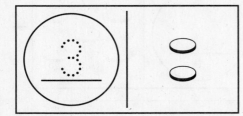

2. 4 in all

3. 7 in all

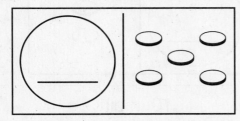

4. 7 in all

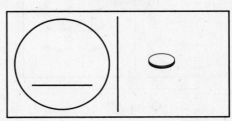

5. 6 in all

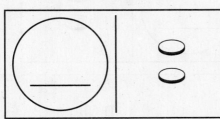

6. 3 in all

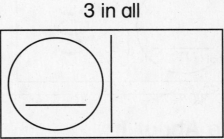

Problem Solving Estimation

7. Work with a friend. Hold some things in a  .

Have your friend estimate how many.

Count them. Take turns.

Notes for Home Your child found how many counters are missing. *Home Activity:* Following the examples on this
sheet, take turns finding how many objects are hidden from a group of 6 things.

Find Missing Parts
Through 10

How many  are under the ?

1. **8 in all** 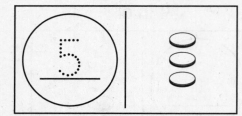	2. **5 in all** 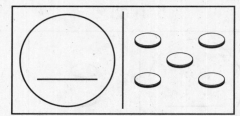
3. **10 in all** 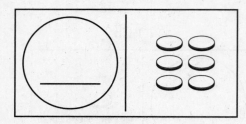	4. **6 in all** 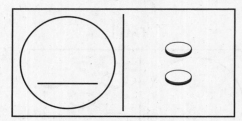
5. **9 in all** 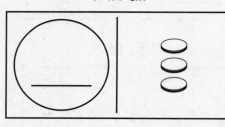	6. **10 in all** 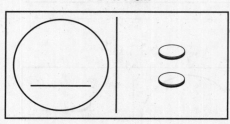

Write About It

Make up your own.

Have a friend solve it.

_____ in all

Notes for Home Your child found the missing counters through 10. *Home Activity:* Ask your child to assemble a group of 10 objects, such as paper clips. Put different number of paper clips in your hand and ask your child to tell how many are missing.

Name _____

Problem Solving: Draw a Picture

Draw a picture to show the problem.

Write how many in all.

1. 2 and 3 is __5__.

2. 1 and 2 is _____.

3. 4 and 3 is _____.

4. 3 and 3 is _____.

Tell a Math Story

5. Draw a picture of 3 ducks and 1 cow.

Tell a math story about your picture.

_____

Notes for Home Your child used the strategy Draw a Picture to solve problems. *Home Activity:* Ask your child to draw a picture of children playing and to tell a number story about the picture.

Name _____

Mixed Practice: Lessons 6–11

1. Use 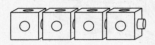.
   Write how many.

   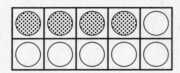

   _____

   Make a train with:

   3 more

   Write how many.

   _____

---

2. Write the numbers

   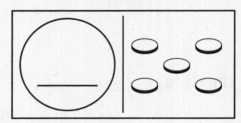

   _____ and _____ is _____.

3. How many are under the ?

   8 in all

Problem Solving

4. Draw a picture to show the problem.

   3 birds flying.
   2 more came.

   Write how many birds in all.

   3 and 2 is _____.

Notes for Home Your child practiced writing number sentences, finding missing numbers, and drawing pictures to solve problems. *Home Activity:* Ask your child to draw a picture to show 3 different ways to make 5.

Name _____

Cumulative Review

Circle the one that belongs.

1.

2. Draw the missing tower. Write how many in each tower.

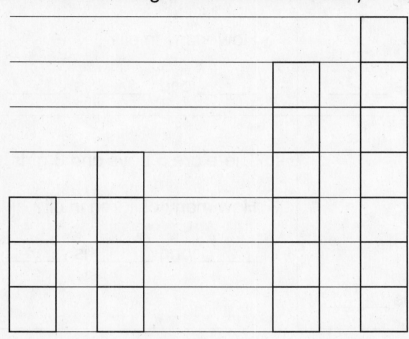

___ ___ ___   ___ ___

Test Prep

3. Use the graph. Fill in the ○ for the correct answer.

How many ☀ ?

2	3	4	5
○	○	○	○

☀	☀	☀	☀			
☁	☁	☁				
1	2	3	4	5	6	7

Notes for Home Your child reviewed counting to 12 and reading a graph. *Home Activity:* Ask your child to make a graph of what he or she had to drink at lunch each day for one week.

Explore Addition

Solve each problem.

You can use ⬭ .

1. There are 3 🐕 .

   2 more 🐕 come.

   How many in all?

   __3__ and __2__ is __5__ .

2. There are 6 🦆 .

   2 more 🦆 come.

   How many in all?

   _____ and _____ is _____ .

3. There are 5 🐈 .

   4 more 🐈 come.

   How many in all?

   _____ and _____ is _____ .

4. There are 5 boys and 3 girls.

   How many children in all?

   _____ and _____ is _____ .

Problem Solving Visual Thinking

5. Draw a picture. Tell a math story about the picture.

_____

Notes for Home Your child solved addition problems. *Home Activity:* Ask your child to tell you a math story about Exercise 1.

Name _____

Show Addition

You can use  and [|] .

Show the parts.

Write the number sentence.

1.  $\underline{3} + \underline{4} = \underline{7}$

2. 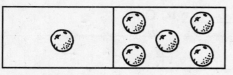 $\underline{} + \underline{} = \underline{}$

3. 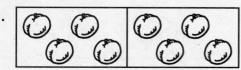 $\underline{} + \underline{} = \underline{}$

4. 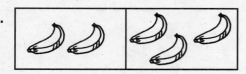 $\underline{} + \underline{} = \underline{}$

5.  $\underline{} + \underline{} = \underline{}$

Tell a Math Story

6. Ask a friend to tell you a
   short math story.
   You can show it
   with ⬭ ⬮ .

Notes for Home Your child used counters and wrote number sentences to show addition. *Home Activity:* Ask your child to show 5 + 4 using common objects, such as buttons or pennies.

Use with pages 93–94. **37**

Name _____

Problem Solving: Use Addition

Use ⬯ to show the story.

Write a number sentence.

Write how many in all.

1. There are 3 🚲 .
   5 more 🚲 come.
   How many now?

   _3_ + _5_ = _8_

   _8_ 🚲

2. There are 4 🚚
   and 2 🚙 .
   How many in all?

   ___ + ___ = ___

   _____ in all

3. There are 2 🚌 .
   3 more 🚌 come.
   How many now?

   ___ + ___ = ___

   _____ in all

4. There are 4 ✈
   and 4 ✈ .
   How many in all?

   ___ + ___ = ___

   _____ ✈

Critical Thinking

5. Write a number sentence
   to go with the picture.

   ___ + ___ = ___

   _____ in all

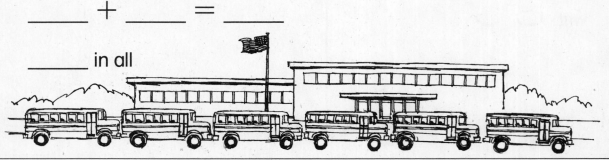

Notes for Home Your child wrote number sentences to solve problems. *Home Activity:* Ask your child to draw a picture of his or her favorite form of transportation to show 7 + 2.

Addition Sentences to 12

Use .

Show some ways to make each number.

Write the number sentences.

1. **8**

$$\underline{3} + \underline{5} = \underline{8}$$
$$\underline{\quad} + \underline{\quad} = \underline{\quad}$$
$$\underline{\quad} + \underline{\quad} = \underline{\quad}$$

2. **10**

$$\underline{\quad} + \underline{\quad} = \underline{\quad}$$
$$\underline{\quad} + \underline{\quad} = \underline{\quad}$$
$$\underline{\quad} + \underline{\quad} = \underline{\quad}$$

3. **12**

$$\underline{\quad} + \underline{\quad} = \underline{\quad}$$
$$\underline{\quad} + \underline{\quad} = \underline{\quad}$$
$$\underline{\quad} + \underline{\quad} = \underline{\quad}$$

4. **6**

$$\underline{\quad} + \underline{\quad} = \underline{\quad}$$
$$\underline{\quad} + \underline{\quad} = \underline{\quad}$$
$$\underline{\quad} + \underline{\quad} = \underline{\quad}$$

Problem Solving Visual Thinking

5. Draw balls to make 5. Complete the number sentences.

$$1 + \underline{\quad} = 5 \qquad 3 + \underline{\quad} = 5 \qquad 4 + \underline{\quad} = 5$$

Notes for Home Your child used counters to write addition sentences. *Home Activity:* Ask your child to tell you a math story using 3 different ways to make 12.

Add in Vertical Form

Write the sums. You can use .

1.

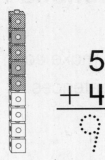

$$\begin{array}{r} 5 \\ +\,4 \\ \hline 9 \end{array}$$

$5 + 4 = \underline{9}$

---

2. $6 + 3 = \underline{}$ $\quad \begin{array}{r} 6 \\ +\,3 \\ \hline \end{array}$

3. $7 + 0 = \underline{}$ $\quad \begin{array}{r} 7 \\ +\,0 \\ \hline \end{array}$

---

4. $6 + 5 = \underline{}$ $\quad \begin{array}{r} 6 \\ +\,5 \\ \hline \end{array}$

5. $4 + 4 = \underline{}$ $\quad \begin{array}{r} 4 \\ +\,4 \\ \hline \end{array}$

---

6. $\begin{array}{r} 6 \\ +\,4 \\ \hline \end{array} \quad \begin{array}{r} 2 \\ +\,9 \\ \hline \end{array} \quad \begin{array}{r} 6 \\ +\,1 \\ \hline \end{array} \quad \begin{array}{r} 9 \\ +\,0 \\ \hline \end{array} \quad \begin{array}{r} 4 \\ +\,3 \\ \hline \end{array} \quad \begin{array}{r} 8 \\ +\,2 \\ \hline \end{array} \quad \begin{array}{r} 7 \\ +\,4 \\ \hline \end{array}$

Problem Solving

Solve each problem.

7. There are 3 + ☐

and 7 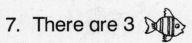.
How many in all?

8. There are 8 . + ☐

4 more come.
How many now?

Notes for Home Your child solved addition problems that were shown both horizontally and vertically.
Home Activity: Write 3 addition sentences horizontally. Ask your child to write them vertically and to solve them.

Name _____

Problem Solving: Draw a Picture

Draw a picture to show the story.
Write a number sentence.

1. 4  are on the track.

   2 more join the train.

   How many are on the track?

   $\underline{4} + \underline{2} = \underline{6}$

2. There are _____ on the ground.

   _____ more fall onto the ground.

   How many are there now?

   _____ + _____ = _____

3. _____ fly.

   _____ more fly with them.

   How many are there?

   _____ + _____ = _____

Journal

Write a problem that could be solved by drawing
a picture.

Notes for Home Your child solved addition problems by drawing a picture. *Home Activity:* Ask your child to write
an addition sentence for a picture in a magazine or book.

Name _____

Mixed Practice: Lessons 1-6

Write a number sentence.

1.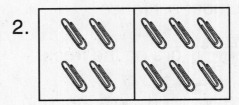

   ____ + ____ = ____

2. ____ + ____ = ____

3. Write the sum. You can use ⬭.

4	5	7	5	2	9	4
+0	+2	+1	+5	+6	+0	+3

Problem Solving

Use ⬭ ⬯ or draw a picture.

Write a number sentence.

4. 4 🐎 run.

   2 more 🐎 come.

   How many 🐎 are there now?

   ____ + ____ = ____ 🐎

Journal

Draw a picture to show a math story for a problem in exercise 3.

Write the number sentence.

___

Notes for Home Your child practiced addition for sums through 12. *Home Activity:* Ask your child to chose 3 addition sentences in Exercise 3, and draw a picture for each.

Name _____

Cumulative Review

How many 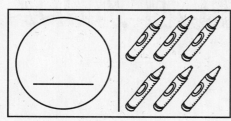 are under the ⌓ ?

1. 9 in all	2. 12 in all

Look at the pattern.

Draw the next two shapes.

3. ☆ ♡ ☆ ♡ ☆ ♡ ☆ ♡ ☆

4. △ ▽ ▽ △ ▽ ▽ △ ▽ ▽

Test Prep

Fill in the ○ for the correct answer.

5. There are 2 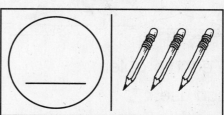 .

4 more  come.

How many are there now?

4	7	6	8
○	○	○	○

6. Jan sees 3 .

She sees 5 .

How many does Jan see?

5	3	7	8
○	○	○	○

Notes for Home Your child reviewed finding missing parts of a number, patterns, and addition. *Home Activity:* Ask your child to draw a pattern using his or her favorite toys.

Explore Subtraction

Solve each problem.
You can use ⬭ .

1. 8 🍓 are on the plate.

   4 🍓 are eaten.

   How many are left on the plate?

   _____ are left.

2. 9 ⫟ are in a box.

   7 ⫟ are taken out.

   How many are left in the box?

   _____ are left.

3. 7 🥛 are on the table.

   2 🥛 are taken away.

   How many are left on
   the table?

   _____ are left.

4. 6 🧒 are eating lunch.

   3 🧒 leave.

   How many are left eating
   lunch?

   _____ are left.

Problem Solving Patterns

5. Draw 🍕 to complete the pattern.

  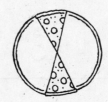 

Notes for Home Your child solved subtraction problems. *Home Activity:* Ask your child draw a picture to show
9 – 6 = 3.

Show Subtraction

Cross out. Subtract.

1.

$8 - 3 = \underline{5}$

2.

$5 - 2 = \underline{}$

Subtract.

3. $12 - 7 = \underline{}$ $7 - 6 = \underline{}$ $9 - 3 = \underline{}$

4. $6 - 4 = \underline{}$ $5 - 2 = \underline{}$ $4 - 4 = \underline{}$

5. $8 - 4 = \underline{}$ $10 - 2 = \underline{}$ $11 - 8 = \underline{}$

Mental Math

6. Use the clues. Write each number.

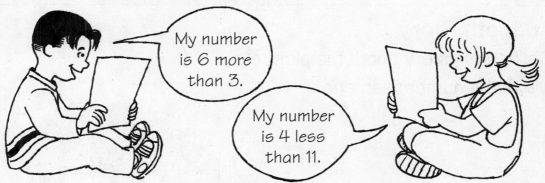

My number is 6 more than 3.

My number is 4 less than 11.

My number is _____.   My number is _____.

Notes for Home Your child subtracted by crossing out objects in a picture and then wrote how many were left.
Home Activity: Ask your child to draw a picture of 12 objects, cross out 2, 3, and 4 of the objects, and write the
subtraction sentence for each. (12 − 2 = 10, 12 − 3 = 9, 12 − 4 = 8)

Name _____

Problem Solving: Use Subtraction

Use ⬭. Show the story.

Write the number sentence.

1. There are 8 .

   6 hop away.

   How many are left?

   __8__ − __6__ = __2__

   _____ are left.

2. There are 6  .

   2 🐍 slide away.

   How many now?

   _____ − _____ = _____

   _____ 🐍 .

3. There are 7 .

   4 🦌 run away.

   How many now?

   _____ − _____ = _____

   _____ 🦌 .

4. There are 12 🐿 .

   3 🐿 run away.

   How many are left?

   _____ − _____ = _____

   _____ are left.

Tell a Math Story

5. Tell a math story about the picture.

   Write the number sentence.

_____ − _____ = _____

Notes for Home Your child read math stories and wrote number sentences to answer the questions.
Home Activity: Ask your child to draw a picture for the number sentence 10 − 9 and then have him or her solve it.

Name _____

Subtract in Vertical Form

You can use to subtract.

1.

$6 - 2 = \underline{4}$

$\begin{array}{r} 6 \\ -2 \\ \hline \end{array}$

2.

$11 - 8 = \underline{}$

$\begin{array}{r} 11 \\ -8 \\ \hline \end{array}$

3.

$7 - 7 = \underline{}$

$\begin{array}{r} 7 \\ -7 \\ \hline \end{array}$

4.

$10 - 9 = \underline{}$

$\begin{array}{r} 10 \\ -9 \\ \hline \end{array}$

5.

$12 - 6 = \underline{}$

$\begin{array}{r} 12 \\ -6 \\ \hline \end{array}$

6.

$\begin{array}{r} 5 \\ -1 \\ \hline \end{array}$
$\begin{array}{r} 12 \\ -1 \\ \hline \end{array}$
$\begin{array}{r} 9 \\ -6 \\ \hline \end{array}$
$\begin{array}{r} 8 \\ -8 \\ \hline \end{array}$
$\begin{array}{r} 10 \\ -2 \\ \hline \end{array}$
$\begin{array}{r} 6 \\ -4 \\ \hline \end{array}$

Problem Solving

Solve the problem.

7. There were 12 .
Now there are 7.
How many were eaten?

_____ were eaten.

8. Kara had 8 .
Now she has 3.
How many did she give away?

_____ were given away.

Notes for Home Your child subtracted in horizontal and vertical forms. *Home Activity:* Ask your child to write the Problem Solving problem in horizontal form and solve it.

Name _____

Relate Addition
and Subtraction

You can use .

Complete the number sentences.

1.

$$\underline{5} + \underline{3} = \underline{8}$$
$$\underline{8} - \underline{3} = \underline{5}$$

2.

$$\underline{\hspace{1cm}} + \underline{\hspace{1cm}} = \underline{\hspace{1cm}}$$
$$9 - \underline{\hspace{1cm}} = \underline{\hspace{1cm}}$$

3.

$$\underline{\hspace{1cm}} + \underline{\hspace{1cm}} = \underline{\hspace{1cm}}$$
$$5 - \underline{\hspace{1cm}} = \underline{\hspace{1cm}}$$

4.

$$\underline{\hspace{1cm}} + \underline{\hspace{1cm}} = \underline{\hspace{1cm}}$$
$$11 - \underline{\hspace{1cm}} = \underline{\hspace{1cm}}$$

Problem Solving Critical Thinking

5. How many ways can you subtract from 2? _____

$$2 - \underline{\hspace{1cm}} = \underline{\hspace{1cm}}$$
$$2 - \underline{\hspace{1cm}} = \underline{\hspace{1cm}}$$
$$2 - \underline{\hspace{1cm}} = \underline{\hspace{1cm}}$$

Notes for Home Your child wrote related addition and subtraction sentences. *Home Activity:* Ask your child write how many ways he or she can subtract from 4. (There are 5 ways: 4 − 0 = 4, 4 − 1 = 3, 4 − 2 = 2, 4 − 3 = 1, 4 − 4 = 0.)

Name _____

Problem Solving:
Choose an Operation

Use ⬭ ⬭ to show the story.
Circle add or subtract. Write the number sentence.

---

1. There are 12 ⬤ .

   3 ⬤ are eaten.

   How many are there now?

   add   (subtract)

   12 ⊖ 3 = 9

---

2. There are 2 🥛 .

   2 more 🥛 are poured.

   How many in all?

   add   subtract

   ___ ◯ ___ = ___

---

3. 4 🥪 are on the plate.

   3 🥪 are taken away.

   How many are on the plate?

   add   subtract

   ___ ◯ ___ = ___

---

4. 5 🧃 on the table.

   Children bring 4 more 🧃 .

   How many are on the table now?

   add   subtract

   ___ ◯ ___ = ___

Journal

Think about 5 things that you have.

Write an addition story.

Write a subtraction story.

Notes for Home Your child read number stories, chose and wrote the addition or subtraction sign, and then solved the problems. *Home Activity:* Ask your child to write an addition and a subtraction story about people who come and go in your family.

Name _____

Mixed Practice: Lessons 7–12

Subtract.

You can use 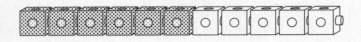 .

1.
$$\begin{array}{r}7\\-5\end{array}\qquad\begin{array}{r}9\\-3\end{array}\qquad\begin{array}{r}11\\-1\end{array}\qquad\begin{array}{r}4\\-4\end{array}\qquad\begin{array}{r}8\\-6\end{array}\qquad\begin{array}{r}7\\-2\end{array}\qquad\begin{array}{r}10\\-5\end{array}$$

2. Write the number sentences.

_____ + _____ = _____

11 − _____ = _____

Problem Solving

Write the number sentence.

3. There are 8  .

6 more  come.

How many are there now?

_____ ◯ _____ = _____

4. There are 6  .

2  fly away.

How many are left?

_____ ◯ _____ = _____

Journal

Write a math story that has the number 5 in it.

Draw a picture.

Write a number sentence for your story.

Notes for Home Your child practiced subtraction concepts, and relating addition and subtraction.
Home Activity: Ask your child to write a math story about a game he or she has played at school.

Cumulative Review

Use 1 or 2 colors.

Color to show 2 ways to make the number.

Write a number sentence.

1.

_____ and _____ is 6.

_____ and _____ is 6.

Draw a picture to match the number sentence.

Write how many in all.

2.

$$3 + 1 = \underline{\hspace{1cm}}.$$

Test Prep

Choose the number sentence.

Fill in the ○ for the correct answer.

3.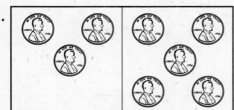

○ $5 - 2 = 3$
○ $3 + 8 = 11$
○ $8 - 3 = 5$
○ $3 + 5 = 8$

4. There are 8

and 2 come.

How many in all?

○ $8 - 2 = 6$
○ $8 + 2 = 10$
○ $10 + 2 = 12$
○ $10 - 2 = 8$

Notes for Home Your child reviewed finding combinations for numbers and drawing a picture to solve a problem.
Home Activity: Ask your child to draw pictures for Exercise 1.

Count On 1 or 2

Count on to add.

1.

$7 + 1 = \underline{8}$

$\begin{array}{r} 7 \\ +\ 1 \\ \hline 8 \end{array}$

2.

$7 + 2 = \underline{\hphantom{0}}$

$\begin{array}{r} 7 \\ +\ 2 \\ \hline \end{array}$

3. $6 + 2 = \underline{\hphantom{0}}$ $3 + 1 = \underline{\hphantom{0}}$ $1 + 2 = \underline{\hphantom{0}}$

4. $4 + 2 = \underline{\hphantom{0}}$ $1 + 1 = \underline{\hphantom{0}}$ $4 + 1 = \underline{\hphantom{0}}$

5. $\begin{array}{r} 5 \\ +\ 1 \\ \hline \end{array}$ $\begin{array}{r} 5 \\ +\ 2 \\ \hline \end{array}$ $\begin{array}{r} 9 \\ +\ 1 \\ \hline \end{array}$ $\begin{array}{r} 9 \\ +\ 2 \\ \hline \end{array}$ $\begin{array}{r} 3 \\ +\ 1 \\ \hline \end{array}$ $\begin{array}{r} 3 \\ +\ 2 \\ \hline \end{array}$

6. $\begin{array}{r} 2 \\ +\ 2 \\ \hline \end{array}$ $\begin{array}{r} 6 \\ +\ 1 \\ \hline \end{array}$ $\begin{array}{r} 7 \\ +\ 2 \\ \hline \end{array}$ $\begin{array}{r} 8 \\ +\ 2 \\ \hline \end{array}$ $\begin{array}{r} 7 \\ +\ 1 \\ \hline \end{array}$ $\begin{array}{r} 8 \\ +\ 1 \\ \hline \end{array}$

Problem Solving Patterns

Complete the pattern.

What pattern do you see?

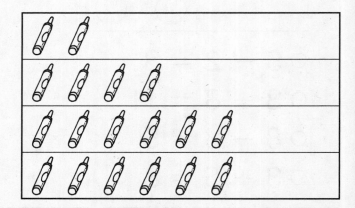

Notes for Home Your child added 1 or 2 to a number. *Home Activity:* Ask your child to draw a small object. Then ask him or her to add 1 or 2 of the objects to the picture several times and to find each total.

Name _____

Explore Turnaround Facts

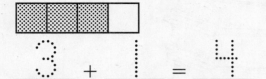   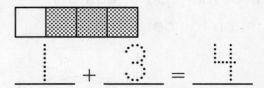

3 + 1 = 4   1 + 3 = 4

1. Make a 6 train. Write 2 turnaround facts.

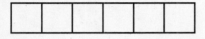   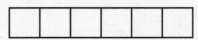

____ + ____ = ____   ____ + ____ = ____

2. Make a 9 train. Write 2 turnaround facts.

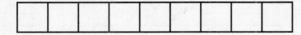   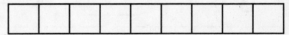

____ + ____ = ____   ____ + ____ = ____

3. Make a 7 train. Write 2 turnaround facts.

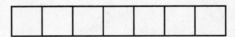

____ + ____ = ____   ____ + ____ = ____

Problem Solving Visual Thinking

4. Tell how the trains are alike and different.

Notes for Home Your child learned that turnaround facts like 1 + 3 and 3 + 1 always have the same sum. *Home Activity:* Ask your child to make an 8 train and show 2 turnaround facts.

Name _____

Count On from Any Number

Think of the greater number.
Count on to add.

1.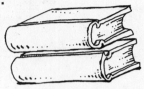

$2 + 3 = \underline{5}$

$$\begin{array}{r} 2 \\ + 3 \\ \hline 5 \end{array}$$

2. $4 + 3 = \underline{\hphantom{00}}$ | $8 + 1 = \underline{\hphantom{00}}$ | $4 + 2 = \underline{\hphantom{00}}$

$3 + 4 = \underline{\hphantom{00}}$ | $1 + 8 = \underline{\hphantom{00}}$ | $2 + 4 = \underline{\hphantom{00}}$

3.
$$\begin{array}{r} 4 \\ + 1 \\ \hline \end{array} \quad \begin{array}{r} 1 \\ + 4 \\ \hline \end{array} \quad \begin{array}{r} 5 \\ + 2 \\ \hline \end{array} \quad \begin{array}{r} 2 \\ + 5 \\ \hline \end{array} \quad \begin{array}{r} 3 \\ + 7 \\ \hline \end{array} \quad \begin{array}{r} 7 \\ + 3 \\ \hline \end{array}$$

4.
$$\begin{array}{r} 6 \\ + 2 \\ \hline \end{array} \quad \begin{array}{r} 2 \\ + 6 \\ \hline \end{array} \quad \begin{array}{r} 1 \\ + 9 \\ \hline \end{array} \quad \begin{array}{r} 9 \\ + 1 \\ \hline \end{array} \quad \begin{array}{r} 1 \\ + 3 \\ \hline \end{array} \quad \begin{array}{r} 3 \\ + 1 \\ \hline \end{array}$$

Tell a Math Story

5. Look at the picture.
   Think of a math story.
   Tell it to a friend.

Notes for Home Your child added 1, 2, or 3 to the greater number. *Home Activity:* Ask your child to choose a number sentence in Exercise 5 and to illustrate it.

Use a Number Line to Count On

$$\overset{0 \quad 1 \quad 2 \quad 3 \quad 4 \quad 5 \quad 6 \quad 7 \quad 8 \quad 9 \quad 10 \quad 11 \quad 12}{\longleftarrow \cdot\cdot\cdot\cdot\cdot\cdot\cdot\cdot\cdot\cdot\cdot\cdot\cdot\cdot\cdot \longrightarrow}$$

You can use the number line. Write the sum.

1. $5 + 2 = \underline{7}$ $4 + 3 = \underline{\hspace{1.5em}}$ $3 + 1 = \underline{\hspace{1.5em}}$

2. $6 + 1 = \underline{\hspace{1.5em}}$ $2 + 3 = \underline{\hspace{1.5em}}$ $8 + 1 = \underline{\hspace{1.5em}}$

3. $4 + 1 = \underline{\hspace{1.5em}}$ $2 + 7 = \underline{\hspace{1.5em}}$ $3 + 5 = \underline{\hspace{1.5em}}$

4.
$$\begin{array}{cccccc} 8 & 3 & 2 & 5 & 1 & 6 \\ +3 & +6 & +3 & +1 & +9 & +2 \\ \hline \end{array}$$

5.
$$\begin{array}{cccccc} 2 & 1 & 7 & 3 & 2 & 1 \\ +4 & +7 & +3 & +3 & +9 & +2 \\ \hline \end{array}$$

Write your own number sentences.

6. $\underline{\hspace{1.5em}} + 1 = \underline{\hspace{1.5em}}$ $\underline{\hspace{1.5em}} + 2 = \underline{\hspace{1.5em}}$

Mental Math

7. What number is 3 more than 6? How can the number line help?

_____

_____

Notes for Home Your child used a number line to add numbers. *Home Activity:* Write 3 addition facts such as 4 + 5, 2 + 7, and 6 + 3, and ask your child to find the sums using a number line.

Add Zero

Add.

1. $3 + 0 =$ ____

2. $\begin{array}{r} 5 \\ + 0 \\ \hline \end{array}$

3. $5 + 2 =$ ____ $3 + 0 =$ ____ $1 + 3 =$ ____

4. $2 + 0 =$ ____ $0 + 0 =$ ____ $0 + 6 =$ ____

5. $\begin{array}{r} 0 \\ + 4 \\ \hline \end{array}$ $\begin{array}{r} 1 \\ + 0 \\ \hline \end{array}$ $\begin{array}{r} 3 \\ + 5 \\ \hline \end{array}$ $\begin{array}{r} 7 \\ + 0 \\ \hline \end{array}$ $\begin{array}{r} 2 \\ + 2 \\ \hline \end{array}$ $\begin{array}{r} 9 \\ + 1 \\ \hline \end{array}$

6. $\begin{array}{r} 8 \\ + 0 \\ \hline \end{array}$ $\begin{array}{r} 9 \\ + 2 \\ \hline \end{array}$ $\begin{array}{r} 0 \\ + 5 \\ \hline \end{array}$ $\begin{array}{r} 2 \\ + 1 \\ \hline \end{array}$ $\begin{array}{r} 6 \\ + 0 \\ \hline \end{array}$ $\begin{array}{r} 0 \\ + 0 \\ \hline \end{array}$

Problem Solving Critical Thinking

Try this super fact.

$800 + 0 =$ ____

Write your own super fact. ____ $+ 0 =$ ____

Notes for Home Your child added zero. *Home Activity:* Ask your child to write and solve 3 addition sentences that include adding zero.

Add with 5

Add.

1. $7 + 5 = \underline{12}$ $5 + 5 = \underline{}$ $1 + 5 = \underline{}$

2.
$$
\begin{array}{r} 2 \\ +5 \\ \hline \end{array}
\qquad
\begin{array}{r} 4 \\ +5 \\ \hline \end{array}
\qquad
\begin{array}{r} 3 \\ +5 \\ \hline \end{array}
\qquad
\begin{array}{r} 0 \\ +5 \\ \hline \end{array}
\qquad
\begin{array}{r} 5 \\ +4 \\ \hline \end{array}
\qquad
\begin{array}{r} 5 \\ +6 \\ \hline \end{array}
$$

Mixed Practice

Add.

3.
$$
\begin{array}{r} 9 \\ +3 \\ \hline \end{array}
\qquad
\begin{array}{r} 7 \\ +0 \\ \hline \end{array}
\qquad
\begin{array}{r} 8 \\ +1 \\ \hline \end{array}
\qquad
\begin{array}{r} 6 \\ +2 \\ \hline \end{array}
\qquad
\begin{array}{r} 5 \\ +5 \\ \hline \end{array}
\qquad
\begin{array}{r} 2 \\ +3 \\ \hline \end{array}
$$

4.
$$
\begin{array}{r} 3 \\ +1 \\ \hline \end{array}
\qquad
\begin{array}{r} 2 \\ +7 \\ \hline \end{array}
\qquad
\begin{array}{r} 4 \\ +1 \\ \hline \end{array}
\qquad
\begin{array}{r} 0 \\ +8 \\ \hline \end{array}
\qquad
\begin{array}{r} 9 \\ +0 \\ \hline \end{array}
\qquad
\begin{array}{r} 1 \\ +5 \\ \hline \end{array}
$$

Problem Solving Critical Thinking

5. Circle what you can buy with and   .

5¢   14¢   20¢

Notes for Home Your child added 5, 0, and 1, 2, or 3. *Home Activity:* Ask your child to draw a picture that shows adding 0.

Problem Solving: Make a List

Choose 2 boxes. Make a list.

1. Your friend wants exactly 12 party favors.

I box of __9__ favors and I box of __3__ favors

I box of _____ favors and I box of _____ favors

I box of _____ favors and I box of _____ favors

2 boxes of _____ favors.

2. You want exactly 9 party favors.

I box of _____ favors and I box of _____ favors

I box of _____ favors and I box of _____ favors

I box of _____ favors and I box of _____ favors

Critical Thinking

3. Add the numbers in circles.
   Add the numbers in triangles.
   Add the numbers in squares.
   What do you find?

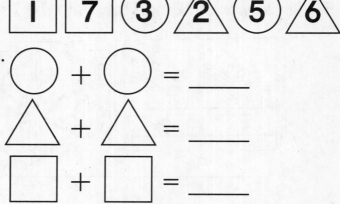

$\bigcirc + \bigcirc = $ _____

$\triangle + \triangle = $ _____

$\square + \square = $ _____

Notes for Home Your child solved problems by choosing numbers to get a given sum. *Home Activity:* Ask your child to list 4 ways to get 10 party favors. (Answers will vary, but may include: 5 + 5, 6 + 4, 8 + 2, 7 + 3.)

Name _____

Mixed Practice: Lessons 1–7

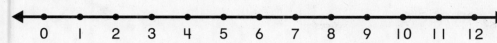

0   1   2   3   4   5   6   7   8   9   10   11   12

Count on to add. You can use the number line.

1. $\begin{array}{r} 6 \\ +3 \\ \hline \end{array}$ $\begin{array}{r} 5 \\ +2 \\ \hline \end{array}$ $\begin{array}{r} 8 \\ +3 \\ \hline \end{array}$ $\begin{array}{r} 7 \\ +1 \\ \hline \end{array}$ $\begin{array}{r} 2 \\ +4 \\ \hline \end{array}$ $\begin{array}{r} 1 \\ +9 \\ \hline \end{array}$

Add.

2. $6 + 2 =$ _____ $0 + 3 =$ _____ $6 + 5 =$ _____

3. $\begin{array}{r} 9 \\ +1 \\ \hline \end{array}$ $\begin{array}{r} 1 \\ +9 \\ \hline \end{array}$ $\begin{array}{r} 0 \\ +8 \\ \hline \end{array}$ $\begin{array}{r} 8 \\ +0 \\ \hline \end{array}$ $\begin{array}{r} 3 \\ +7 \\ \hline \end{array}$ $\begin{array}{r} 7 \\ +3 \\ \hline \end{array}$

Problem Solving

4. Miguel wants exactly 9 apples. Make a list.

I bag of _____ apples and I bag of _____ apples

I bag of _____ apples and I bag of _____ apples

I bag of _____ apples

Journal

5. Draw pictures to show ways to make 8.

Notes for Home Your child practiced addition facts to 12. *Home Activity:* Ask your child to list 3 ways to make 2 groups of food items, such as eggs, that make 12. (Answers will vary, but may include: 10 + 2, 6 + 6, 4 + 8.)

Name _____

Cumulative Review

Write the missing numbers.

1. 1 ___ ___ 4 ___ 6 7 8 9 ___

2. 10 9 ___ 7 6 ___ ___ ___ 2 1

Write the number sentence.

3.

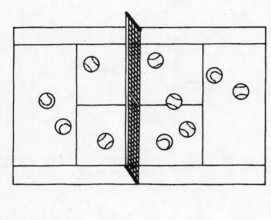

___ + ___ = ___

4.

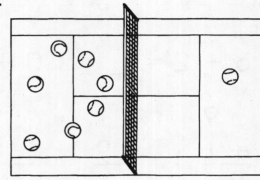

___ + ___ = ___

Test Prep

Fill in the ○ for the correct answer.

Solve.

5.

5 − 2 = ___

1	2	3	4
○	○	○	○

6. 4 🎾 play.
3 more come.
How many now?

5	8	7	6
○	○	○	○

Notes for Home Your child reviewed ordering numbers, addition, and subtraction. *Home Activity:* Ask your child to create and solve 4 addition sentences using the fingers of each hand to show the addends.

Name _____

Use a Number Line to Count Back

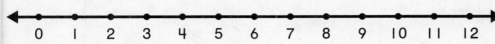

```
←•——•——•——•——•——•——•——•——•——•——•——•——•→
  0   1   2   3   4   5   6   7   8   9  10  11  12
```

You can use the number line.

Write the difference.

1. $6 - 1 = \underline{5}$ $5 - 1 = \underline{\quad}$ $7 - 2 = \underline{\quad}$

2. $9 - 1 = \underline{\quad}$ $8 - 2 = \underline{\quad}$ $5 - 3 = \underline{\quad}$

3.
$$\begin{array}{ccccccc} 5 & 8 & 10 & 6 & 7 & 4 \\ -2 & -1 & -2 & -2 & -1 & -1 \\ \hline \end{array}$$

4.
$$\begin{array}{ccccccc} 9 & 3 & 8 & 3 & 2 & 2 \\ -2 & -1 & -2 & -2 & -1 & -2 \\ \hline \end{array}$$

Write your own number sentences.

5. $\underline{\quad} - 1 = \underline{\quad}$ 6. $\underline{\quad} - 1 = \underline{\quad}$

7. $\underline{\quad} - 2 = \underline{\quad}$ 8. $\underline{\quad} - 2 = \underline{\quad}$

Mental Math

9. Start at 12.
   Count back 2.
   Write the answer. _____

$12 - 2 = \underline{\quad}$

Notes for Home Your child subtracted by counting back. *Home Activity:* Ask your child to use the number line to show you how to solve the Mental Math problem.

Name _____

Count Back 1 or 2

Count back to subtract.

1.

$3 - 1 = \underline{2}$

$\begin{array}{r} 3 \\ -1 \\ \hline 2 \end{array}$

2.

$5 - 2 = \underline{}$

$\begin{array}{r} 5 \\ -2 \\ \hline \end{array}$

3. $8 - 1 = \underline{}$ $9 - 2 = \underline{}$ $4 - 1 = \underline{}$

4. $6 - 2 = \underline{}$ $9 - 1 = \underline{}$ $11 - 2 = \underline{}$

5. $\begin{array}{r} 10 \\ -1 \\ \hline \end{array}$ $\begin{array}{r} 4 \\ -2 \\ \hline \end{array}$ $\begin{array}{r} 12 \\ -2 \\ \hline \end{array}$ $\begin{array}{r} 9 \\ -1 \\ \hline \end{array}$ $\begin{array}{r} 3 \\ -2 \\ \hline \end{array}$ $\begin{array}{r} 11 \\ -1 \\ \hline \end{array}$

6. $\begin{array}{r} 8 \\ -2 \\ \hline \end{array}$ $\begin{array}{r} 10 \\ -2 \\ \hline \end{array}$ $\begin{array}{r} 6 \\ -1 \\ \hline \end{array}$ $\begin{array}{r} 7 \\ -2 \\ \hline \end{array}$ $\begin{array}{r} 12 \\ -1 \\ \hline \end{array}$ $\begin{array}{r} 11 \\ -2 \\ \hline \end{array}$

Problem Solving

Solve.

7. There are 11  in a . 2 fly off.

How many are left? _____

8. There are 8 on a . 1 walks away.

How many are left? _____

Notes for Home Your child counted back 1 or 2 to subtract. *Home Activity:* Ask your child to use 9 of his or her favorite toys. Have your child tell you a math story about them by counting back 1 and then 2.

Name _____

Subtract All and Subtract Zero

Solve.

1. There are 5 🍌.
All are eaten.
How many are left?

$5 \quad -5 \over 0$

$5 - 5 = \underline{0}$

2. There are 8 🍒.
No one ate any.
How many are left?

$8 \over -0$

$8 - 0 = \underline{}$

Subtract.

3. $9 - 0 = \underline{} \qquad 9 - 9 = \underline{} \qquad 11 - 0 = \underline{}$

4.
$7 \over -7 \qquad 7 \over -0 \qquad 5 \over -5 \qquad 6 \over -6 \qquad 12 \over -0 \qquad 12 \over -12$

Mixed Practice Subtract.

5. $6 - 1 = \underline{} \qquad 5 - 2 = \underline{} \qquad 2 - 0 = \underline{}$

6.
$1 \over -1 \qquad 9 \over -2 \qquad 10 \over -1 \qquad 6 \over -6 \qquad 8 \over -2 \qquad 4 \over -3$

Problem Solving Critical Thinking

7. Try this super fact. $200 - 0 = \underline{}$

Write your own super fact. $\underline{} - 0 = \underline{}$

Notes for Home Your child subtracted all or 0. *Home Activity:* Have your child use small objects, such as beans, to show show you 8 − 0 and 8 − 8.

Use with pages 155–156. **63**

Name _____

Subtract with 5

Subtract.

1.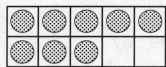

$8 - 5 = \underline{3}$

2.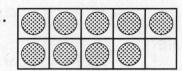

$9 - 5 = \underline{}$

3. $6 - 5 = \underline{}$ $10 - 5 = \underline{}$ $7 - 5 = \underline{}$

4.
$$\begin{array}{cc} 9 \\ -5 \\ \hline \end{array} \quad \begin{array}{cc} 11 \\ -5 \\ \hline \end{array} \quad \begin{array}{cc} 12 \\ -5 \\ \hline \end{array} \quad \begin{array}{cc} 8 \\ -5 \\ \hline \end{array} \quad \begin{array}{cc} 5 \\ -5 \\ \hline \end{array} \quad \begin{array}{cc} 10 \\ -5 \\ \hline \end{array}$$

Mixed Practice Subtract.

5.
$$\begin{array}{cc} 10 \\ -0 \\ \hline \end{array} \quad \begin{array}{cc} 6 \\ -3 \\ \hline \end{array} \quad \begin{array}{cc} 12 \\ -5 \\ \hline \end{array} \quad \begin{array}{cc} 11 \\ -1 \\ \hline \end{array} \quad \begin{array}{cc} 8 \\ -8 \\ \hline \end{array} \quad \begin{array}{cc} 9 \\ -2 \\ \hline \end{array}$$

6.
$$\begin{array}{cc} 7 \\ -2 \\ \hline \end{array} \quad \begin{array}{cc} 11 \\ -2 \\ \hline \end{array} \quad \begin{array}{cc} 5 \\ -0 \\ \hline \end{array} \quad \begin{array}{cc} 9 \\ -1 \\ \hline \end{array} \quad \begin{array}{cc} 10 \\ -10 \\ \hline \end{array} \quad \begin{array}{cc} 12 \\ -2 \\ \hline \end{array}$$

Problem Solving

7. There are 9 in all.
   How many are in the bag?

   _____

Notes for Home Your child subtracted with 5, counted back 1 or 2, and subtracted 0. *Home Activity:* Write 3 subtraction sentences on a piece of paper. Ask your child to solve each subtraction sentence and to draw pictures representing each sentence.

Practice
4-12

Problem Solving:
Write a Number Sentence

You can use ⬭ 🍪 and ▭▭ to show the story.
Write a number sentence.

1. 7 🍐 are on a plate.

   All 7 🍐 are eaten.

   How many are left?

   _____

2. 8 children put their ✏ in a box.

   2 more children put their ✏ in the box.

   How many are in the box?

   _____

3. Michele has 5 🚗 .

   She gives 2 🚗 away.

   How many are left?

   _____

4. Joshua has 3 🍕 .

   He eats all 3 🍕 .

   How many are left?

   _____

Write About It

Here is a number sentence. $9 - 8 = 1$

You write the story. _____

_____

_____

Notes for Home Your child wrote number sentences to solve problems. *Home Activity:* Ask your child to draw a picture to illustrate the story they told in Write About It.

Name _____

Mixed Practice: Lessons 8–12

```
0  1  2  3  4  5  6  7  8  9  10  11  12
```

Count back to subtract.

1.
9	10	7	5	9	12
−2	−2	−1	−2	−1	−1

Subtract.

2.
10	10	6	6	8	8
−0	−10	−6	−0	−8	−0

Problem Solving

You can use ▭▭ and ⬭ ◉ to show the story.
Write the number sentence.

3. There are 2 .

   5 more 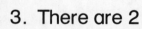 join them.
   How many are there?

   _____

4. There are 3 .

   Tom and Paul take 3 .
   How many are left?

   _____

Journal

5. Write a math story and a number sentence.

___

Notes for Home Your child practiced subtraction and problem solving. *Home Activity:* Ask your child to use small food items, such as raisins or crackers, to show subtraction problems by eating 1 or 2 of them.

Cumulative Review

Add.

1.
2	9	4	6	4	1	10
+7	+2	+5	+4	+4	+8	+0

Problem Solving

Use the graph. Write the number.

2. How many more than ? _____ more

3. How many fewer than ? _____ fewer

Test Prep

Fill in the ○ for the correct answer.

You can use the number line to count on.

| 0 1 2 3 4 5 6 7 8 9 10 11 12 |

4. 8 + 2 = ____

9	10	11	12
○	○	○	○

5. 6 + 3 = ____

8	9	10	11
○	○	○	○

Notes for Home Your child reviewed using a graph and addition. *Home Activity:* Ask your child to solve the problem 8 + 3. (11)

Name _____

Explore Solids

pyramid   rectangular   cube
         prism

sphere   cylinder   cone

These can stack and slide.   These are round and curved. They roll.

Draw a solid that belongs.

Draw a solid that does not belong.

	belongs	does not belong
1.		
2.		

Problem Solving Patterns

Circle the solid that comes next.

3.

4. 

Notes for Home Your child identified and described differences between solid shapes. *Home Activity:* Ask your child to point to kitchen objects that have shapes similar to those in Exercise 1.

Faces of Solids

Kim drew around these solids.
Find the shape she made.

1.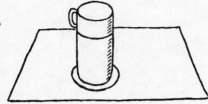

2.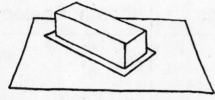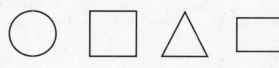

3.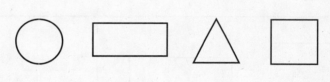

4.

Problem Solving Critical Thinking

5. How many faces do these solids have?

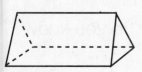   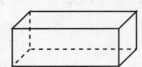

_____   _____   _____   _____

Notes for Home Your child predicted the shape that would be made by tracing around each solid. *Home Activity:* Ask your child to point to solids with 6 sides on this worksheet. (Possible answers: rectangular prism; cube)

Explore Shapes

circle

0 flat sides
0 corners

triangle

3 sides
3 corners

square

4 sides
4 corners

rectangle

4 sides
4 corners

Draw a shape that belongs.

Draw a shape that does not belong.

	belongs	does not belong
1. 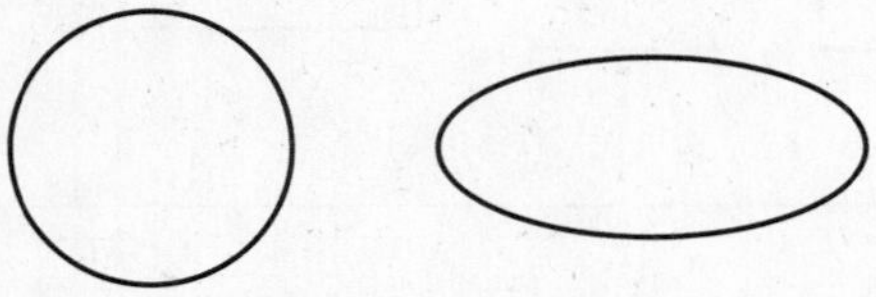		
2. 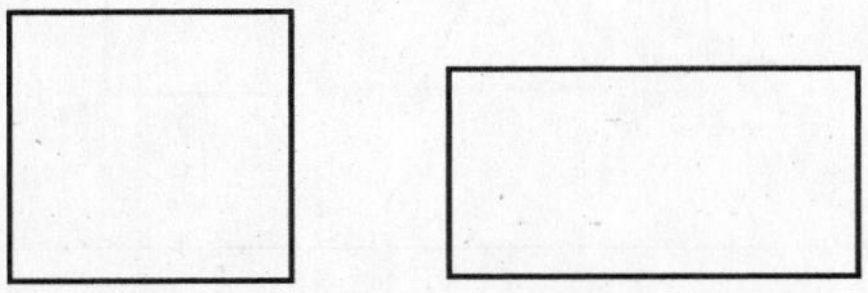		
3. 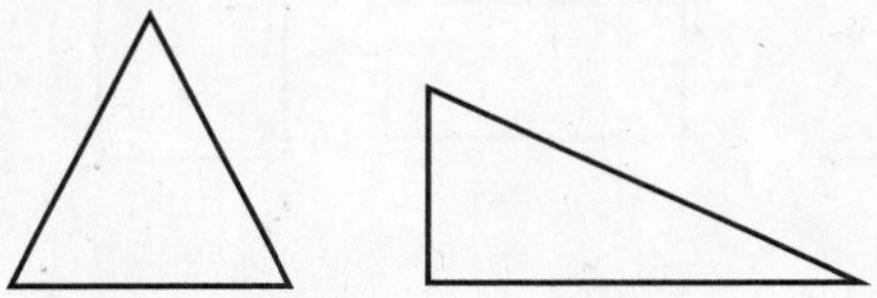		

Problem Solving Critical Thinking

4. If a shape has 0 flat sides, how many corners will it have? How many corners does a shape with 3 sides have? How do you know?

_____

_____

Notes for Home Your child compared shapes to find similarities and differences. *Home Activity:* Ask your child to point to 5 objects in a room that have a square or rectangular shape.

Same Size and Shape

Circle the ones that are the same size and shape.

1.
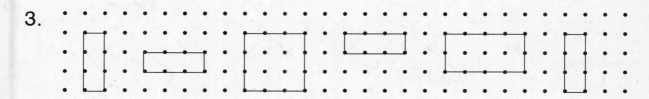

2.
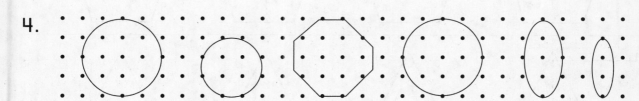

3.

4.

Write About It

5. Draw a shape. Now draw another one
that is the same size and shape.

Notes for Home Your child identified figures that have the same sizes and shapes. *Home Activity:* Ask your child
to draw shapes with 3, 4, and 5 sides.

Symmetry

Practice 5-5

Circle the shapes if the parts match when you fold on the line.

1.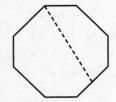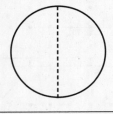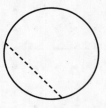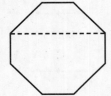

2.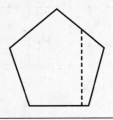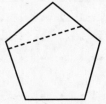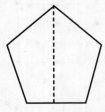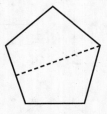

3.

4. (triangles)

Problem Solving Visual Thinking

5. Draw to make two parts that match.

Notes for Home Your child identified lines of symmetry. *Home Activity:* Point to different symmetrical objects in your home such as doors, plates, or windows. Ask your child to draw the object and to add a line to each drawing to create two parts that match.

72 Use with pages 183–184.

Problem Solving: Make a Table

Use pattern blocks.

How many ways
can you make this shape?

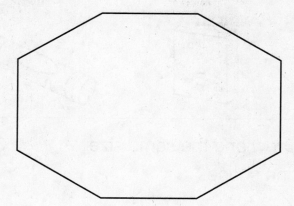

Record the blocks
you used.

Shapes I used	⏢	▢	△	▱
1st way	2	2	0	0
2nd way				
3rd way				
4th way				
5th way				

Patterns

Draw what comes next.

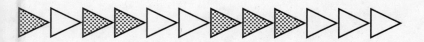

Name _____

Mixed Practice: Lessons 1–6

1. Circle the things that can roll.

 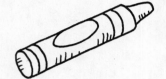

2. Draw one the same size and shape.

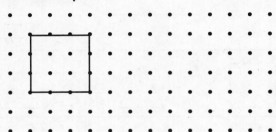

3. Circle the shape if both parts match when you fold on the line.

Problem Solving

4. How many of each shape are there? Record the numbers in the table.

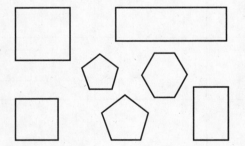

	4 sides	5 sides	6 sides
Number of Shapes			

Journal

5. Write about the shape of a box.

Notes for Home Your child identified shapes. *Home Activity:* Ask your child to count the number of objects in the kitchen that have 4 or more sides.

Name _____

Cumulative Review

Count on to add.

1. $2 + 5 =$ _____

   $5 + 2 =$ _____

2. $1 + 8 =$ _____

   $8 + 1 =$ _____

Subtract.

3.
$$\begin{array}{ccccccc} 6 & 8 & 9 & 10 & 7 & 5 & 4 \\ -2 & -1 & -6 & -8 & -2 & -4 & -4 \\ \hline \end{array}$$

Problem Solving

4. Draw a picture to match the number sentence.

   Write how many in all.

$2 + 7 =$ _____	$9 - 7 =$ _____

Test Prep

Fill in the ◯ for the correct answer.

Add or subtract.

5. $\begin{array}{r} 8 \\ -8 \\ \hline \end{array}$ ◯ 8 ◯ 1 ◯ 12 ◯ 0

6. $\begin{array}{r} 3 \\ +2 \\ \hline \end{array}$ ◯ 3 ◯ 4 ◯ 5 ◯ 6

7. $\begin{array}{r} 1 \\ +0 \\ \hline \end{array}$ ◯ 0 ◯ 1 ◯ 2 ◯ 10

Notes for Home Your child reviewed the concepts learned in Chapters 1–5. *Home Activity:* Ask your child to draw a picture to match the number sentence in Exercise 6.

Name _____

Fair Shares

Draw lines to show fair shares.

1.

2.

3.

4.

5.

6.

Problem Solving

Solve.

7. Jon, Pablo, and Tania want to share some pie.
   There are 6 pieces of pie. How can they make fair shares?

_____

Notes for Home Your child made fair shares of items. *Home Activity:* Ask your child to explain his or her reasoning.

Halves

Color to show one half.

1.

2.

3.

4.

5.

6.

7.

8.

Tell a Math Story

9. Tell a story about a time you
   gave a friend half of something.

Notes for Home Your child colored to show halves of shapes. *Home Activity:* Ask your child to name 3 things that can be shared fairly by two people.

Fourths

Color to show $\frac{1}{4}$.

1.

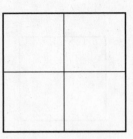

2.

3.

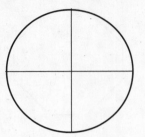

4.

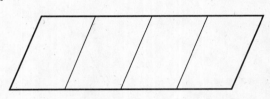

5.

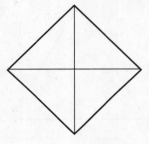

6.

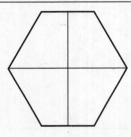

Problem Solving Visual Thinking

7. Show different ways to show fourths.

Notes for Home Your child colored to show fourths of shapes. *Home Activity:* Ask your child to tell you how he or she would divide a pizza between 4 people.

Name _____

Thirds

Color to show $\frac{1}{3}$.

1.

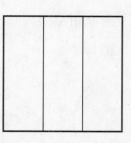

2.

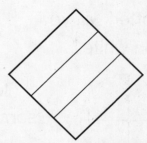

3.

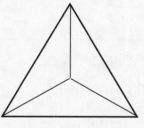

4.

Write your own examples of $\frac{1}{3}$.

5.

6.

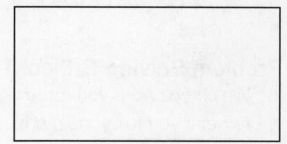

Problem Solving Estimation

7. About how much is gone?
   Circle the best estimate.

   $\frac{1}{2}$ $\frac{1}{4}$ $\frac{1}{3}$

Notes for Home Your child colored thirds of whole shapes. *Home Activity:* Ask your child to cut a piece of bread to show thirds.

Name _____

Explore Probability

What will happen if you use the spinner? Circle the word.

1. How often will you
   land on white?

   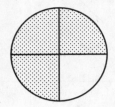

   always
   sometimes
   never

2. How often will you
   land on gray?

   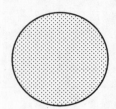

   always
   sometimes
   never

3. How likely are you
   to land on gray?

   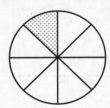

   more likely
   less likely

4. How likely are you
   to land on white?

   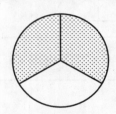

   more likely
   less likely

Problem Solving Critical Thinking

5. Which color are you more likely
   to get if you take one marble
   from this bag? Why?

6. Which size are you more likely
   to get if you take one marble
   from this bag? Why?

Notes for Home Your child described how likely it was to get a given color on a spinner or marble. *Home Activity:*
Flip a coin several times and ask your child to tell you whether you are more likely to flip heads or tails. (Neither is
more likely than the other.)

Name _____

Fractions and Probability

1. Make your own spinner. Use 3 colors.

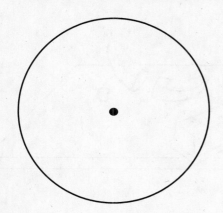

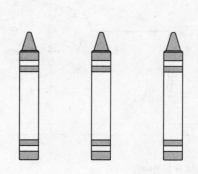

Is your spinner fair? _____

2. Make 20 spins.
   Color to show what you get.

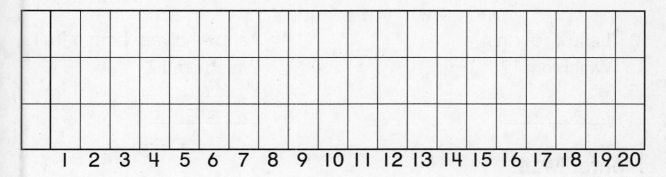

1 2 3 4 5 6 7 8 9 10 11 12 13 14 15 16 17 18 19 20

Problem Solving
Solve.

3. Tad got 3 blue, 1 red, and 2 green. How many times did he spin?

4. Anne got 5 red and 3 green. How many times did she spin?

_____   _____

Notes for Home Your child colored spinners in thirds and made a table to show the results of 20 spins.
Home Activity: Hide a small object, such as a button or paper clip, in one hand. Ask your child to guess the hand.
Repeat several times and record the number of correct guesses.

Problem Solving:
Use Data from a Picture

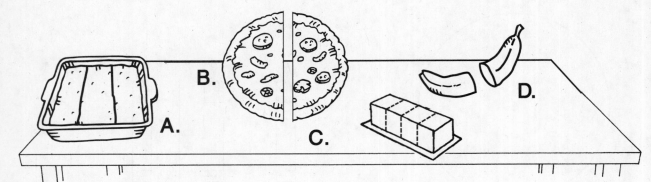

Answer the riddles.

1. I show halves. I am round.
   Which am I?

   _____

2. I show thirds.
   Which am I?

   _____

3. I show fourths.
   Which am I?

   _____

4. I show halves. I am a fruit.
   Which am I?

   _____

Mental Math

5. The girls are going to eat the ⬡.

   Kendra has $\frac{1}{4}$ of the ⬡. Rhea has $\frac{1}{4}$ of the ⬡.

   Is there any of the ⬡ left for Alicia? Why or why not?

   _____

   _____

Notes for Home Your child used a picture to answer riddles about fractions. *Home Activity:* Cut a fruit (or vegetable) into 2, 3, or 4 equal pieces. Ask your child to tell if the fruit has been cut into halves (2 pieces), thirds (3 pieces), or fourths (4 pieces).

Name _____

Mixed Practice: Lessons 7–13

Draw a line to show 2 fair shares.

1.

2.

Color to show the fraction.

3.
   $\dfrac{1}{3}$

4.
   $\dfrac{1}{2}$

5.
   $\dfrac{1}{2}$

Circle the answer.

6. Pick a frog.

certain
impossible

7. Pick a coin.

certain
impossible

Problem Solving

8. Look at the animals. Circle the correct answer.

   I show fourths. Which animals am I?

Journal

9. Draw objects you see that show fourths.

Notes for Home Your child used fractions and probability concepts. *Home Activity:* Ask your child to design 2 different spinners, one that is fair and one that is not fair.

Cumulative Review

1. Add.

$$\begin{array}{r} 3 \\ +5 \\ \hline \end{array} \qquad \begin{array}{r} 6 \\ +4 \\ \hline \end{array} \qquad \begin{array}{r} 7 \\ +4 \\ \hline \end{array}$$

2. Subtract.

$$\begin{array}{r} 8 \\ -5 \\ \hline \end{array} \qquad \begin{array}{r} 9 \\ -4 \\ \hline \end{array} \qquad \begin{array}{r} 6 \\ -3 \\ \hline \end{array}$$

Problem Solving

Solve. Write a number sentence.

3. 2 and 6 .

How many in all?

___ + ___ = ___

4. 7 . 3 walk away.

How many are left?

___ − ___ = ___

Test Prep

Fill in the ○ for the correct answer.

Add or subtract.

5. $11 - 3 =$ _____

   8   3   1   9
   ○   ○   ○   ○

6. $10 + 2 =$ _____

   8   6   11   12
   ○   ○   ○   ○

7. $6 + 3 =$ _____

   8   4   9   10
   ○   ○   ○   ○

8. $9 - 2 =$ _____

   9   7   2   10
   ○   ○   ○   ○

Notes for Home Your child reviewed the concepts taught in Chapters 1– 5. *Home Activity:* Ask your child to draw pictures to show 4 + 1 = 5 and 5 – 1 = 4.

Add with Doubles

Write the sum. Use the doubles to help.

1. $6 + 6 = \underline{12}$ $2 + 2 = \underline{}$ $0 + 0 = \underline{}$

2.
$$
\begin{array}{cccccccc}
3 & 6 & 0 & 5 & 4 & 1 & 3 \\
+3 & +6 & +0 & +5 & +4 & +1 & +3 \\
\hline
\end{array}
$$

Mixed Practice Write the sum. Circle the doubles.

3.
$$
\begin{array}{cccccccc}
3 & 7 & 2 & 5 & 2 & 9 & 2 \\
+3 & +3 & +3 & +5 & +4 & +2 & +2 \\
\hline
\end{array}
$$

4.
$$
\begin{array}{cccccccc}
4 & 3 & 3 & 5 & 9 & 6 & 5 \\
+4 & +1 & +4 & +2 & +1 & +6 & +6 \\
\hline
\end{array}
$$

Problem Solving Critical Thinking

5. Can you use doubles to make 11? Why not? _____

_____

Notes for Home Your child solved addition facts to 12. *Home Activity:* Write these facts on a piece of paper: 3 + 4, 4 + 4, 0 + 0, 5 + 4. Ask your child to solve the problems and to identify the doubles. (3 + 4 = 7, 4 + 4 = 8 is a doubles fact, 0 + 0 = 0 is a doubles fact, 5 + 4 = 9)

Explore Adding Doubles Plus One

Use a doubles fact to add
other facts.

  $2 + 3 = 5$

Write the doubles fact that helps.
Add.

1.
$$\begin{array}{r} 1 \\ + 2 \\ \hline 3 \end{array}$$
$$\begin{array}{r} 1 \\ + 1 \\ \hline 2 \end{array}$$

2.
$$\begin{array}{r} 6 \\ + 5 \\ \hline \end{array}$$
+

3.
$$\begin{array}{r} 3 \\ + 4 \\ \hline \end{array}$$
+

Add.

4. $5 + 6 = \underline{\quad}$ $5 + 5 = \underline{\quad}$ $4 + 5 = \underline{\quad}$

5.
$$\begin{array}{r} 4 \\ + 4 \\ \hline \end{array}$$
$$\begin{array}{r} 6 \\ + 3 \\ \hline \end{array}$$
$$\begin{array}{r} 1 \\ + 2 \\ \hline \end{array}$$
$$\begin{array}{r} 3 \\ + 5 \\ \hline \end{array}$$
$$\begin{array}{r} 7 \\ + 4 \\ \hline \end{array}$$
$$\begin{array}{r} 6 \\ + 4 \\ \hline \end{array}$$
$$\begin{array}{r} 2 \\ + 3 \\ \hline \end{array}$$

Tell a Math Story

6. Use doubles to make up a
   math story about these dogs.
   Retell the story using
   doubles plus one.

Notes for Home Your child learned that facts like 3 + 4 = 7 are 1 more than a doubles fact (3 + 3 = 6).
Home Activity: Say a doubles fact like 5 + 5 = 10 and ask your child to name a fact that is 1 more.
(5 + 6 = 11 or 6 + 5 = 11)

Add with Doubles Plus One

Add.

1. $5 + 5 =$ __10__ $5 + 6 =$ ___ $6 + 5 =$ ___

2. $3 + 3 =$ ___ $3 + 4 =$ ___ $4 + 3 =$ ___

3.
$$
\begin{array}{cc}
2 & 2 & 3 \\
+2 & +3 & +2 \\
\end{array}
$$

4.
$$
\begin{array}{cc}
0 & 0 & 1 \\
+0 & +1 & +0 \\
\end{array}
$$

5.
$$
\begin{array}{cccccc}
3 & 0 & 5 & 6 & 4 & 2 & 1 \\
+3 & +0 & +5 & +6 & +4 & +2 & +1 \\
\end{array}
$$

6.
$$
\begin{array}{cccccc}
4 & 3 & 1 & 5 & 1 & 6 & 4 \\
+5 & +2 & +0 & +6 & +2 & +5 & +3 \\
\end{array}
$$

Problem Solving Critical Thinking

7. Billy Bee threw 3 darts.

His total score was 9.

Circle the 3 numbers he scored.

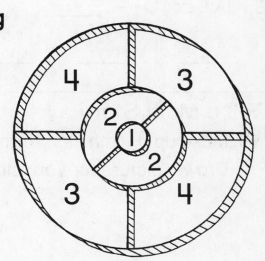

Notes for Home Your child used doubles plus one. *Home Activity:* Ask your child to find 5 numbers on the dart board that equal 11 when added. (3 + 3 + 2 + 2 + 1)

Use Doubles to Subtract

Add or subtract.

1. $6 - 3 = \underline{3}$

   $3 + 3 = \underline{6}$

2. $10 - 5 = \underline{}$

   $5 + 5 = \underline{}$

3. $12 - 6 = \underline{}$

   $6 + 6 = \underline{}$

4. $8 - 4 = \underline{}$

   $4 + 4 = \underline{}$

Subtract. Write the addition facts that help.

5. $\begin{array}{r} 8 \\ -4 \\ \hline 4 \end{array}$ $\begin{array}{r} 4 \\ + 4 \\ \hline 8 \end{array}$

6. $\begin{array}{r} 6 \\ -3 \\ \hline \end{array}$ $\begin{array}{r} \\ + \\ \hline \end{array}$

7. $\begin{array}{r} 12 \\ -6 \\ \hline \end{array}$ $\begin{array}{r} \\ + \\ \hline \end{array}$

8. $10 - 5 = \underline{}$

   $\underline{} + \underline{} = \underline{}$

9. $8 - 4 = \underline{}$

   $\underline{} + \underline{} = \underline{}$

Tell a Math Story

10. Make up a math story using $6 - 3$.

    Draw a picture for your story.

Notes for Home Your child used addition and subtraction to find answers. *Home Activity:* Ask your child to say a subtraction fact for things found around your home that come in doubles, such as 4 windowpanes minus 2 windowpanes is 2 windowpanes.

Name _____

Problem Solving:
Collect and Use Data

Mrs. Shah's class went
for a walk outside.
Here is what they saw.

Critters	Tally	Total
Dogs	IIII	4
Cats	III	3
Birds	⊬⊬ III	8
Worms	⊬⊬ II	7
Insects	⊬⊬ ⊬⊬	10

Write your own questions.
Use the chart to write 3 questions.
Trade papers. Answer each other's questions.

1. _____

_____

2. _____

_____

3. _____

_____

Patterns Algebra Readiness

4. Complete the pattern.
   Draw the towers.
   Write the number.

  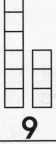

3   **6**   **9**   _____   _____

Notes for Home Your child used a tally chart to answer questions. *Home Activity:* Ask your child to show you how
to make a tally chart. You may wish to count the number of forks, spoons, and knives in a drawer. Then ask *"Which
do we have the fewest of?" "Which do we have the most of?"*

Name _____

Mixed Practice: Lessons 1-5

Add. Use doubles when you can.

1.
$$\begin{array}{cccccccc} 2 & 2 & 5 & 5 & 0 & 0 & 1 \\ +2 & +3 & +5 & +6 & +0 & +1 & +1 \end{array}$$

2. $3 + 3 = \underline{}$ $3 + 4 = \underline{}$ $5 + 6 = \underline{}$

Subtract.

3.
$$\begin{array}{ccccccc} 8 & 0 & 2 & 12 & 10 & 6 & 4 \\ -4 & -0 & -1 & -6 & -5 & -3 & -2 \end{array}$$

Problem Solving

Write the totals.
Use the chart to solve.

4. How many chose green? _____

5. Which one did the
   most children choose? _____

Favorite Colors		
Color	Tally	Total
Green	ЖHT I	_____
Blue	ЖHT IIII	_____
Yellow	III	_____

Journal

6. Draw a picture to show a double for 3.
   Write an addition and a subtraction sentence for the picture.

Notes for Home Your child added and subtracted through 12. *Home Activity:* Ask your child to circle all the problems on this page that use doubles to add or subtract, such as 3 + 3 and 8 − 4. Then have him or her write and solve two more different doubles problems.

Name _____

Cumulative Review

Add or subtract.

1. $\begin{array}{r} 8 \\ -4 \\ \hline \end{array}$ $\begin{array}{r} 6 \\ +6 \\ \hline \end{array}$ $\begin{array}{r} 7 \\ +2 \\ \hline \end{array}$ $\begin{array}{r} 5 \\ -2 \\ \hline \end{array}$ $\begin{array}{r} 3 \\ +5 \\ \hline \end{array}$ $\begin{array}{r} 9 \\ -2 \\ \hline \end{array}$ $\begin{array}{r} 12 \\ -7 \\ \hline \end{array}$

2. $\begin{array}{r} 0 \\ +1 \\ \hline \end{array}$ $\begin{array}{r} 10 \\ -5 \\ \hline \end{array}$ $\begin{array}{r} 6 \\ -4 \\ \hline \end{array}$ $\begin{array}{r} 4 \\ +5 \\ \hline \end{array}$ $\begin{array}{r} 3 \\ +3 \\ \hline \end{array}$ $\begin{array}{r} 9 \\ -6 \\ \hline \end{array}$ $\begin{array}{r} 10 \\ +2 \\ \hline \end{array}$

Problem Solving

Write a number sentence. Solve.

3. Martin has 5 stickers.
   Josh gives him 6 more.
   How many stickers
   does he have?

   _____ stickers

4. Ellen has 11 marbles.
   She gives 6 to her brother.
   How many marbles
   are left?

   _____ marbles

Test Prep

Fill in the ○ for the correct answer.

Choose the fraction for the shaded part shown.

5.

   $\frac{1}{3}$ ○ $\frac{1}{5}$ ○ $\frac{1}{4}$ ○

6.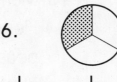

   $\frac{1}{3}$ ○ $\frac{1}{5}$ ○ $\frac{1}{4}$ ○

7.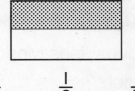

   $\frac{1}{3}$ ○ $\frac{1}{2}$ ○ $\frac{1}{4}$ ○

Notes for Home Your child reviewed adding 1, 2, and 3 and subtracting 1 and 2; and identifying fractions.
Home Activity: Ask your child to explain how he or she determined the fraction for the shaded parts shown in
Exercises 5 – 7.

Relate Addition and Subtraction

Add or subtract. You can use ⬭ ▨ .

1.
$$3 \quad\quad 7$$
$$\underline{+4} \quad \underline{-3}$$
$$7$$

2.
$$5 \quad\quad 11$$
$$\underline{+6} \quad \underline{-5}$$

3.
$$6 \quad\quad 9$$
$$\underline{+3} \quad \underline{-3}$$

4.
$$7 \quad\quad 12$$
$$\underline{+5} \quad \underline{-5}$$

5.
$$4 \quad\quad 5$$
$$\underline{+1} \quad \underline{-1}$$

6.
$$2 \quad\quad 7$$
$$\underline{+5} \quad \underline{-5}$$

7.
$$4 \quad\quad 9$$
$$\underline{+5} \quad \underline{-5}$$

8.
$$6 \quad\quad 10$$
$$\underline{+4} \quad \underline{-4}$$

9. $3 + 7 = $ _____ $\quad\quad$ $10 - 7 = $ _____

10. $6 + 1 = $ _____ $\quad\quad$ $7 - 1 = $ _____

11. $6 + 3 = $ _____ $\quad\quad$ $9 - 3 = $ _____

Problem Solving
Solve.

12. Mark had 5 peas on his plate. He took 7 more. How many peas does Mark have on his plate?

_____ peas

13. Mark had 12 peas on his plate. He ate 7 peas. How many peas does Mark have on his plate?

_____ peas

Notes for Home Your child used addition facts to help solve subtraction facts. *Home Activity:* Ask your child to explain how he or she can use the fact 3 + 4 = 7 to find 7 - 3 and 7 - 4. (Possible answer: since 3 + 4 = 7, I can subtract either 3 or 4 from 7 and get the other number for the answer.)

Fact Families

Complete the fact family. You can use ⬚ .

1. $3 + \underline{7} = \underline{}$ $\underline{10} - \underline{3} = \underline{}$

   $\underline{7} + \underline{3} = \underline{}$ $\underline{10} - \underline{7} = \underline{}$

2. $5 + \underline{} = \underline{11}$ $\underline{} - \underline{} = \underline{}$

   $\underline{} + \underline{} = \underline{}$ $\underline{} - \underline{} = \underline{}$

Write your own fact family. Draw a picture to go with it.

3.

$\underline{} + \underline{} = \underline{}$ $\underline{} - \underline{} = \underline{}$

$\underline{} + \underline{} = \underline{}$ $\underline{} - \underline{} = \underline{}$

Problem Solving Critical Thinking

4. There are 7 ladybugs.

   6 bees join them.

   How many ladybugs are there? _____

Notes for Home Your child wrote number sentences to show the number relationships in addition and subtraction. *Home Activity:* Ask your child to use objects such as 5 dry beans and 6 dry macaroni to show the four related number sentences for 5 + 6, 6 + 5, 11 − 5, and 11 − 6.

Think Addition to Subtract

Use addition to help you subtract.

1.

$$10 - 6 = \boxed{4}$$

$$6 + \boxed{4} = 10$$

2.

$$9 - 3 = \boxed{}$$

$$3 + \boxed{} = 9$$

Mixed Practice Add or subtract.
Draw lines to match related facts.

3.

$$3 + 8 \quad 3 + 6 \quad 7 + 4$$

$$11 - 4 \quad 11 - 3 \quad 9 - 6$$

4.

$$2 + 9 \quad 4 + 3 \quad 7 + 1$$

$$7 - 3 \quad 8 - 1 \quad 11 - 9$$

Problem Solving Critical Thinking

Solve the riddle.

Write your own riddle.

5. First double me.
   Then subtract 4.
   You will get 8.
   What number am I? _____

6. _____
   _____
   _____

Notes for Home Your child used addition to check subtraction. *Home Activity:* Write a subtraction sentence such as 11 − 6 = ____. Ask your child to write the answer, then write an addition fact that can help check the subtraction. (Answers may include: 5 + 6 = 11 and 6 + 5 = 11.)

Name _____

Fact Families for 10

Practice 6-9

Complete the fact family for 10.

1.

3 + ___ = ___   ___ − ___ = ___

___ + ___ = ___   ___ − ___ = ___

Mixed Practice Add or subtract.

Draw lines to match related facts.

3.
$$2 + 7$$ $$4 + 6$$ $$7 + 4$$

$$11 - 4$$ $$10 - 4$$ $$9 - 7$$

4.
$$2 + 10$$ $$3 + 6$$ $$6 + 1$$

$$9 - 6$$ $$7 - 1$$ $$12 - 2$$

Problem Solving Visual Thinking

5. There are 7 in all.

How many are in the water?

_____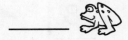

Notes for Home Your child added and subtracted with 10. *Home Activity:* Show your child 10 small objects, such as paper clips. Cover 7 of them. Have your child say an addition and a subtraction sentence to tell about the objects. (Answers may include: 7 + 3 = 10, 3 + 7 = 10, 10 − 7 = 3.)

Problem Solving: Guess and Check

Use ⬭ ⬯.

Guess. Then check to find the answer.

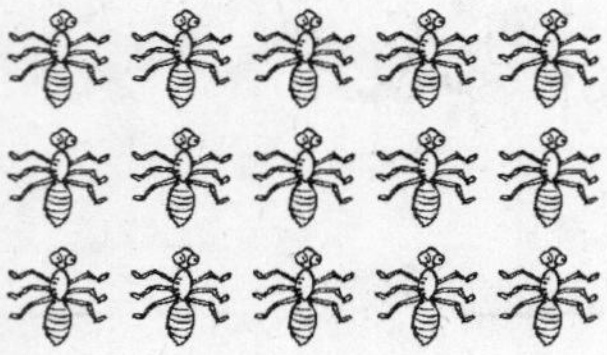

1. Try _____ $6 + \underline{\hspace{1cm}} = \underline{\hspace{1cm}}$

   Try _____ $6 + \underline{\hspace{1cm}} = \underline{\hspace{1cm}}$

15 in all

2. Try _____ $5 + \underline{\hspace{1cm}} = \underline{\hspace{1cm}}$

   Try _____ $5 + \underline{\hspace{1cm}} = \underline{\hspace{1cm}}$

9 in all

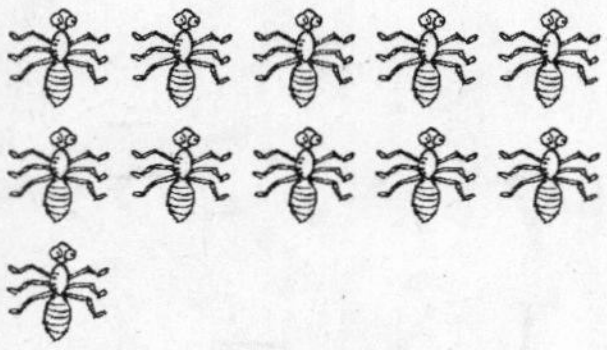

3. Try _____ $9 + \underline{\hspace{1cm}} = \underline{\hspace{1cm}}$

   Try _____ $9 + \underline{\hspace{1cm}} = \underline{\hspace{1cm}}$

11 in all

Mental Math

4. Circle numbers that are odd numbers less than 16.

| 12 | 15 | 17 | 14 |

| 3 | 10 | 4 | 1 | 8 |

| 9 | 6 | 7 | 11 |

Notes for Home Your child solved addition and subtraction problems by using the Guess and Check strategy.
Home Activity: Ask your child to find the even numbers in the Mental Math activity. (4, 6, 8, 10, 12, 14)

Name _____

Mixed Practice: Lessons 6–10

Use . Complete the fact family.

1.

$4 + $ _____ $ = $ _____   _____ $ - $ _____ $ = $ _____

_____ $ + $ _____ $ = $ _____   _____ $ - $ _____ $ = $ _____

Add or subtract.

2.
$$\begin{array}{cc} 4 \\ +2 \\ \hline \end{array} \qquad \begin{array}{cc} 9 \\ +3 \\ \hline \end{array} \qquad \begin{array}{cc} 5 \\ -5 \\ \hline \end{array} \qquad \begin{array}{cc} 12 \\ -8 \\ \hline \end{array} \qquad \begin{array}{cc} 2 \\ +7 \\ \hline \end{array} \qquad \begin{array}{cc} 9 \\ -8 \\ \hline \end{array}$$

3.
$$\begin{array}{cc} 2 \\ +2 \\ \hline \end{array} \qquad \begin{array}{cc} 6 \\ +2 \\ \hline \end{array} \qquad \begin{array}{cc} 12 \\ -3 \\ \hline \end{array} \qquad \begin{array}{cc} 5 \\ +6 \\ \hline \end{array} \qquad \begin{array}{cc} 9 \\ -2 \\ \hline \end{array} \qquad \begin{array}{cc} 6 \\ -5 \\ \hline \end{array}$$

Problem Solving

4. Guess. Then check to find the answer. You can use ⬭ ⬭ .

	Guess	Check
	Try _____	$7 + $ _____ $ = $ _____
12 in all	Try _____	$7 + $ _____ $ = $ _____

Journal

5. Take a total of 9 in two colors. Draw a picture of the cubes.
   Write the fact family.

Notes for Home Your child practiced addition and subtraction facts through 12 and problem solving.
Home Activity: Ask your child to make up one addition and one subtraction problem for you to solve.
Work together to check your answers.

Cumulative Review

Add or subtract.

1. $8 + 3$ $8 - 5$ $7 + 0$ $4 + 5$ $3 + 5$ $4 + 4$ $10 - 2$

2. $5 - 1$ $6 + 4$ $6 - 4$ $5 + 2$ $3 - 0$ $9 - 5$ $3 + 7$

3. $7 + 4 =$ ___ $11 - 8 =$ ___ $12 - 4 =$ ___

Problem Solving

Write a number sentence.

4. Frank has 8 marbles.
   Martha gives him 4 more.
   How many does Frank have now?

5. Alice had 6 books.
   She gave away 2.
   How many are left?

_____   _____

Test Prep

Fill in the ○ for the correct answer.

6. Which shows a circle and a triangle?

○   ○   ○   ○

Notes for Home Your child reviewed addition and subtraction, writing number sentences, and identifying shapes.
Home Activity: Ask your child to tell you how he or she found the answer to Exercise 4.

Numbers to 19

Write the numbers.

1. 17 seventeen

___10___ and ___7___ is ___17___.

2. 13 thirteen

___10___ and _____ is _____.

3. 11 eleven

___10___ and _____ is _____.

4. 19 nineteen

___10___ and _____ is _____.

5. 15 fifteen

___10___ and _____ is _____.

6. 12 twelve

___10___ and _____ is _____.

7. 16 sixteen

___10___ and _____ is _____.

8. 14 fourteen

___10___ and _____ is _____.

Problem Solving

9. These are José's trucks.

Tell how you found how many he has.

Notes for Home Your child wrote numbers 11–19 as 10 and ones. *Home Activity:* Ask your child to complete this sentence for 19: ____ and ____ is ____. (10 and 9 is 19.)

Name _____

Tens

Write the number.

1. 20 and 10 is .

2. 40 and 10 is _____.

3. 30 and 10 is _____.

4. 60 and 10 is _____.

5. 70 and 10 is _____.

6. 80 and 10 is _____.

Each  has 10  . How many in all?

7. _____

8. _____

9. _____

10. _____

Problem Solving

11. This is one page in Scott's picture book.

    How many photos are on 6 pages? _____ photos

Notes for Home Your child counted groups of 10. *Home Activity:* Ask your child "How many 10s are in 50?" (5)

Numbers to 60

Circle groups of 10. Write the numbers.

1. ☆☆☆☆☆☆☆☆☆☆☆☆
☆☆☆☆☆☆☆☆☆☆☆☆
☆☆☆☆☆☆☆☆☆☆☆☆
☆☆☆☆☆☆☆☆☆☆☆

_____ tens and _____ extra is _____.

2. **Write your own** problem.

Draw a lot of things.

Circle groups of 10. Write the numbers.

_____ tens and _____ extra is _____.

Estimation

3. About how many are in the middle bowl?

Circle the number.

20   40   10

 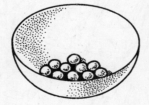 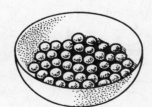

4. Why do you think so?

Notes for Home Your child put things into groups of ten and wrote the number. *Home Activity:* Have your child count a handful of pennies by putting them in groups of 10.

Explore Estimation

Take a lot of counters. Do not count yet.

Estimate how many there are.

Let your partner count how many.

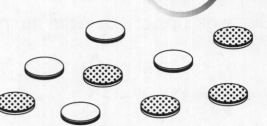

	Estimate.	Draw. Circle tens.	How many in all?
1.			
2.			
3.			

Journal

4. Look at cars in a parking lot.

   About how many cars are in the lot?

Notes for Home Your child worked with another child to estimate an amount and to check how good the estimate was. *Home Activity:* While in the grocery store, ask your child to count 10 cans on a shelf. Then ask him or her to estimate how many cans there are on the whole shelf.

Estimation

Estimate how many. Circle the number.

1.

about   10   30   50

2.

about   20   40   60

3. **Write your own** problem.
   Draw some things.
   Ask a friend to estimate
   how many.

Mental Math

Solve.

4. Chelsea has 40 stickers on one page.
   She also has 10 stickers on another page.
   How many stickers does she have on both pages? _____

Problem Solving:
Use Data from a Graph

This graph shows how many paper apples the children have made.

Paper Apples We Made			
Sean	Della	Perry	Patty

Read the graph.

1. Patty made 13 paper apples.
   Complete the graph to show this.

2. Who has more apples than Perry? _____

3. How many more apples does Della have than Perry? _____

4. How many more apples does Sean need to have 30? _____

Tell a Math Story

5. Make up your own math story about paper apples.
   Tell it to a friend.

Notes for Home Your child practiced using a graph to find information. *Home Activity:* Ask your child to use the graph to answer "*Who has the most apples?*" (Della)

Name _____

Mixed Practice: Lessons 1-6

Write the number.

1. 10 and 6 is _____.

2. 10 and 9 is _____.

3. 40 and 10 is _____.

4. 30 and 10 is _____.

5. Estimate how many. Circle the number.

about   10   20   40

Problem Solving

Read the graph.

Seashells collected	
Jennifer	🐚🐚🐚🐚 🐚🐚🐚🐚🐚 🐚🐚🐚🐚 🐚🐚🐚🐚 🐚🐚🐚🐚🐚 🐚🐚🐚🐚
Bart	🐚🐚🐚🐚🐚 🐚🐚🐚🐚🐚 🐚🐚🐚🐚🐚 🐚🐚🐚🐚🐚 🐚🐚🐚🐚🐚 🐚🐚🐚🐚🐚 🐚

---

6. How many does Jennifer have? _____

Journal

7. What are some things you might count by tens? Why?

Notes for Home Your child practiced counting groups of numbers to 60. *Home Activity:* Ask your child to tell how many toes three people have in all. (30)

Cumulative Review

1. Circle the one that comes next in this pattern.

Problem Solving

Write the number sentence.

2. I had 9 stamps.

    I got 3 more.

    How many do I have now?

    _____ + _____ = _____

3. Nell had 7 cards.

    She gave away 3.

    How many are left?

    _____ − _____ = _____

Test Prep

Fill in the ○ for the correct answer.

4. How many ◯ ?

    ○   ○   ○   ○
    3   4   5   6

5. How many △ ?

    ○   ○   ○   ○
    3   4   5   6

Notes for Home Your child reviewed concepts taught in Chapters 1-7. *Home Activity:* Ask your child to tell you how he or she solved Exercise 3.

Count by 2s and 10s

1. How many fingers? Count by 10s.

<u>10</u> <u>___</u> <u>___</u> <u>40</u> <u>___</u> <u>___</u> <u>___</u>

2. Count by 10s. You can use a 🖩.

Press	Display
	0
+ 1 0 =	
+ 1 0 =	
+ 1 0 =	

Press	Display
+ 1 0 =	
+ 1 0 =	
+ 1 0 =	
+ 1 0 =	

Problem Solving Patterns

Use a 🖩. Press the buttons shown below.

3. Count by 2s.

+ 2 = = =

4. Count by 10s.

+ 1 0 = = =

5. What happens each time you press = ?

_____

_____

Notes for Home Your child counted by 2s and 10s. *Home Activity:* Ask your child to count how many ears there are in your family.

Name _____

Count by 2s, 5s, and 10s

Count by 5s.

1. 10, 15, 20, _____, _____, _____, _____, 45

2. 35, _____, _____, _____, 55, _____, 65, _____

3. 55, 60, _____, _____, 75, 80, _____, _____

Count by 2s.

4. 10, 12, _____, _____, 18, _____, 22, _____

5. 46, 48, 50, _____, _____, _____, _____, 60

6. 72, 74, _____, 78, 80, 82, _____, _____

Count by 10s.

7. 30, _____, 50, _____, _____, _____

Write your own counting pattern.

8. _____, _____, _____, _____, _____, _____

Problem Solving Visual Thinking

9. Look at the picture.
   Count by 10s.
   How many muffins
   will be baked?

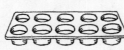

   _____ muffins

Notes for Home Your child practiced counting by 10s, 5s, and 2s. *Home Activity:* Ask your child to count by 2s from 8 to 20. (8, 10, 12, 14, 16, 18, 20)

Ordinals

1. Color the shelves.

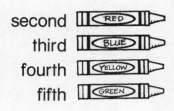

second ▯▯▯ RED
third ▯▯▯ BLUE
fourth ▯▯▯ YELLOW
fifth ▯▯▯ GREEN

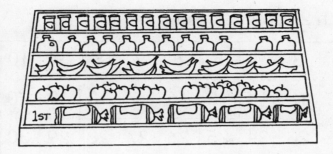

2. Color the cars.

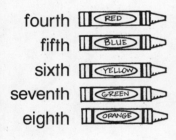

fourth ▯▯▯ RED
fifth ▯▯▯ BLUE
sixth ▯▯▯ YELLOW
seventh ▯▯▯ GREEN
eighth ▯▯▯ ORANGE

Problem Solving Visual Thinking

3. How many cars are in this tunnel?

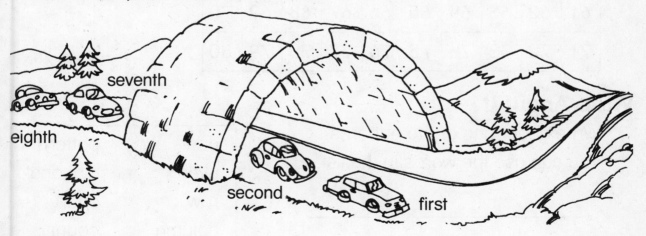

Write how many. _____

Notes for Home Your child used number words from *first* through *tenth* to identify position. *Home Activity:* Ask your child to arrange 5 things in a line and show you the ones that are first, third, and fifth.

Problem Solving: Look for a Pattern

Color the charts to continue the pattern.

1. Start with 2. Count by 2s.

1	2	3	4	5	6	7	8	9	10
11	12	13	14	15	16	17	18	19	20
21	22	23	24	25	26	27	28	29	30

2. Start with 10. Count by 10s.

1	2	3	4	5	6	7	8	9	10
11	12	13	14	15	16	17	18	19	20
21	22	23	24	25	26	27	28	29	30
31	32	33	34	35	36	37	38	39	40
41	42	43	44	45	46	47	48	49	50
51	52	53	54	55	56	57	58	59	60
61	62	63	64	65	66	67	68	69	70
71	72	73	74	75	76	77	78	79	80

Write About It

3. Write about one of the patterns.
   You can use the words in the list.

odd	pattern
even	diagonal
row	chart
column	count

_____

_____

Notes for Home Your child continued patterns on a chart. *Home Activity:* Ask your child to tell you which numbers he or she would color if each chart had another row. (32, 34, 36, 38, 40; 90)

Mixed Practice: Lessons 7-10

1. Count by 2s.   6, _____, _____, 12, _____, _____, 18, _____

2. Count by 5s.   10, 15, 20, _____, _____, _____, _____, 45

3. Count by 10s.   20, _____, 40, _____, _____, _____

4. Color the tops.

   fifth   ▭ blue ▷

   sixth   ▭ orange ▷

   seventh ▭ yellow ▷

Problem Solving

5. Color to continue the pattern.

1	2	3	4	5	6	7	8	9	10
11	12	13	14	15	16	17	18	19	20
21	22	23	24	25	26	27	28	29	30
31	32	33	34	35	36	37	38	39	40
41	42	43	44	45	46	47	48	49	50
51	52	53	54	55	56	57	58	59	60

Journal

6. Write about how you count by 2s, 5s, or 10s to find
   how much money is in a pile of nickels and dimes.

Notes for Home Your child practiced counting by 2s, 5s, and 10s, and matching numbers to positions in line.
Home Activity: Ask your child to count aloud by 2s from 10 to 30. (10, 12, 14, 16, 18, 20, 22, 24, 26, 28, 30)

Cumulative Review

Count on to add.

1. $8 + 2 =$ _____ $4 + 8 =$ _____ $6 + 3 =$ _____

2.
$$\begin{array}{cccccc} 8 & 3 & 5 & 10 & 5 & 4 & 1 \\ +1 & +7 & +4 & +2 & +3 & +2 & +9 \end{array}$$

---

3. Draw 3 more 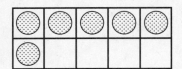.
   Write the sum.

   $6 + 3 =$ _____

4. Cross out 3 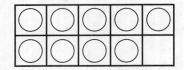.
   Write the difference.

   $9 - 3 =$ _____

Test Prep

Fill in the ○ for the correct answer.

Add or subtract.

5.
$$\begin{array}{r} 10 \\ +0 \\ \hline \end{array}$$

   ○   ○   ○   ○
   7   8   9   10

6. $7 - 0 =$ _____

   ○   ○   ○   ○
   7   8   9   10

Notes for Home Your child reviewed basic addition and subtraction facts. *Home Activity:* Ask you child to explain how he or she used a ten frame to solve Exercise 3.

Name _____

Explore Tens and Ones

Use [○] and [tens | ones].

Take a lot of [○].

Use the [tens | ones] to help make train of 10 [○].
Record how many tens and ones.

1.
tens	ones

2.
tens	ones

3.
tens	ones

4.
tens	ones

5.
tens	ones

6.
tens	ones

Journal

Draw something that has more than 10 parts or pieces.

Write how many tens and ones.

Notes for Home Your child used snap cubes to make groups of tens and ones and recorded the number of tens and ones. *Home Activity:* Have your child use between 10 and 19 pennies to show you how to make a group of ten and ones.

Name _____

Tens and Ones to 60

Use 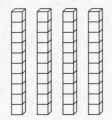 and ⊞ .

Count how many tens and ones. Write the number.

1.

tens	ones
4	5

___

2.

tens	ones

___

Write your own example. Show with ▭ ▯ .

3.

tens	ones

___

4.

tens	ones

___

Problem Solving

5. Solve.

Sam has 34 carrots.

He buys 10 more.

How many does he have now?

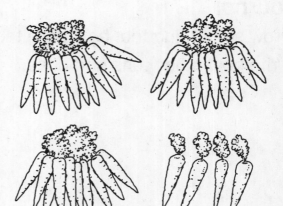

 ___

Notes for Home Your child modeled tens, then wrote the number. *Home Activity:* Have your child use objects such as pencils to represent tens and paper clips to represent ones to solve problems such as "*Ana has 25 stickers. She buys 10 more. How many does she have now?*" (25 + 10 = 35 stickers)

Numbers More than Ten

How many tens and ones? Write the number.

1.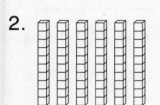

tens	ones
8	7

_____

2.

tens	ones

_____

3.

tens	ones

_____

4.

tens	ones

_____

5.

tens	ones

_____

Problem Solving Critical Thinking

What are some ways you can show 80 using ▭ ▱ ?

Notes for Home Your child used place-value blocks and wrote numbers up to 99. *Home Activity:* Find page numbers up to 99 in a book, and as you point to different pages, ask your child to tell you the number of tens and ones.

Name _____

Estimation

Estimate.   Count.

Make groups of 10.   Write the number.

1.

tens	ones

About   50   70   90

_____

2.

tens	ones

About   50   70   90

_____

Problem Solving Visual Thinking

3. About how many 🌀 are in Sue's bowl?

Circle your estimate.

less than 30

more than 30

10

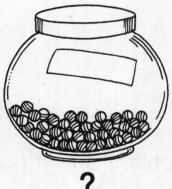

?

Notes for Home Your child estimated the number of objects in a large group by looking for groups of 10. *Home Activity:* Ask your child to estimate the number of books on a shelf or in a bookcase, or the number of glasses in a kitchen cabinet.

Name _____

10 Ones Make 1 Ten

Use ▭▭▭▭▭▭▭▭▭▭ ▭

and | tens | ones |
|---|---|

Show this many.

	Add 2 more. Do you need to make a trade? Circle yes or no.	Write how many tens and ones.
1. 4 tens 6 ones	yes no	**tens** / **ones** 4 / 8
2. 6 tens 9 ones	yes no	tens / ones
3. 9 tens 0 ones	yes no	tens / ones
4. 8 tens 8 ones	yes no	tens / ones

Problem Solving Estimate

4. Jake has these blocks.
   He needs 80. About how
   many more does he need?

   _____

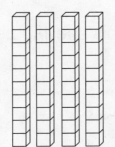

Notes for Home Your child traded 10 ones for 1 ten. *Home Activity:* Have your child explain how he or she solved Exercise 4. Then ask if a trade would be needed if 1 one were added to 8 tens and 8 ones, and to explain why or why not. (No, you would have 8 tens and 9 ones, and you do not trade 9 ones for 1 ten.)

Problem Solving: Use Objects

Use ⬚⬚⬚⬚⬚⬚⬚⬚ ⬚ and

tens	ones

Trade if you need to.

1. The Blues won these points in the spelling bee.

   What is their final score?

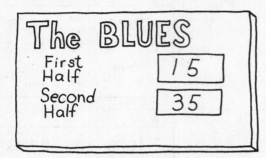

The BLUES
First Half   15
Second Half   35

tens	ones
5	0

Final score: _____

2. The Reds won these points in the spelling bee.

   What is their final score?

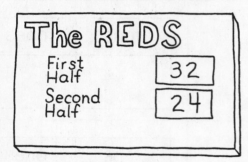

The REDS
First Half   32
Second Half   24

Final score: _____

3. Look at the team's scores.

   Circle the team that won the spelling bee.   The Blues   The Reds

Tell a Math Story

Tell a math story about this spelling bee.

How will it end?

Which team will win?

What will the final score be?

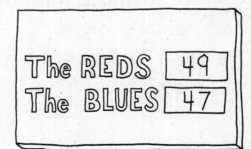

The REDS   49
The BLUES   47

Notes for Home Your child solved problems using place-value blocks. *Home Activity:* Point to the results of some game scores in a newspaper. Ask your child to tell who won each game and to explain how they know. (Possible answer: The Knicks won. They had 9 tens and 6 ones. The other team had 8 tens and 9 ones.)

Name _____

Mixed Practice: Lessons 1–6

Write the number.

1. Estimate how many. Make groups of 10.

About   **30   50   70**   _____ tens   _____ ones

---

2. Count how many.	Add 2 more. Do you need to make a trade? Circle yes or no.	Write how many tens and ones.
	yes no	tens | ones

Problem Solving

Use  . Trade if you need to.

3. What is the Honey Bees final score?

The HONEY BEES
First Half 31
Second Half 19

Final Score: _____

Journal

Draw a picture that shows 2 tens and 7 ones.

Write the number.

Notes for Home Your child practiced estimating, counting numbers to 99, and problem solving. *Home Activity:* Have your child look for numbers displayed on products in your home. Ask your child to explain what the numbers show. (Answer might include the dates of a month on a calendar, weights on food packaging, etc.)

Cumulative Review

Complete the fact family.

1. $8 + 3 =$ _____

$3 + 8 =$ _____

$11 - 8 =$ _____

$11 - 3 =$ _____

2. $6 + 7 =$ _____

$7 + 6 =$ _____

$13 - 6 =$ _____

$13 - 7 =$ _____

Write a number sentence.

3. 12 children played tag.
3 left to play ball.
How many play tag now?

_____

4. Maya found 7 shells.
Ellie found 5 shells.
How many shells do they
have all together?

_____

Test Prep

Fill in the ○ for the correct answer.
Do the parts match when you fold on the line?

7.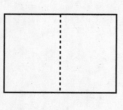

○ yes   ○ no

8.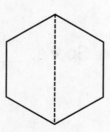

○ yes   ○ no

9.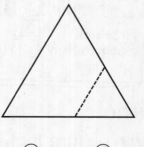

○ yes   ○ no

Notes for Home Your child reviewed fact families and finding shapes with parts that match. *Home Activity:* Ask your child to use objects such as pennies to model an addition and a subtraction problem on the page.

Compare Numbers

Use ⟨▭▭▭▭▭▭▭⟩ ▱ and | tens | ones | .

Write the tens and ones. Circle the number that is less.

1. 73 __7__ tens __3__ ones

   48 __4__ tens __8__ ones

2. 24 ____ tens ____ ones

   49 ____ tens ____ ones

3. 56 ____ tens ____ ones

   85 ____ tens ____ ones

4. 90 ____ tens ____ ones

   67 ____ tens ____ ones

5. 36 ____ tens ____ ones

   63 ____ tens ____ ones

6. 17 ____ tens ____ ones

   71 ____ tens ____ ones

Write your own numbers. Circle the number that is less.

7. ____ ____ tens ____ones

   ____ ____ tens ____ones

8. ____ ____ tens ____ones

   ____ ____ tens ____ones

Problem Solving Visual Thinking

Circle the one that is less.

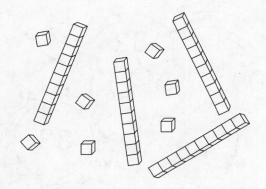
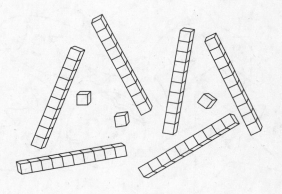

Notes for Home Your child compared two numbers to tell which is less. *Home Activity:* Show your child two page numbers from a newspaper. Ask him or her to tell you which number is less.

Order Numbers to 100

Write the number that comes after.

1. 82 _____

2. 39 _____

3. 71 _____

4. 68 _____

5. 42 _____

6. 94 _____

Write the numbers that come before.

7. _____ 20

8. _____ 57

9. _____ 88

10. _____ 65

11. _____ 42

12. _____ 79

Write the numbers that come between.

13. 68, _____, _____, 71

14. 87, _____, _____, 90

15. 49, _____, _____, 52

16. 75, 76, _____, _____, 79

Problem Solving Critical Thinking

17. Al picked three of these stickers.
    They were odd numbers between 77 and 85.
    Circle the stickers he picked.

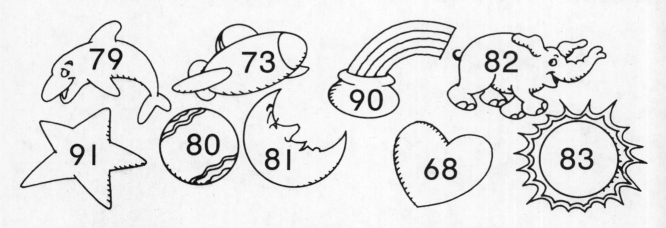

Notes for Home Your child learned about numbers that come before, after, and between. *Home Activity:* Point to different page numbers in a newspaper or magazine and ask your child to tell you the numbers before and after.

Name _____

Patterns on the 100 Chart

Write the missing numbers.

1.

37	38	39
	48	49

2.

21	22	23
31	32	33

3.

	82	83
91		

4.

		54	55
	63	64	65

5.

11	12	
	22	

6.

64	65		
	75		77

7.

	46	
55	56	

8.

	78	79	
87			

Problem Solving Patterns

9. What comes next?

Circle the next shape in the pattern.

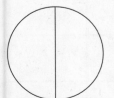  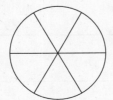  

Notes for Home Your child used the patterns in a 100 chart to help find missing numbers. *Home Activity:* Ask your child to write 3 numbers to extend the following pattern: 5, 10, 15. (20, 25, 30)

Name _____

Problem Solving:
Collect and Use Data

1. Put your name where it belongs.

   Ask 6 friends to put their names in the circles.

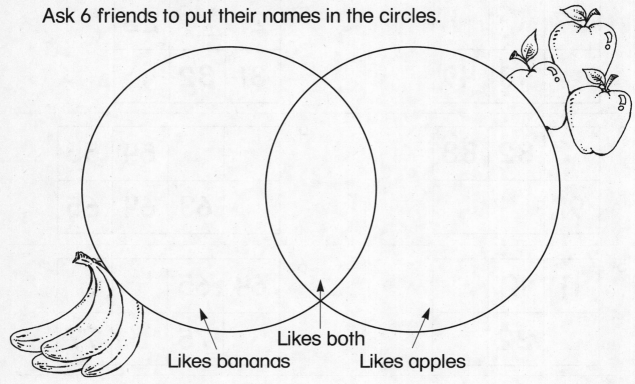

Likes both

Likes bananas   Likes apples

Write About It

2. Which children put their names in the left circle?

   _____

3. What do you know about the children whose names belong in both circles?

   _____

   _____

Notes for Home Your child made a diagram and answered questions about it. *Home Activity:* Have your child explain the diagram to you and other family members, and ask them to put their names in the circles where they belong.

Name _____

Mixed Practice: Lessons 7 - 10

1. Write the missing numbers.

71	72				76				80
		84	85				88		
91						97			100

Write the missing numbers.

2. 45, 46, _____   3. 29, _____, 31   4. _____, 50, 51

5. 92, _____, 94   6. _____, 61, 62   7. 18, 19, _____

Problem Solving

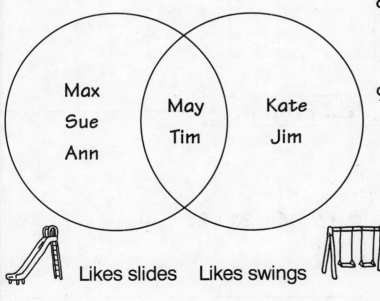

Max
Sue
Ann

May
Tim

Kate
Jim

Likes slides   Likes swings

8. How many children like swings? _____

9. Who likes both slides and swings? _____

Journal

Which is greater, 69 or 72? How do you know?

Notes for Home Your child practiced using numbers to 99 and reading a diagram to solve problems.
Home Activity: Ask your child to tell you whether more children like swings or slides. (More children like slides.)

Cumulative Review

Subtract.

1.
$$6 \atop +4$$
$$10 \atop -4$$

2.
$$12 \atop -5$$
$$7 \atop +5$$

3.
$$5 \atop +6$$
$$11 \atop -6$$

4. $3 + 4 =$ ___   5. $1 + 11 =$ ___   6. $8 + 4 =$ ___

$7 - 4 =$ ___ $12 - 1 =$ ___ $12 - 4 =$ ___

Problem Solving

7. Circle the shape that shows $\frac{1}{3}$.

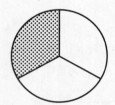 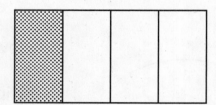

Test Prep

What number comes next?

Fill in ○ for the correct answer.

8. 3   6   9   12 ____   ○ 15

                          ○ 13

9. 15   20   25   30 ____   ○ 32

                            ○ 35

Notes for Home Your child reviewed basic addition and subtraction facts, problem solving, and skip counting.
Home Activity: Ask your child to find something in the kitchen that he or she can count by 2s.

Nickels and Pennies

Circle the coins you need.

1.

2.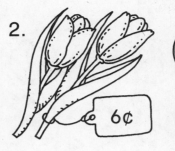

3.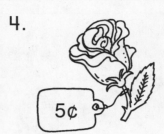

4.

5.

Problem Solving Patterns

6. Is there enough money to buy the apples?   Yes

   Count the nickels by 5s.

   Circle Yes or No.   No

 5¢ 10¢ 15¢ ___ ___

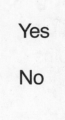

Notes for Home Your child practiced counting groups of nickels and pennies. *Home Activity:* Ask your child to show you how to make 9¢ with pennies, and then with nickels and pennies. (9 pennies, and 1 nickel and 4 pennies)

Dimes and Pennies

Circle the coins you need.

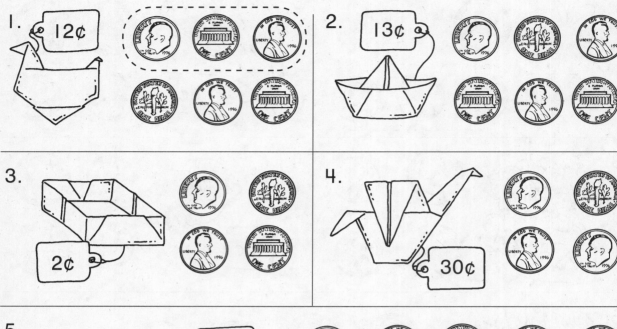

1. 12¢

2. 13¢

3. 2¢

4. 30¢

5. 16¢

Problem Solving Critical Thinking

6. Mia has one coin.
Sam has 6 coins.
Each has 10¢.
What coins do
they have?
Draw their coins.

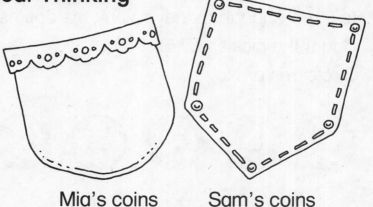

Mia's coins   Sam's coins

Notes for Home Your child practiced counting groups of dimes and pennies. *Home Activity:* Using dimes and pennies, ask your child to show you how to make 15¢. (1 dime and 5 pennies)

128 Use with pages 335–336.

Dimes, Nickels, and Pennies

Count. Write the amount.

1.   22 ¢

__5__, __10__, _____, _____, _____, _____

2.   _____ ¢

_____, _____, _____, _____, _____, _____

3.   _____ ¢

_____, _____, _____, _____, _____, _____

Problem Solving

4. Who has more money?
   Write the amount each child has.
   Circle the amount that is more.

_____   _____

Count Mixed Coins

Circle the coins you need.

1.

2.

3.

4.

Mental Math

5. Juan bought a present.
   It cost more than 2 dimes
   but less than 6 nickels.
   Circle what Juan bought.

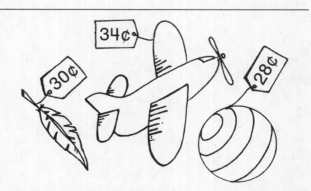

Notes for Home Your child decided which coins are needed to buy an item. *Home Activity:* Ask your child to show you how he or she counted the coins in Exercise 4. (10¢, 20¢, 25¢, 30¢, 35¢, 36¢)

130 Use with pages 341–342.

Problem Solving:
Use Data from a Picture

Use the picture of items at a yard sale. Count the money.
Write the amount. Circle the item you can buy.

1. You have

$$\underline{32}¢$$

 or

 or

2. You have

_____¢

 or

 or

Write About It

3. Choose one thing to buy at
   the yard sale. Circle it.
   Draw the coins you can use.

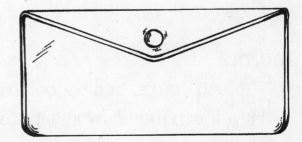

Notes for Home Your child practiced solving problems using information in a picture. *Home Activity:* With your child, look at the prices on grocery items that cost less than 50¢. Ask your child how many dimes, nickels, and pennies he or she would need to buy each one.

Name _____

Mixed Practice: Lessons 1–5

Count the money. Write the amount.

1.   _18_ ¢

   _5_ , _10_ , _15_ , _16_ , _17_ , _18_

2.   _____ ¢

   _____ , _____ , _____ , _____ , _____ , _____

Problem Solving

3. Count your money. Write the amount.

   _____ ¢

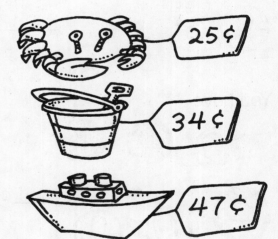

25¢

34¢

47¢

Circle what you can buy.

Journal

4. Pretend you go to a school fair. What would you buy?
   How much money would it cost?

Notes for Home Your child practiced counting groups of dimes, nickels, and pennies. *Home Activity:* Arrange an assortment of dimes, nickels, and pennies on a table. Ask your child to use some of the coins to show you how to sort and count them.

Name _____

Cumulative Review

Write the number.

1. _____

2. _____

Add or Subtract.

3.

$$\begin{array}{c} 4 \\ +6 \end{array} \qquad \begin{array}{c} 3 \\ -2 \end{array} \qquad \begin{array}{c} 12 \\ -9 \end{array} \qquad \begin{array}{c} 5 \\ +7 \end{array} \qquad \begin{array}{c} 9 \\ -6 \end{array} \qquad \begin{array}{c} 8 \\ +0 \end{array} \qquad \begin{array}{c} 10 \\ -7 \end{array}$$

Problem Solving

Complete the number sentence.

4. Jamie made 12 snacks.
   He gave 3 to Ben.
   How many snacks are left?

   $12 - \_\_\_ = \_\_\_$

5. Sarah baked four pies.
   Then she baked 7 pies.
   How many pies did she bake?

   $4 + \_\_\_ = \_\_\_$

Test Prep

Fill in the ○ for the correct answer.

6. Which number is less
   than 32?

   ○   ○   ○   ○
   38   63   35   23

7. Which number is greater
   than 89?

   ○   ○   ○   ○
   39   88   94   72

Notes for Home Your child reviewed counting to 50, using addition and subtraction, and comparing numbers.
Home Activity: Ask your child to name another number that is less than 32 and another that is greater than 89.

Explore Quarters

10,   20,   21,   22,   23,   24,   25   25¢

Circle the coins that show 25¢.

1.

2.

3.

Problem Solving

4. You have 25¢ to spend.

   You have 4 coins.

   Draw the coins you have.

Notes for Home Your child practiced counting groups of coins that equal 25¢. *Home Activity:* Give your child 2 dimes, 5 nickels, and 5 pennies. Ask him or her to show you different ways to make 25¢.

Name _____

Quarter, Dimes, Nickels, and Pennies

Count the money. Write the amount.

1.

25, 35, 40, 45, 46, 47 _____ ¢

2.

_____, _____, _____, _____, _____ _____ ¢

3.

_____, _____, _____, _____, _____ _____ ¢

Problem Solving Critical Thinking

You have 30¢. Write what you can buy.

cherries	banana	apple	pear	watermelon

20¢	5¢	15¢	10¢	25¢

4. _____ and _____.

5. _____ and _____ and _____.

Notes for Home Your child counted mixed groups of coins. *Home Activity:* Ask your child to name 2 fruits he or she could buy and spend exactly one quarter. (grapes and banana, or apple and pear)

Problem Solving: Make a List

Susie gets 25¢ to spend at the zoo.

What coins might Susie get?

Use

to find all the ways to make 25¢.

Make a list.

Journal

What would you buy at the zoo

for 20¢ or 25¢?

Notes for Home Your child made a list of all the ways to make 25¢ with dimes, nickels, and pennies.
Home Activity: Ask your child to solve this riddle: *What coins do I use to make the same amount with 25 coins or 1 coin?* (25 pennies and 1 quarter)

Mixed Practice: Lessons 6–8

1. Circle the coins that show 30¢.

2. Count the money. Write the amount.

       _____ ¢

Problem Solving

3. Amy buys a toy for 25¢.

   She has no pennies.

   Find the ways she can pay 25¢.

   Make a list.

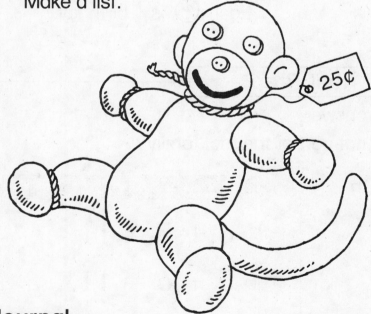

25¢

Journal

4. Do you think it is easier to pay for a toy
   with 25 pennies or 5 nickels? Why?

Notes for Home Your child practiced counting groups of coins and solving a problem by making a list.
Home Activity: Ask your child what is the fewest number of coins needed to buy something for 30¢. (1 quarter
and 1 nickel)

Cumulative Review

Add or subtract.

1.
$$9 + 3 \quad 10 - 3 \quad 12 - 6 \quad 7 + 7 \quad 5 + 4 \quad 11 - 7 \quad 8 - 5$$

Problem Solving

2. Read the graph.
   How many birthdays are

   in July? _____

   How many more birthdays
   does August need to

   match July? _____

Summer Birthdays	
June	☺☺☺☺☺☺☺☺
July	☺☺☺☺☺☺☺☺☺
August	☺☺☺☺☺☺

Each ☺ is 1 birthday.

Test Prep

Fill in the ○ for the correct answer.

Which number sentence is not part of the fact family?

3. ○ 7 + 2 = 9
   ○ 9 − 2 = 7
   ○ 9 + 2 = 11
   ○ 2 + 7 = 9

4. ○ 6 + 5 = 11
   ○ 5 + 6 = 11
   ○ 11 − 5 = 6
   ○ 6 − 5 = 1

Notes for Home Your child reviewed addition and subtraction facts, reading a graph, and finding facts in a fact family. *Home Activity:* Ask your child how many birthdays there are in the months of July and August. (15)

Explore Time

A clock shows time. Where can you see a clock?

Here are places you could see a clock.

Draw a clock you could see in each place.

in the kitchen		outside
in a bedroom	at home	in another room

Talk About It

Name three places you think a clock would be useful.

Explain your choices.

Notes for Home Your child talked about and drew pictures of clocks. *Home Activity:* Ask your child to point out clocks inside or outside the home.

Clocks

Write the time.

1.

_12__ o'clock

2.

_____ o'clock

3.

_____ o'clock

4.

_____ o'clock

5.

_____ o'clock

6.

_____ o'clock

Problem Solving Visual Thinking

Write the time.

7.

_____ o'clock

8.

_____ o'clock

9.

_____ o'clock

Notes for Home Your child read a clock and wrote the time to the hour. *Home Activity:* Ask your child to tell you the time on the next hour. What time will it be on the following hour?

Name _____

Write Time to the Hour

Match the clocks that show the same time.

1.

| 4:00 | 8:00 | 12:00 | 3:00 |

Write the time.

2.  3.  4.  5.

___:___   ___:___   ___:___   ___:___

Write About It

6. Write a note to someone that includes a time.

_____

_____

_____

Mom called.
She will
be home at 7:00.

Notes for Home Your child read and wrote time to the hour. *Home Activity:* Ask your child to write the time it is on the next hour and the time at the following hour.

Write Time to the Half Hour

Write the time.

1.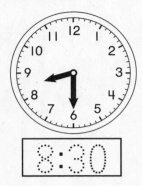

8:30

2.

☐ : ☐

3.

☐ : ☐

4.

☐ : ☐

5.

☐ : ☐

6.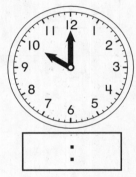

☐ : ☐

Problem Solving Visual Thinking

7. Complete the Saturday sports schedule.

Soccer

Baseball

Basketball

Hockey

Saturday Sports
____:_____ Soccer
____:_____ Baseball
____:_____ Basketball
____:_____ Hockey

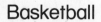

Notes for Home Your child read and wrote time to the half hour. *Home Activity:* Help your child write a schedule for a Saturday or Sunday afternoon. For example: clean room 1:30, pull weeds 3:00, shopping 3:30, visit family 4:00.

Tell Time

1.

☐ : ☐

☐ : ☐

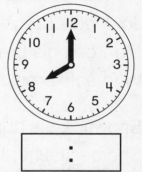

☐ : ☐

2.

☐ : ☐

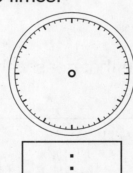

☐ : ☐

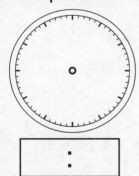

☐ : ☐

3. **Write your own** time problem.
Draw pictures. Write the times.

☐ : ☐   ☐ : ☐   ☐ : ☐

Problem Solving

Solve.

4. At school, lunch starts at
12:00. It lasts for 1 hour.
What time does lunch end?

_____

5. Swimming began at 3:30.
It ended at 4:30.
How long did it take?

_____

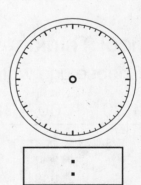

Notes for Home Your child wrote time to the hour and half hour. *Home Activity:* Ask your child: *Choir practice began at 1:30. It ended at 2:30. How long did it last?* (1 hour)

Problem Solving: Logical Reasoning

Solve.

1. Sean is first in line.

   Jim is behind Sean.

   Tasha is in front of Jim.

   Who is last in line?   _____

2. Kisha eats breakfast at 8:30.

   Jane eats breakfast at 7:00.

   Monroe eats breakfast at 7:30.

   Who eats breakfast last?   _____

3. Shawna gets home from school at 3:30.

   She begins her homework after she

   eats her snack. She eats a snack at 4:00.

   After what time does she begin her homework? _____

Critical Thinking

4. Choose and write the time that goes with each picture.

   4:30   4:00   3:30

   __ : __   __ : __   __ : __

Notes for Home   Your child solved problems. *Home Activity:* Ask your child to explain his or her reasoning in solving Problem 1.

Name _____

Mixed Practice: Lessons 1-6

Write the time.

1.

_____ o'clock

2.

_____ o'clock

3.

_____ o'clock

4.

[:]

5.

[:]

6.

[:]

7.

[:]

8.

[:]

9.

[:]

Problem Solving

10. Solve.

Anya has a flute lesson at 4:30. Her sister
Laryssa has a lesson at 5:30. Joseph has a
lesson before Anya. Who has the last lesson?   _____

Journal

11. Draw something you do at 12:00. Add a clock to your picture.

Notes for Home Your child practiced telling time to the hour and half hour and solved problems about time.
Home Activity: Ask your child to read the time on a face clock and write the time as it would appear on a
digital clock.

Cumulative Review

1. Add or subtract.

10	11	7	8	6	10	5
-4	-6	$+4$	$+2$	$+6$	-3	$+4$

Problem Solving

2. Make a picture graph. Color a picture for each ☐ and △.

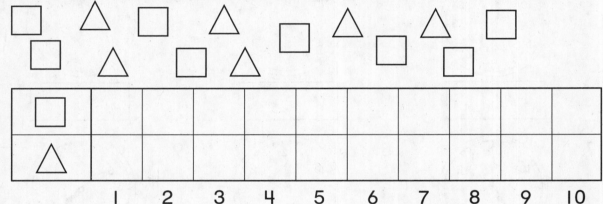

Test Prep

Fill in the O for the correct answer.

Choose the number that tells how many.

3.

45   46   37   36
○   ○   ○   ○

4.

47   48   58   59
○   ○   ○   ○

Notes for Home Your child reviewed addition and subtraction, graphing, and tens and ones. *Home Activity:* Ask your child to explain how he or she solved Exercise 4.

Order Events

Write 1st, 2nd, 3rd to put the pictures in order.

1. | | | |
|---|---|---|
| _____ | _____ | _____ |

2. | | | |
|---|---|---|
| _____ | _____ | _____ |

Write your own order problem.

3. | | | |
|---|---|---|
| _____ | _____ | _____ |

Problem Solving Critical Thinking

4. Write 1st, 2nd, and 3rd to show the order the students arrived.

The children arrive at Taft School
at different times in the morning.
The bus dropped Kisha off on time.
Jonathan arrived before Kisha.
Pablo arrived late.

Kisha _____

Jonathan _____

Pablo _____

Notes for Home Your child reordered events into the correct sequence using 1st, 2nd, and 3rd. *Home Activity:* Ask your child to write or draw pictures in order to show the events of a special day.

Estimate Time

Circle the time it takes.

1.

about 1 minute   about 1 hour

2.

about 1 minute   about 1 hour

3.

about 1 minute   about 1 hour

4.

about 1 minute   about 1 hour

5. **Draw your own** time problem.

Tell a Math Story

6. Tell about something you did yesterday.

   Tell what time you started and what time you stopped.

Notes for Home Your child estimated times for familiar activities. *Home Activity:* Do one of the activities shown in Exercises 1–5 with your child and time how long it takes.

Name _____

Calendar

1. Make a calendar for this month.

			Month: _____			
Sunday	Monday	Tuesday	Wednesday	Thursday	Friday	Saturday

Use your calendar.

2. Today is _____.

3. The day before yesterday was _____.

4. In five more days it will be _____.

5. The day after tomorrow is _____.

Problem Solving Patterns

6. What is the number date of the Monday of next week? _____

Notes for Home Your child completed a calendar for the current month. *Home Activity:* Mark your family calendar with special days of family members and friends. Ask your child to tell you the month, date, and day of the week for each event.

Name _____

Problem Solving:
Too Much Information

Cross out what you do not need. Solve.

1. Stacy bought 9 stickers on Monday.
   She likes those with animals.
   Stacy gave away 3 stickers on Tuesday.
   How many stickers does Stacy have now?   _____

2. Mark collected 11 soup can labels.
   Debbie collected 5 labels. The school
   will buy a new computer with the labels.
   How many labels do they have in all?   _____

3. There are 14 children in Peggy's
   music class. There are 5 boys and 9 girls.
   6 of the children also take a dance class.
   How many children in the music class
   do not take a dance class?   _____

Problem Solving Visual Thinking

What does each clock show? Write the time.

4.

   __ : __

5.

   __ : __

6.

   __ : __

Notes for Home Your child solved problems that give too much information. *Home Activity:* Ask your child to tell you about a time when he or she had more information than was needed to solve a problem or perform an activity.

Name _____

Mixed Practice: Lessons 7-10

Write 1st, 2nd, and 3rd to put the pictures in order.

1.

Use the calendar to answer the question.

July

2.

Thursday	Friday	Saturday
4	5	6
11	12	13
18	19	20

Circle the correct day.

July 20	Saturday	Sunday
July 4	Wednesday	Thursday
July 19	Friday	Saturday
July 13	Friday	Saturday

Problem Solving

Cross out what you do not need.

Solve.

3. Jack went to the store at 3:30 with his brother.

They bought 4 apples.

Jack bought 6 bananas.

His brother bought 5 oranges.

How many pieces of fruit did they buy?   _____

Journal

Write about something you do that takes less time

than it takes to brush your teeth.

Notes for Home Your child practiced ordering events, reading a calendar, and solving problems. *Home Activity:*
Ask your child to look at the calendar on this page and tell you the date of the first Sunday. (7)

Cumulative Review

1. Circle the shape that belongs.

Problem Solving

2. Count your money.
   Circle what you can buy.

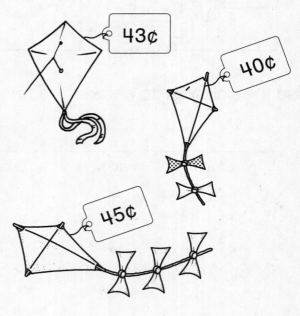

43¢

40¢

45¢

Write the amount. _____¢

Test Prep

Fill in the ○ for the correct answer. Add.

3. $6 + 4 = \underline{\quad}$	4. $4 + 6 = \underline{\quad}$
○ 9 ○ 10 ○ 11 ○ 12	○ 12 ○ 11 ○ 10 ○ 9
5. $5 + 7 = \underline{\quad}$	6. $7 + 5 = \underline{\quad}$
9 10 11 12 ○ ○ ○ ○	12 11 10 9 ○ ○ ○ ○

Notes for Home Your child reviewed sorting, using money, and addition. *Home Activity:* Ask your child how much more money is needed to buy the 45¢ kite in exercise 2. (3¢)

Explore Measuring with Nonstandard Units

How wide is your desk?

Estimate. Then use a  and a  to measure.

How wide?

Use.	Estimate.	Measure.
1.	about _____	about _____
2.	about _____	about _____

How tall is your desk?

Use.	Estimate.	Measure.
1.	about _____	about _____
2.	about _____	about _____

Talk About It Did you use fewer or fewer ?
Why do you think that happened?

Notes for Home Your child estimated and measured length using books and pencils. *Home Activity:* Ask your child to choose an object from his or her room, and measure three different objects or areas in that room.

Estimate, Measure, and Compare Lengths

Make a train of 10 . Use it to estimate the length.

Measure with □.	Does it look longer than 10 □?	How many □ long?
1.	yes no	about _____ □
2.	yes no	about _____ □
3.	yes no	about _____ □

4. Choose an object.
   Draw it.
   Estimate its length.
   Measure its length.

Problem Solving Estimate

Circle the best answer.

5. Sarah and Susan are partners for folk dancing
   Sarah is about 45 □ tall. How tall is Susan?

   Susan is about   40   45   50   55   □ tall.

Notes for Home Your child used Snap Cubes to measure lengths of classroom objects. *Home Activity:* Give your child an object such as a spoon. Then ask your child to think of some things that are longer than 10 spoons and shorter than 10 spoons. Measure with the spoon to check.

Name _____

Estimate and Measure with Inches

About how long? Estimate. Measure. Use your  .

1.

Estimate. _____ inches

Measure. _____ inches

2.

Estimate. _____ inches

Measure. _____ inches

3.

Estimate. _____ inches

Measure. _____ inch

Start at the dot.

4. Draw a line that is about 3 inches long.

●

5. Draw another line.

Make it longer than 3 inches and shorter than 6 inches.

●

Problem Solving Visual Thinking

6. Circle the best answer.

Joan is putting books on the bookshelf.

Which book will fit on the top shelf?

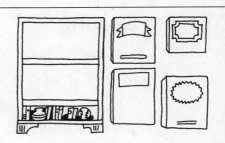

Notes for Home Your child estimated and measured lengths of objects on the page with an inch ruler.
Home Activity: Show your child three different objects. Ask your child to use a ruler to measure the length
of the objects in inches.

Compare to One Foot

How long would each object be? Circle the best answer.

1.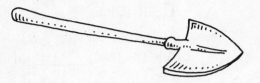

shorter than I foot
about I foot
longer than I foot

2.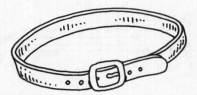

shorter than I foot
about I foot
longer than I foot

3.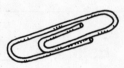

shorter than I foot
about I foot
longer than I foot

4.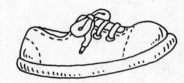

shorter than I foot
about I foot
longer than I foot

5.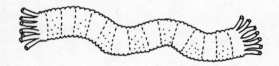

shorter than I foot
about I foot
longer than I foot

6.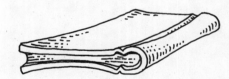

shorter than I foot
about I foot
longer than I foot

Problem Solving

7. Albert measured the longest watermelon in his garden.
   He found that it was about one foot and five inches long.

   How many inches long was the watermelon? _____ inches

Notes for Home Your child identified whether an object is about 1 foot, shorter than 1 foot, or longer than 1 foot.
Home Activity: Ask your child to find objects in your home that are longer than 1 foot and shorter than 1 foot.
Measure them and compare your measurements.

Estimate and Measure
with Centimeters

About how long? Estimate. Measure. Use your ⌷⌷⌷⌷⌷⌷⌷⌷⌷⌷.
                                             1 2 3 4 5 6 7 8 9 10

1.

Estimate. _____ centimeters

Measure. _____ centimeters

2.

Estimate. _____ centimeters

Measure. _____ centimeters

3.

Estimate. _____ centimeters

Measure. _____ centimeters

Start at the dot.

4. Draw a line. Make it longer than 10 centimeters
and shorter than 15 centimeters.

•

Problem Solving Critical Thinking

5. Solve.

Rover is taller than Rex.

Princess is taller than Rover.

Spot is shorter than Rex.

Who is the shortest? _____

Notes for Home Your child estimated and measured lengths of objects with a centimeter ruler.
Home Activity: Have your child select 4 small kitchen utensils. Ask your child to guess and then measure
the length of these objects in centimeters.

Name _____

Problem Solving:
Group Decision Making

Work with your group. Choose an object in the classroom to measure.
Write the answers.

1. Your group has only paper clips and a centimeter ruler.
   Talk about how you can used these to measure your object.
   Draw what you will do.

   _____

2. Estimate. How big around does the group think your object is?

   _____

3. Measure. How big around is it?

   _____

4. Talk it over. Were paper clips a good thing to use? Why or why not?

   _____

Journal

Write about your group. How did you work together?

Would you do something differently the next time? Why or why not?

If you would change something, what would it be?

_____

Notes for Home Your child worked with a group to choose tools and carry out a measurement project.
Home Activity: Work with your child to measure around some large things in your home, such as the refrigerator,
a bookcase, or a television set.

Name _____

Mixed Practice: Lessons 1–6

Use the rulers to measure length. Write the answer.

1.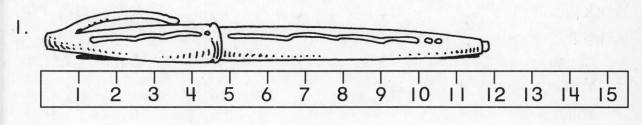

about _____ centimeters

2.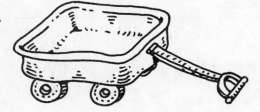

about _____ inches

How long would the wagon be? Circle the best answer.

3.

shorter than 1 foot
about 1 foot
longer than 1 foot

Problem Solving

4. Susie's mother needs to know how big the living room is. She wants to buy new carpeting. Should she measure the room in inches or feet?

_____

Journal

What is something you would measure in feet?
Draw a picture of it.
Estimate how long it is.

Notes for Home Your child worked with centimeters, inches and feet. *Home Activity:* Ask your child to find something in your home that you would measure in inches. Measure it together.

Cumulative Review

1. Add or subtract.

$$\begin{array}{r} 5 \\ +6 \\ \hline \end{array} \quad \begin{array}{r} 9 \\ -5 \\ \hline \end{array} \quad \begin{array}{r} 7 \\ +3 \\ \hline \end{array} \quad \begin{array}{r} 8 \\ +4 \\ \hline \end{array} \quad \begin{array}{r} 12 \\ -9 \\ \hline \end{array} \quad \begin{array}{r} 3 \\ +3 \\ \hline \end{array} \quad \begin{array}{r} 11 \\ -9 \\ \hline \end{array}$$

2. Circle the correct estimate.

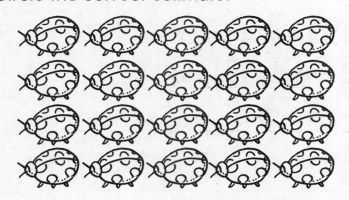

about
10   20   30

Test Prep

Fill in the O for the correct answer.
Read the graph.

3. How many buttons does
   Mike have?

   20   40   50
   ○   ○   ○

4. How many fewer buttons
   does Kathy have than Mike?

   5   10   15
   ○   ○   ○

Buttons We Have	
Mike	Kathy
○ ○ ○ ○ ○ ○ ○ ○ ○ ○	○ ○ ○ ○ ○ ○ ○ ○ ○ ○
○ ○ ○ ○ ○ ○ ○ ○ ○ ○	○ ○ ○ ○ ○ ○ ○ ○ ○ ○
○ ○ ○ ○ ○ ○ ○ ○ ○ ○	○ ○ ○ ○ ○
○ ○ ○ ○ ○ ○ ○ ○ ○ ○	

Notes for Home Your child reviewed addition and subtraction, estimation, and graphing. *Home Activity:* Ask your child to solve 7 + 2 = (9) and 12 – 5 = (7).

Explore Weight

Compare these weights. Write **more**, **less**, or **same**.

1.

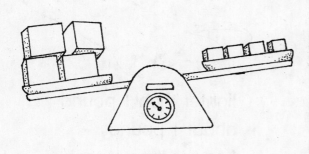

_____ _____

2.

_____ _____

3.

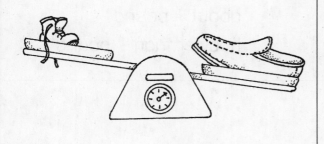

_____ _____

4.

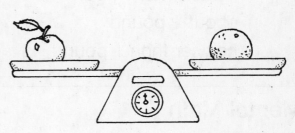

_____ _____

Talk About It What are some other ways
you compare how heavy two things are?

Notes for Home Your child compared the weights of objects. *Home Activity:* Have your child select two objects
and hold one in each hand. Ask him or her to tell which one weighs more and which one weighs less.

Compare to One Pound

How heavy would each be?
Circle the best answer.

1.

   lighter than I pound
   about I pound
   heavier than I pound

2.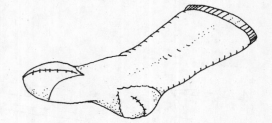

   lighter than I pound
   about I pound
   heavier than I pound

3.

   lighter than I pound
   about I pound
   heavier than I pound

4.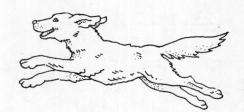

   lighter than I pound
   about I pound
   heavier than I pound

Mental Math

5. Count by tens to solve.

   Elana is buying green apples for her grandmother.

   The apples costs 10¢ a pound.

   Grandma needs 9 pounds of apples for her pies.

   How much will the apples cost?

   _____ ¢

Notes for Home Your child compared the weights of objects to one pound. *Home Activity:* Find a food product, such as a box of crackers or a bag of fruit, that weighs one pound. Have your child compare other objects to it. Which weighs more? Which weighs less?

Compare to One Kilogram

How heavy would each object be?
Circle the best answer.

1.

lighter than I kilogram
about I kilogram
heavier than I kilogram

2.

lighter than I kilogram
about I kilogram
heavier than I kilogram

3.

lighter than I kilogram
about I kilogram
heavier than I kilogram

4.

lighter than I kilogram
about I kilogram
heavier than I kilogram

Problem Solving Critical Thinking

5. Is a kilogram of playground sand
heavier than a kilogram of marbles?
Explain.

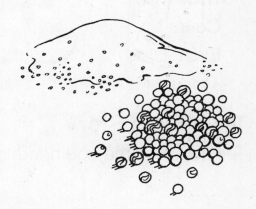

_____

Notes for Home Your child estimated whether things are heavier or lighter than one kilogram. *Home Activity:* Ask
child to make a list of things in your home or neighborhood that are heavier than one kilogram.

Compare Cups, Pints, and Quarts

Circle the things that could hold less than 1 cup.

Mark an X on the things that hold more than 1 cup.

1.

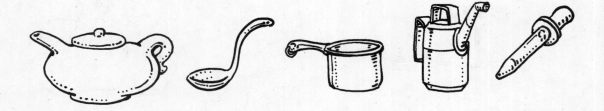

2.

Circle the things that could hold less than 1 quart.

Mark an X on the things that hold more than 1 quart.

3.

Tell a Math Story

Tell about a time you needed to measure using a cup, pint, or quart.

Notes for Home Your child identified containers that hold more or less than 1 cup, 1 pint, and 1 quart. *Home Activity:* Ask your child to find some containers in your kitchen that hold more than a quart. Use a measuring cup to check.

Name _____

Compare to One Liter

Check how much each container could hold.

	Container	Less than 1 liter	About 1 liter	More than 1 liter
1.				
2.				
3.				
4.				
5.				

Mental Math

6. Tanya went to the store to buy juice for a party. She bought 6 bottles of juice. Each bottle holds two liters. How many liters of juice did she buy? _____

I can count by 2s.

Notes for Home Your child checked whether various containers hold more or less than 1 liter.
Home Activity: Ask your child to explore the capacity of your kitchen containers. Often containers have capacities marked on the container, like a measuring cup. Show these markings to your child. Discuss how it might make it easier to choose a container to store leftovers.

Name _____

Use a Thermometer

Look at the .

Draw a picture to show how it looks outside.

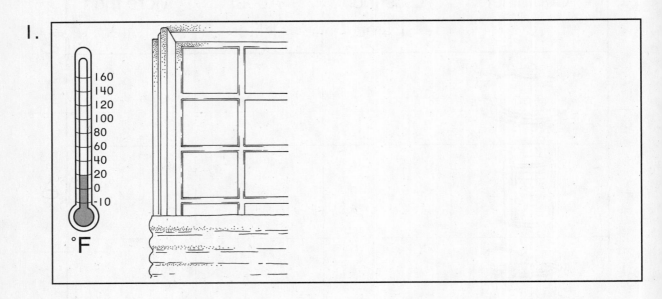

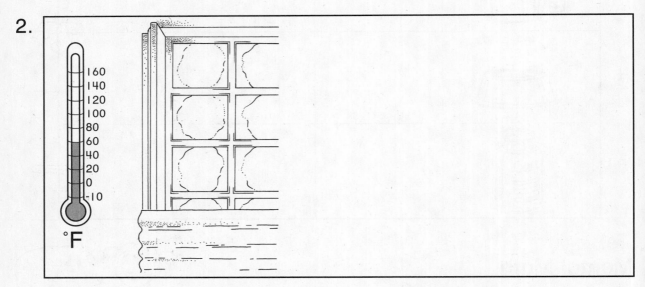

Journal

Write about some things you like to do outside when it is warm.

Write about some things you like to do outside when it is cool.

Notes for Home Your child drew pictures to show understanding of the temperature shown on a thermometer.
Home Activity: Help your child look in the newspaper for today's high temperature. Have your child draw a picture
of a thermometer showing the correct temperature.

Name _____

Problem Solving: Logical Reasoning

Circle the tool that you need to answer each question.

---

1. How heavy is it?

---

2. How warm is it?

---

3. How much water does it hold?

---

4. How long is it?

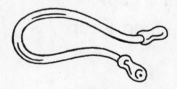

Tell a Math Story

5. Richard is baking a cake with his father.

   Tell a story about how they follow the recipe.

   Talk about measuring the ingredients.

   Tell about choosing a container for mixing and baking.

   Tell about baking the cake.

Notes for Home Your child chose tools of measurement to measure length, weight, and capacity.
Home Activity: Ask your child to find objects in his or her bedroom to measure. Help your child identify the correct tool to measure each object and tell why he or she chose it.

Mixed Practice: Lessons 7–13

Circle the words that tell about the object.

1. The kitten weighs

less than I kilogram.
about I kilogram.
more than I kilogram.

2. The bananas weigh

less than I pound.
about I pound.
more than I pound.

3. The watering can holds

less than I liter.
about I liter.
more than I liter.

4. The glass holds

less than I cup.
about I cup.
more than I cup.

Problem Solving

Circle the tool you need to answer the question.

5. Is your dog heavier than your cat?

Journal

Choose an object and record as many things as you can about it.

Notes for Home Your child estimated weight and capacity measures. *Home Activity:* Ask your child to tell you why you might use a cup to measure baking materials.

Name _____

Cumulative Review

Add.

1. $3 + 3 =$ ___ $3 + 4 =$ ___ $4 + 3 =$ ___

2. $2 + 2 =$ ___ $2 + 3 =$ ___ $3 + 2 =$ ___

Problem Solving

Write a number sentence.

3. Jonathan had 11 sports cards. He gave 3 to Tom. How many are left?

_____

4. Ellen had 6 pennies. Her mother gave her 5 more. How many pennies does Ellen have?

_____

Test Prep

Fill in the O for the correct answer.

What time does the clock show?

5.
   - ○ 3:30
   - ○ 4:30
   - ○ 5:30

6.
   - ○ 10:00
   - ○ 11:00
   - ○ 12:00

7.
   - ○ 6:00
   - ○ 7:00
   - ○ 8:00

8.
   - ○ 11:30
   - ○ 12:30
   - ○ 1:30

Notes for Home Your child reviewed addition, writing a number sentence, and telling time. *Home Activity:* Ask your child to tell you what time it will be on the next half hour and the next hour.

Name _____

Add Doubles to 18

Write the sum.

1. $4 + 4 =$ __8__ $6 + 6 =$ ___ $8 + 8 =$ ___

2. $5 + 5 =$ ___ $7 + 7 =$ ___ $9 + 9 =$ ___

Mixed Practice Write the sum. Circle the doubles.

3.
$$\begin{array}{c} 2 \\ +8 \\ \hline 10 \end{array} \quad \begin{array}{c} 4 \\ +4 \\ \hline \end{array} \quad \begin{array}{c} 7 \\ +7 \\ \hline \end{array} \quad \begin{array}{c} 3 \\ +8 \\ \hline \end{array} \quad \begin{array}{c} 5 \\ +5 \\ \hline \end{array} \quad \begin{array}{c} 1 \\ +6 \\ \hline \end{array} \quad \begin{array}{c} 8 \\ +7 \\ \hline \end{array}$$

4.
$$\begin{array}{c} 6 \\ +6 \\ \hline \end{array} \quad \begin{array}{c} 9 \\ +3 \\ \hline \end{array} \quad \begin{array}{c} 4 \\ +8 \\ \hline \end{array} \quad \begin{array}{c} 9 \\ +9 \\ \hline \end{array} \quad \begin{array}{c} 5 \\ +7 \\ \hline \end{array} \quad \begin{array}{c} 8 \\ +8 \\ \hline \end{array} \quad \begin{array}{c} 7 \\ +3 \\ \hline \end{array}$$

Problem Solving Visual Thinking

5. Jacob sets the table for dinner.
   One plate goes on each mat.
   One bowl goes on each mat, too.
   How many dishes will Jacob use?

   _____ dishes

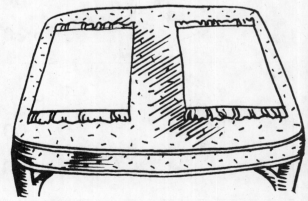

Notes for Home Your child added doubles facts such as 6 + 6, 7 + 7, 8 + 8, and 9 + 9. *Home Activity:* Set out two equal groups of kitchen utensils and ask how many in all. (Possible answer: 6 forks + 6 forks = 12 forks.)

Add Doubles Plus One

Write the sum.

1.
$$\begin{array}{r} 4 \\ +4 \\ \hline 8 \end{array} \qquad \begin{array}{r} 4 \\ +5 \\ \hline \end{array} \qquad \begin{array}{r} 5 \\ +4 \\ \hline \end{array}$$

2.
$$\begin{array}{r} 5 \\ +5 \\ \hline \end{array} \qquad \begin{array}{r} 5 \\ +6 \\ \hline \end{array} \qquad \begin{array}{r} 6 \\ +5 \\ \hline \end{array}$$

3.
$$\begin{array}{r} 9 \\ +9 \\ \hline \end{array} \qquad \begin{array}{r} 9 \\ +10 \\ \hline \end{array} \qquad \begin{array}{r} 10 \\ +9 \\ \hline \end{array}$$

4.
$$\begin{array}{r} 8 \\ +8 \\ \hline \end{array} \qquad \begin{array}{r} 8 \\ +9 \\ \hline \end{array} \qquad \begin{array}{r} 9 \\ +8 \\ \hline \end{array}$$

5. $6 + 6 = $ _____ $1 + 2 = $ _____ $8 + 9 = $ _____

6. $6 + 5 = $ _____ $8 + 8 = $ _____ $7 + 8 = $ _____

7. $7 + 6 = $ _____ $4 + 3 = $ _____ $7 + 7 = $ _____

Problem Solving

Solve. Write the number sentence.

8. Meg made an ant farm.
   She put in 8 red ants.
   She put in 9 black ants.
   How many ants did Meg put in?

   _____ + _____ = _____

   _____ ants

9. A fish had 6 teeth on the top.
   It had 5 teeth on the bottom.
   How many teeth did the fish have?

   _____ + _____ = _____

   _____ teeth

Notes for Home Your child added using a doubles fact, such as 6 + 6 = 12, to solve other facts.
Home Activity: Have your child line up shoes to show a doubles plus one fact.

Name _____

Add 3 Numbers

Use a paper clip and pencil. Spin.
Write the number in the box. Add.

1.
```
  4          3          ☐
  5         ☐          6
+ ☐       + 2        + 0
___        ___         ___
```
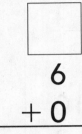

2.
```
  3          6          ☐          1
  7         ☐          2          5
+ ☐       + 7        + 4        + ☐
___         ___        ___        ___
```

3.
```
  ☐          1          5          6          2
  4          8          5         ☐         ☐
+ 6        + ☐       + ☐       + 3        + 1
___        ___        ___        ___        ___
```

Mental Math

4. Coach had 3 bags of soccer balls.
   He had 16 balls in all.
   Color the 3 bags Coach had.

Notes for Home Your child added three numbers. *Home Activity:* Ask your child to separate a pile of 18 rocks into 3 groups. Have them write a number sentence to show how they would add the groups. (Possible answer: 5 + 5 + 8 = 18. I would add the doubles first and then add on 8 more.)

Explore Making 10 to Add 7, 8, or 9

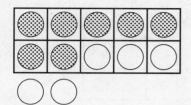

$7 + 5 = \underline{12}$

$10 + 2 = \underline{12}$

Use ⬭ ⬭ and ▦ .

Write the sum. Match.

3.
$$\begin{array}{c} 8 \\ +6 \\ \hline 14 \end{array} \quad \begin{array}{c} 7 \\ +3 \\ \hline \end{array} \quad \begin{array}{c} 9 \\ +3 \\ \hline \end{array} \quad \begin{array}{c} 7 \\ +7 \\ \hline \end{array} \quad \begin{array}{c} 8 \\ +8 \\ \hline \end{array} \quad \begin{array}{c} 9 \\ +2 \\ \hline \end{array} \quad \begin{array}{c} 7 \\ +8 \\ \hline \end{array}$$

4.
$$\begin{array}{c} 10 \\ +0 \\ \hline \end{array} \quad \begin{array}{c} 10 \\ +4 \\ \hline 14 \end{array} \quad \begin{array}{c} 10 \\ +4 \\ \hline \end{array} \quad \begin{array}{c} 10 \\ +1 \\ \hline \end{array} \quad \begin{array}{c} 10 \\ +2 \\ \hline \end{array} \quad \begin{array}{c} 10 \\ +6 \\ \hline \end{array} \quad \begin{array}{c} 10 \\ +5 \\ \hline \end{array}$$

Problem Solving

3. Pedro has 9 rocks.
   He found 5 more.
   How many rocks does
   he have now?

_____ rocks

How many rocks will not fit in the box?

_____ rocks

Notes for Home Your child matched facts such as 7 + 5 = 12 and 10 + 2 = 12. *Home Activity:* Ask your child to tell you a story problem for 8 + 8. Help him or her draw a ten frame to solve the problem.

Make 10 When Adding 7, 8, or 9

Draw 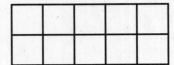 to show the number sentence. Add.

1.

$8 + 7 = 15$

$10 + \underline{} = \underline{}$

2.

$9 + 3 = \underline{}$

$10 + \underline{} = \underline{}$

Add. You can use 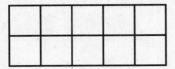 and ▭.

3.
$\begin{array}{r} 7 \\ +4 \\ \hline \end{array}$
$\begin{array}{r} 8 \\ +6 \\ \hline \end{array}$
$\begin{array}{r} 9 \\ +3 \\ \hline \end{array}$
$\begin{array}{r} 5 \\ +9 \\ \hline \end{array}$
$\begin{array}{r} 8 \\ +5 \\ \hline \end{array}$
$\begin{array}{r} 4 \\ +8 \\ \hline \end{array}$
$\begin{array}{r} 7 \\ +6 \\ \hline \end{array}$

4.
$\begin{array}{r} 9 \\ +5 \\ \hline \end{array}$
$\begin{array}{r} 8 \\ +3 \\ \hline \end{array}$
$\begin{array}{r} 7 \\ +5 \\ \hline \end{array}$
$\begin{array}{r} 5 \\ +7 \\ \hline \end{array}$
$\begin{array}{r} 7 \\ +7 \\ \hline \end{array}$
$\begin{array}{r} 4 \\ +9 \\ \hline \end{array}$
$\begin{array}{r} 4 \\ +9 \\ \hline \end{array}$

Problem Solving Visual Thinking

5. Each hive can hold 10 bees.

   How many more bees will fit in each hive?

 more bees

 more bees

 more bees

---

Notes for Home Your child added 7, 8, or 9 to another number by making a 10 first. *Home Activity:* Ask your child to write a number sentence for each bee hive problem. (7 + 3 = 10, 9 + 1 = 10, 8 + 2 = 10)

Problem Solving:
Choose a Strategy

Solve. Use  and ⊞ or draw a picture.

1. A hen has 4 yellow chicks.

   She has 9 tan chicks, too.

   How many chicks does the hen have?

   _____ chicks

2. 19 seals go fishing.

   13 seals catch fish.

   How many seals do not catch fish?

   _____ seals

3. A zoo has 6 lions.

   It has 4 tigers.

   6 leopards live there, too.

   How many big cats are at the zoo?

   _____ big cats

Tell a Math Story

4. Tell a math story about the picture.

Notes for Home Your child solved problems by drawing a picture or using objects. *Home Activity:* Ask your child to use pennies or other objects to retell the math story.

Name _____

Mixed Practice: Lessons 1–6

Write the sum. Circle the doubles.

1.
$\begin{array}{r} 5 \\ +6 \\ \hline \end{array}$
$\begin{array}{r} 4 \\ +4 \\ \hline \end{array}$
$\begin{array}{r} 6 \\ +7 \\ \hline \end{array}$
$\begin{array}{r} 7 \\ +5 \\ \hline \end{array}$
$\begin{array}{r} 9 \\ +9 \\ \hline \end{array}$
$\begin{array}{r} 8 \\ +9 \\ \hline \end{array}$
$\begin{array}{r} 4 \\ +5 \\ \hline \end{array}$

2.
$\begin{array}{r} 7 \\ +8 \\ \hline \end{array}$
$\begin{array}{r} 9 \\ +4 \\ \hline \end{array}$
$\begin{array}{r} 5 \\ +5 \\ \hline \end{array}$
$\begin{array}{r} 4 \\ +7 \\ \hline \end{array}$
$\begin{array}{r} 6 \\ +9 \\ \hline \end{array}$
$\begin{array}{r} 7 \\ +7 \\ \hline \end{array}$
$\begin{array}{r} 3 \\ +3 \\ \hline \end{array}$

Add.

3.
$\begin{array}{r} 2 \\ 1 \\ +6 \\ \hline \end{array}$
$\begin{array}{r} 4 \\ 3 \\ +5 \\ \hline \end{array}$
$\begin{array}{r} 3 \\ 5 \\ +3 \\ \hline \end{array}$
$\begin{array}{r} 1 \\ 4 \\ +7 \\ \hline \end{array}$
$\begin{array}{r} 6 \\ 2 \\ +8 \\ \hline \end{array}$
$\begin{array}{r} 5 \\ 3 \\ +6 \\ \hline \end{array}$
$\begin{array}{r} 4 \\ 2 \\ +9 \\ \hline \end{array}$

Problem Solving

Solve. Use and ⊞ or draw a picture.

4. Marcy found 14 paper clips in her desk.

   She gave 9 to Martha.

   How many paper clips does

   Marcy have now?

   _____ paper clips

Journal

5. Draw a picture to show a doubles fact. Write the fact.

Notes for Home Your child practiced adding two and three numbers and solving problems by drawing a picture or using objects. *Home Activity:* Ask your child how she or he could use 6 + 6 = 12 to help find the answer for 6 + 7. (13)

Name _____

Cumulative Review

Add or subtract.

1. 6 + 3 = ____ | 4 + 9 = ____ | 5 + 6 = ____

    9 − 6 = ____ | 13 − 9 = ____ | 11 − 5 = ____

Problem Solving

Count these coins. Record the coins in the table.

2.

	Pennies	Nickels	Dimes
How many coins?			

Test Prep

Fill in the ○ for the correct answer.

Count the money.

3.

   39¢   31¢   41¢   45¢
   ○   ○   ○   ○

4.

   74¢   40¢   27¢   47¢
   ○   ○   ○   ○

Notes for Home Your child reviewed addition and subtraction, making a table, and counting money.
Home Activity: Ask your child to make a table to show the number of shapes he or she can find in the kitchen.

Relate Addition and Subtraction

Add. Use the addition fact to help you subtract.

You can use ⬤ ⬭ .

1. $\begin{array}{r} 5 \\ +6 \\ \hline \end{array}$ $\begin{array}{r} 11 \\ -5 \\ \hline \end{array}$

2. $\begin{array}{r} 7 \\ +4 \\ \hline \end{array}$ $\begin{array}{r} 11 \\ -4 \\ \hline \end{array}$

3. $\begin{array}{r} 9 \\ +2 \\ \hline \end{array}$ $\begin{array}{r} 11 \\ -9 \\ \hline \end{array}$

4. $\begin{array}{r} 11 \\ +0 \\ \hline \end{array}$ $\begin{array}{r} 11 \\ -11 \\ \hline \end{array}$

5. $\begin{array}{r} 7 \\ +5 \\ \hline \end{array}$ $\begin{array}{r} 12 \\ -7 \\ \hline \end{array}$

6. $\begin{array}{r} 9 \\ +3 \\ \hline \end{array}$ $\begin{array}{r} 12 \\ -9 \\ \hline \end{array}$

Add or subtract.

Draw a line to match an addition with a subtraction fact.

7. $8 + 4 =$ _____ $12 - 8 =$ _____

8. $3 + 9 =$ _____ $11 - 7 =$ _____

9. $7 + 4 =$ _____ $12 - 3 =$ _____

Write About It

10. Complete the number sentences.

Draw or write a story to go with them.

$3 + 8 =$ _____

$11 - 3 =$ _____

Notes for Home Your child used an addition fact such as 8 + 4 = 12 to solve a related subtraction fact such as 12 - 8 = 4. *Home Activity:* Ask your child to name a subtraction fact that uses the same numbers as 6 + 5 = 11. (11 - 5 = 6 or 11 - 6 = 5)

Use Doubles to Subtract

Add or subtract.

1. $6 + 6 =$ 12 $5 + 5 =$ ___ $8 + 8 =$ ___

   $12 - 6 =$ ___ $10 - 5 =$ ___ $16 - 8 =$ ___

2. $4 + 4 =$ ___ $9 + 9 =$ ___ $7 + 7 =$ ___

   $8 - 4 =$ ___ $18 - 9 =$ ___ $14 - 7 =$ ___

Subtract. Write the addition fact that helps.

3. $\begin{array}{r} 6 \\ -\ 3 \\ \hline \end{array}$ $\begin{array}{r} 3 \\ +\ 3 \\ \hline 6 \end{array}$

4. $\begin{array}{r} 18 \\ -\ 9 \\ \hline \end{array}$ $\begin{array}{r} \ \\ +\ \\ \hline \end{array}$

5. $\begin{array}{r} 12 \\ -\ 6 \\ \hline \end{array}$ $\begin{array}{r} \ \\ +\ \\ \hline \end{array}$

Problem Solving Patterns

6. Draw the missing dots
   on the last domino.
   Tell how you solved
   the puzzle.

   _____

   _____

   _____

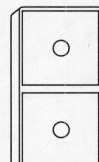
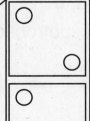
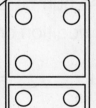
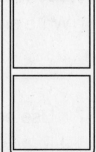

Subtraction Facts for 13 and 14

Subtract. Write the addition fact that helps.

1.
$$\begin{array}{r} 13 \\ -\ 8 \\ \hline \boxed{5} \end{array}$$
$$\begin{array}{r} \boxed{8} \\ +\ \boxed{5} \\ \hline 13 \end{array}$$

2.
$$\begin{array}{r} 14 \\ -\ 5 \\ \hline \boxed{} \end{array}$$
$$\begin{array}{r} 5 \\ +\ \boxed{} \\ \hline 14 \end{array}$$

3.
$$\begin{array}{r} 14 \\ -\ 8 \\ \hline \boxed{} \end{array}$$
$$\begin{array}{r} 8 \\ +\ \boxed{} \\ \hline 14 \end{array}$$

$$\begin{array}{r} 14 \\ -\ 2 \\ \hline \boxed{} \end{array}$$
$$\begin{array}{r} 2 \\ +\ \boxed{} \\ \hline 14 \end{array}$$

$$\begin{array}{r} 13 \\ -\ 6 \\ \hline \boxed{} \end{array}$$
$$\begin{array}{r} 6 \\ +\ \boxed{} \\ \hline 13 \end{array}$$

Subtract.

4. $13 - 5 = \underline{}$ $13 - 7 = \underline{}$ $13 - 9 = \underline{}$

5. $14 - 4 = \underline{}$ $14 - 9 = \underline{}$ $14 - 1 = \underline{}$

Tell a Math Story

6. Use these numbers: 8, 6, 14.

   Write an addition and subtraction fact.

   _____ + _____ = _____   _____ − _____ = _____

7. Use each fact to tell a math story.

Notes for Home Your child subtracted facts from 13 and 14. *Home Activity:* Ask your child to tell how the math stories in Exercise 7 are alike and different.

Subtraction Facts for 15 to 18

Complete the addition fact.

Write the subtraction facts.

You can use  .

1. $7 + 9 = \underline{16}$

$16 - \underline{} = \underline{9}$

$16 - \underline{} = \underline{7}$

Mixed Practice

Subtract.

2.
$$\begin{array}{ccccccc} 12 & 13 & 14 & 15 & 17 & 17 & 18 \\ -3 & -5 & -7 & -9 & -9 & -8 & -9 \end{array}$$

3.
$$\begin{array}{ccccccc} 13 & 16 & 16 & 15 & 14 & 16 & 18 \\ -7 & -7 & -8 & -6 & -5 & -9 & -0 \end{array}$$

Problem Solving Critical Thinking

5. Mark the coins to buy 2 bags of elephant food.

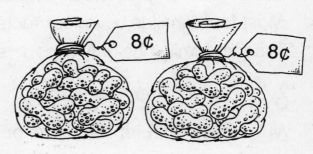

How much money will you have left? _____ ¢

Notes for Home Your child subtracted facts such as 15 − 7 = 8 and 15 − 8 = 7. *Home Activity:* Ask
your child to use real money to show how much they would have left if they bought only one bag of food in
Exercise 4. (11¢)

Fact Families

Complete the fact family. You can use 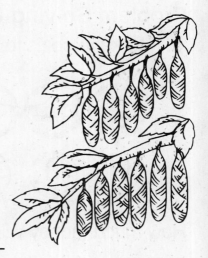 .

1. $9 + 3 =$ _____ $12 - 3 =$ _____

   $3 + 9 =$ _____ $12 - 9 =$ _____

2. $8 + 7 =$ _____ $15 - 8 =$ _____

   $7 + 8 =$ _____ $15 - 7 =$ _____

3. $6 + 8 =$ _____ $14 - 6 =$ _____

   $8 + 6 =$ _____ $14 - 8 =$ _____

4. **Write your own** fact family.

   _____ + _____ = _____   _____ − _____ = _____

   _____ + _____ = _____   _____ − _____ = _____

Problem Solving Critical Thinking

5. Most fact families have four facts.
   This fact family has only two facts. Why?

   $6 + 6 = 12$ $12 - 6 = 6$

   Which other fact families have only two facts?

   _____

Notes for Home Your child added and subtracted using fact families. *Home Activity:* Ask your child to draw a picture to illustrate the fact family in Exercise 3.

Problem Solving:
Choose an Operation

Circle add or subtract.

Complete the number sentence. Solve.

1. 12 penguins are on a hill.

    4 slide down the hill.

    How many are left?

    There are __8__ penguins left.

    add　　**subtract**

    12 ◯ ____ = ____

___

2. 6 brown cows come into the barn.

    7 tan cows came in too.

    How many cows are in the barn?

    There are ____ cows in the barn.

    add　　**subtract**

    ____ ◯ ____ = ____

___

3. 8 bats are in a cave.

    8 more bats fly in.

    How many bats are there all together?

    There are ____ bats.

    add　　**subtract**

    ____ ◯ ____ = ____

Tell a Math Story

4. Use the picture to tell a math story.

    Write a number sentence to go with your story.

    _____

___

Name _____

Mixed Practice: Lessons 7−12

Add or subtract.

1. $\begin{array}{r} 8 \\ +7 \\ \hline \end{array}$ $\begin{array}{r} 15 \\ -7 \\ \hline \end{array}$ 2. $\begin{array}{r} 14 \\ -5 \\ \hline \end{array}$ $\begin{array}{r} 14 \\ -9 \\ \hline \end{array}$ 3. $\begin{array}{r} 6 \\ +7 \\ \hline \end{array}$ $\begin{array}{r} 13 \\ -6 \\ \hline \end{array}$

Subtract.

4. $\begin{array}{r} 18 \\ -9 \\ \hline \end{array}$ $\begin{array}{r} 15 \\ -8 \\ \hline \end{array}$ $\begin{array}{r} 16 \\ -8 \\ \hline \end{array}$ $\begin{array}{r} 13 \\ -5 \\ \hline \end{array}$ $\begin{array}{r} 14 \\ -8 \\ \hline \end{array}$ $\begin{array}{r} 17 \\ -8 \\ \hline \end{array}$ $\begin{array}{r} 14 \\ -7 \\ \hline \end{array}$

Problem Solving

Circle add or subtract.

Complete the number sentence. Solve.

5. Mother bear picked 15 berries.   **add   subtract**
   She gave her cub 6 berries.
   How many are left for Mother?

   Mother bear has ____ berries.   ____ ◯ ____ = ____

Journal

6. Write or draw a math story about 15 penguins.
   Write a number sentence for your story.

Cumulative Review

1.
$$\begin{array}{r} 3 \\ 2 \\ +3 \\ \hline \end{array}$$
$$\begin{array}{r} 6 \\ 1 \\ +1 \\ \hline \end{array}$$
$$\begin{array}{r} 2 \\ 3 \\ +5 \\ \hline \end{array}$$
$$\begin{array}{r} 1 \\ 3 \\ +7 \\ \hline \end{array}$$
$$\begin{array}{r} 4 \\ 0 \\ +8 \\ \hline \end{array}$$
$$\begin{array}{r} 5 \\ 5 \\ +1 \\ \hline \end{array}$$
$$\begin{array}{r} 3 \\ 3 \\ +3 \\ \hline \end{array}$$

Problem Solving

2. Count the money. _____

3. Circle what you can buy.

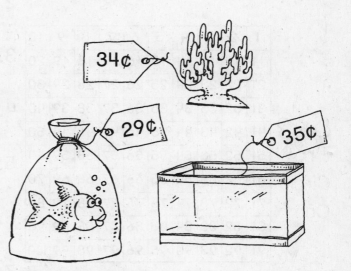

Test Prep

Fill in the ○ for the correct answer.

4.

    2 inches   3 inches   4 inches
      ○   ○   ○

Notes for Home Your child reviewed adding three numbers, counting money, and measurement. *Home Activity:* Ask your child to show you a group of real coins equal to the price of each object in Exercise 3.

Explore Adding Tens

46 and 3 tens more is 76.

Use a to add tens to these numbers.

	Find	Add	Sum
1.	27	2 tens	47
2.	12	3 tens	_____
3.	54	1 ten	_____
4.	75	2 tens	_____
5.	39	4 tens	_____
6.	70	1 ten	_____
7.	66	3 tens	_____

1	2	3	4	5	6	7	8	9	10
11	12	13	14	15	16	17	18	19	20
21	22	23	24	25	26	27	28	29	30
31	32	33	34	35	36	37	38	39	40
41	42	43	44	45	46	47	48	49	50
51	52	53	54	55	56	57	58	59	60
61	62	63	64	65	66	67	68	69	70
71	72	73	74	75	76	77	78	79	80
81	82	83	84	85	86	87	88	89	90
91	92	93	94	95	96	97	98	99	100

Problem Solving Critical Thinking

8. Jed's hamster eats 10 seeds at each meal.
   How many seeds will it eat in 5 meals?   _____ seeds

9. How many meals will it take the hamster to eat
   70 seeds?   _____ meals

Notes for Home Your child explored adding tens using a 100 chart. *Home Activity:* Ask your child to count by tens starting with his or her age. (Possible answer: 6, 16, 26, 36, 46, 56, 66, 76, 86, 96.)

Name _____

Add Tens

Add. Use [tens | ones] and | □ □ .

1.	tens	ones		2.	tens	ones		3.	tens	ones		4.	tens	ones
	2	0			4	5			1	0			5	1
+	3	4		+	4	0		+	5	2		+	3	0
	5	4												

5.
$$26 + 10 \qquad 44 + 40 \qquad 16 + 50 \qquad 30 + 22 \qquad 40 + 57 \qquad 60 + 17$$

6.
$$80 + 14 \qquad 60 + 26 \qquad 49 + 10 \qquad 23 + 20 \qquad 50 + 31 \qquad 12 + 20$$

7.
$$50 + 23 \qquad 14 + 20 \qquad 17 + 40 \qquad 30 + 62 \qquad 40 + 28 \qquad 55 + 10$$

Problem Solving Patterns

8. Brian uses a [calculator] to find the
total for these packets of seeds.
He presses these keys once:
[2] [5] [+] [1] [0]
He presses [=] 4 times.
He sees 35, 45, 55, 65.
What pattern did Brian use to add? _____

Seeds for Brian's Garden
25 tomato seeds
40 carrot seeds

Notes for Home Your child added two-digit numbers and tens. *Home Activity:* Set out a small sum of coins.
Ask your child to add 2, 3, or 4 dimes to the coins and to calculate the total amount.

Add Tens and Ones

Add. Use [tens | ones] and [│].

1.

tens	ones
2	4
+ 1	5

tens	ones
5	1
+ 2	6

tens	ones
1	6
+ 5	2

tens	ones
6	3
+ 3	2

2.

$$41 + 21$$ $$36 + 11$$ $$50 + 5$$ $$61 + 28$$ $$22 + 23$$ $$18 + 31$$

3.

$$81 + 4$$ $$28 + 41$$ $$13 + 33$$ $$15 + 53$$ $$34 + 43$$ $$32 + 22$$

4.

$$94 + 4$$ $$27 + 51$$ $$38 + 50$$ $$40 + 8$$ $$25 + 52$$ $$15 + 40$$

Problem Solving Critical Thinking

5. Use [tens | ones] and [│] to find 4 ways to get the sum of 56.

tens	ones
□	□
+ 4	4
5	6

tens	ones
□	□
+ 3	5
5	6

tens	ones
□	□
+ 5	2
5	6

tens	ones
□	□
+ 2	3
5	6

Notes for Home Your child added numbers like 36 + 12. *Home Activity:* Look at a calendar. Ask your child to add the number of days in his two favorite months.

Regroup with Addition

Use [tens | ones] and |.

	Show this many.	Add this many.	Do you need to regroup?	Solve.
1.	24	3	yes (no)	$24 + 3 = 27$
2.	56	7	yes no	$56 + 7 = \underline{\quad}$
3.	44	5	yes no	$44 + 5 = \underline{\quad}$
4.	19	4	yes no	$19 + 4 = \underline{\quad}$
5.	67	8	yes no	$67 + 8 = \underline{\quad}$
6.	35	6	yes no	$35 + 6 = \underline{\quad}$

Mental Math

What's My Rule? What number does each robot add?

7. $32 + \underline{\quad} = 36$

$14 + \underline{\quad} = 18$

$55 + \underline{\quad} = 59$

This robot adds _____.

8. $21 + \underline{\quad} = 27$

$60 + \underline{\quad} = 66$

$43 + \underline{\quad} = 49$

This robot adds _____.

Notes for Home Your child combed materials to find sums for number sentences like 28 + 6.
Home Activity: Ask your child to explain how they know when to regroup ones when adding. (Regroup when there are ten or more ones.)

Name _____

Problem Solving: Use Objects

Use | tens | ones | and ▯ .

Write the number sentence. Solve.

1. 26 sparklers lit the sky.

   3 firecrackers made a BOOM!

   How many fireworks did Jimmy see? $26 + 3 = 29$ _____ fireworks

2. 40 flags are on top of a float.

   Then 14 more flags are put around it.

   How many flags are there now? _____ flags

3. One band has 17 drums.

   Another band has 30 drums.

   How many drums are there in all? _____ drums

4. 31 children ate tomato soup at lunch.

   6 children ate chicken soup.

   How many children ate soup? _____ children

Visual Thinking

Solve.

5. 25 stars are on this quilt.

   How many are on the back?

   _____ stars

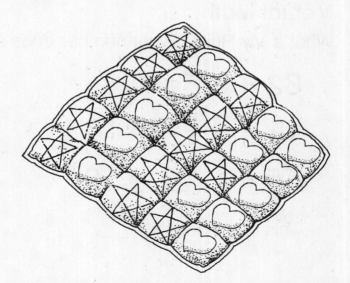

Notes for Home Your child solved problems involving addition. *Home Activity:* Ask your child to use beans, rocks or other small objects to check their answer to Exercise 4. (31 children + 6 children = 37 children)

Name _____

Mixed Practice: Lessons 1–5

Use | tens | ones | and | . Add.

1.
$$50 + 16 \qquad 40 + 41 \qquad 14 + 30 \qquad 47 + 20 \qquad 85 + 10 \qquad 60 + 16$$

$$42 + 46 \qquad 35 + 24 \qquad 27 + 42 \qquad 24 + 13 \qquad 51 + 22 \qquad 73 + 12$$

Circle yes or no to tell if you need to regroup. Solve.

2. $37 + 2 =$ _____ yes no   3. $24 + 7 =$ _____ yes no

4. $15 + 6 =$ _____ yes no   5. $74 + 3 =$ _____ yes no

Problem Solving

Use | . Write the number sentence. Solve.

6. 26 frogs jump in a pond.
   13 more frogs jump in.
   How many frogs are in
   the pond now? _____

   _____ frogs

7. 44 girls go to camp.
   27 boys go to camp.
   How many children go
   to camp? _____

   _____ children

Journal

8. Write an addition math story using 10 and 17.

Notes for Home Your child practiced the concepts, skills, and problem solving taught in lessons 1-5.
Home Activity: Ask your child to use dimes and pennies to solve Exercise 3. Remind them to regroup
10 pennies as 1 dime when possible. (2 dimes and 4 pennies + 7 pennies = 3 dimes and 1 penny, or 31¢.)

Use with pages 503. **191**

Cumulative Review

How many tens and ones?

1. 51 _____ tens _____ one

2. 60 _____ tens _____ ones

3. 97 _____ tens _____ ones

4. 34 _____ tens _____ ones

5. 46 _____ tens _____ ones

6. 23 _____ tens _____ ones

7. 15 _____ ten _____ ones

8. 78 _____ tens _____ ones

Problem Solving

Write a number sentence.

9. The boys flew 13 kites.
   5 kites got caught in trees.
   How many kites are left?

   _____

10. One kite had 7 tails.
    Kim added 7 more.
    How many tails are are left?

    _____

Test Prep

Fill in the O for the correct answer.

Add.

11.
$$\begin{array}{r} 5 \\ 3 \\ +2 \\ \hline \end{array}$$
○ 9
○ 10
○ 11

12.
$$\begin{array}{r} 3 \\ 4 \\ +6 \\ \hline \end{array}$$
○ 13
○ 14
○ 15

13.
$$\begin{array}{r} 2 \\ 5 \\ +8 \\ \hline \end{array}$$
○ 13
○ 14
○ 15

14.
$$\begin{array}{r} 9 \\ 6 \\ +1 \\ \hline \end{array}$$
○ 16
○ 17
○ 18

Notes for Home Your child reviewed place value concepts, problem solving, and addition skills.
Home Activity: Ask your child to name 5 numbers that have no ones. (Possible answers include: 10, 20, 30, 40, 50.)

Subtract Tens

Subtract.

Use and |.

1.

tens	ones
4	7
− 2	0
2	7

tens	ones
2	5
− 1	0

tens	ones
6	3
− 4	0

tens	ones
8	1
− 3	0

2.

25	37	43	56	68	72
− 10	− 20	− 10	− 20	− 30	− 10

Problem Solving

3. **Write your own** problem.

Write a problem about the carrots and rabbits in the picture.

Tell if you add or subtract. Write a number sentence. Solve.

_____

_____

_____

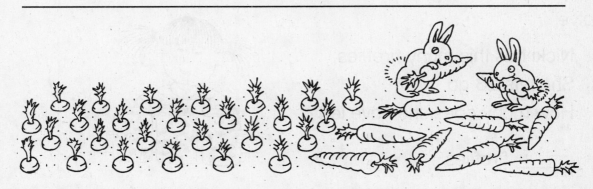

Name _____

Subtract Tens and Ones

Use | tens | ones | and ▯. Subtract.

1.

tens	ones
4	5
− 2	1
2	4

tens	ones
8	3
− 1	2

tens	ones
9	2
− 3	2

tens	ones
5	6
−	5

2.

24	36	52	47	85	74
− 11	− 14	− 31	− 22	− 54	− 42

Mixed Practice Add or subtract.

3.

23	37	47	58	62	75
− 10	− 6	− 31	− 20	− 51	− 14

4.

23	37	47	58	62	75
+ 16	+ 42	+ 50	+ 21	+ 22	+ 13

Problem Solving

Solve.

5. Nicki has this many fireflies.

   She lets 23 go.

   How many does she have left?

   _____ fireflies

Notes for Home Your child subtracted number sentences like 34 − 22. *Home Activity:* Ask your child to tell a subtraction math story about something that recently happened to him or her.

Name _____

Regroup with Subtraction

Use  and ▯.

	Show this many.	Subtract this many.	Do you need to regroup?	Solve.
1.	24	3	yes (no)	24 − 3 = ____
2.	56	7	yes no	56 − 7 = ____
3.	44	5	yes no	44 − 5 = ____
4.	19	4	yes no	19 − 4 = ____
5.	62	6	yes no	62 − 6 = ____
6.	35	7	yes no	35 − 7 = ____
7.	71	8	yes no	71 − 8 = ____

Problem Solving

Write a number sentence. Solve.

8. Mark's soccer team has 21 players.

5 are sick on game day.

How many players can play?

_____ players

Notes for Home Your child worked with tens and ones to find differences for number sentences like 23 − 7.
Home Activity: Ask your child to explain when they need to regroup in subtraction. (You must regroup tens and ones when there are not enough ones to subtract from.)

Name _____

Problem Solving:
Choose an Operation

Circle add or subtract.

Write a number sentence.

1. Brett picked up 46 shells at the beach.

   He found 12 more.

   How many shells did he find in all?

   add   **subtract** _____ shells

2. 38 crabs dug in the sand.

   22 turtles were digging, too.

   How many more crabs than

   turtles are in the sand?

   add   **subtract** _____ crabs

3. We made 68 muffins.

   We sold 40 at the bake sale.

   How many muffins are left?

   add   **subtract** _____ muffins

Estimation

4. Circle the best estimate.

   Fish jump 31 big waves

   and 58 little waves.

   About how many waves were jumped?

   70   80   90

Notes for Home Your child continued solving problems involving addition and subtraction. *Home Activity:* Ask your child to name words that are used in subtraction math stories. (Answers may include: how many more, left, away, and take away.)

Name _____

Mixed Practice: Lessons 6–9

Subtract. Use [tens | ones] and ▯ .

1. 38   55   92   17   47   29
  − 20 − 30 − 40 − 10 − 30 − 10

2. 97   84   26   34   75   28
  − 61 − 44 − 13 − 22 − 53 − 14

Circle yes or no to tell if you need to regroup. Solve.

3. 37 − 5 = ____ yes no   4. 21 − 7 = ____ yes no

5. 14 − 6 = ____ yes no   6. 50 − 2 = ____ yes no

7. 45 − 4 = ____ yes no   8. 33 − 3 = ____ yes no

Problem Solving

Circle add or subtract. Write a number sentence.

9. K.T. has 32¢.   **add**   **subtract**
   Pizza costs 75¢.
   How much more does K.T.
   need to buy pizza?   _____

Journal

10. Write a number story for 25¢ − 10¢.

Notes for Home Your child practiced the concepts, skills, and problem solving taught in lessons 6-9.
Home Activity: Ask your child to share a time when they used subtraction to solve a problem at home.

Name _____

Cumulative Review

Use the ruler to measure. Write the length.

1.

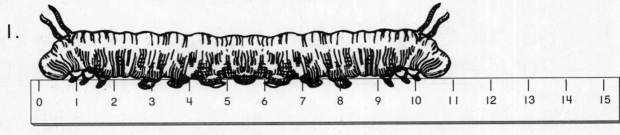

about _____ centimeters

Add.

2. $30 + 10 =$ _____ $20 + 40 =$ _____ $30 + 50 =$ _____

Problem Solving

Solve.

3. Liz sees 13 caterpillars.
   5 turn into cocoons. How
   many caterpillars are left?

   _____ caterpillars

4. 17 butterflies are blue.
   3 are red. How many
   more are blue than red?

   _____ butterflies

Test Prep

Fill in the ○ for the correct answer.
Subtract.

5. $\begin{array}{r} 14 \\ -7 \\ \hline \end{array}$
   ○ 7
   ○ 8
   ○ 9
   ○ 10

6. $\begin{array}{r} 15 \\ -9 \\ \hline \end{array}$
   ○ 4
   ○ 5
   ○ 6
   ○ 7

7. $\begin{array}{r} 12 \\ -8 \\ \hline \end{array}$
   ○ 4
   ○ 5
   ○ 6
   ○ 7

Notes for Home Your child reviewed measurement, subtraction facts, and problem solving. *Home Activity:* Ask your child to check their answers for Exercises 5-7 by adding. (14 - 7 = 7 and 7 + 7 = 14, 15 – 9 = 6 and 9 + 6 = 15, 12 – 8 = 4 and 8 + 4 = 12)

Numbers 1, 2, 3

Write 1, 2, and 3.

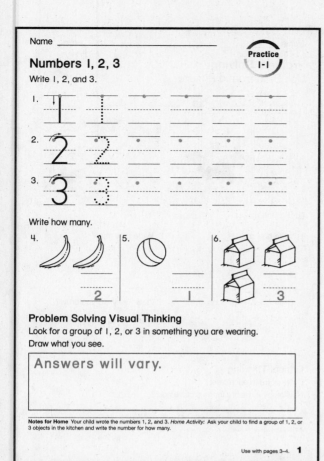

1. 1
2. 2
3. 3

Write how many.

4. 2
5. 1
6. 3

Problem Solving Visual Thinking

Look for a group of 1, 2, or 3 in something you are wearing.
Draw what you see.

Answers will vary.

Notes for Home Your child wrote the numbers 1, 2, and 3. *Home Activity:* Ask your child to find a group of 1, 2, or 3 objects in the kitchen and write the number for how many.

Use with pages 3–4. **1**

Numbers 4, 5, 6

Write 4, 5, and 6.

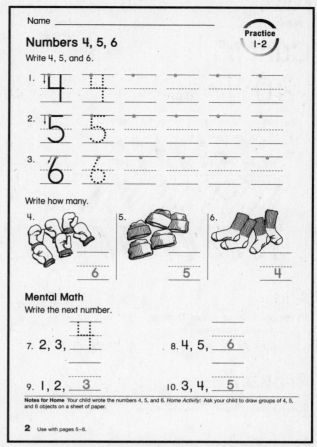

1. 4
2. 5
3. 6

Write how many.

4. 6
5. 5
6. 4

Mental Math

Write the next number.

7. 2, 3, 4

8. 4, 5, 6

9. 1, 2, 3

10. 3, 4, 5

Notes for Home Your child wrote the numbers 4, 5, and 6. *Home Activity:* Ask your child to draw groups of 4, 5, and 6 objects on a sheet of paper.

2 Use with pages 5–6.

Numbers 7, 8, 9

Write 7, 8, and 9.

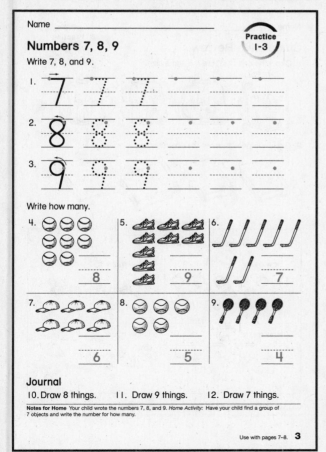

1. 7
2. 8
3. 9

Write how many.

4. 8
5. 9
6. 7

7. 6
8. 5
9. 4

Journal

10. Draw 8 things.   11. Draw 9 things.   12. Draw 7 things.

Notes for Home Your child wrote the numbers 7, 8, and 9. *Home Activity:* Have your child find a group of 7 objects and write the number for how many.

Use with pages 7–8. **3**

Zero

Write 0.

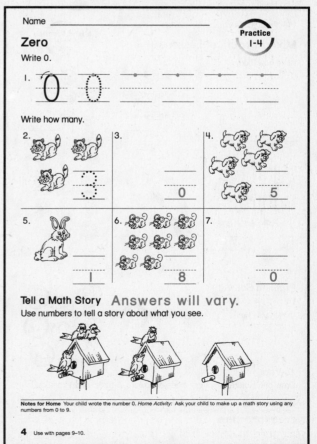

1. 0

Write how many.

2. 3
3. 0
4. 5

5. 1
6. 8
7. 0

Tell a Math Story Answers will vary.

Use numbers to tell a story about what you see.

Notes for Home Your child wrote the number 0. *Home Activity:* Ask your child to make up a math story using any numbers from 0 to 9.

4 Use with pages 9–10.

199

Name _____

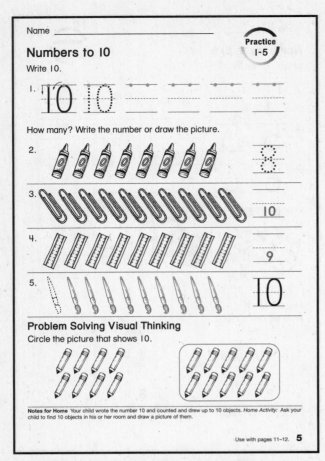

Numbers to 10

Write 10.

1. 10 10 · · · · · · ·

How many? Write the number or draw the picture.

2. 8

3. 10

4. 9

5. 10

Problem Solving Visual Thinking
Circle the picture that shows 10.

Notes for Home Your child wrote the number 10 and counted and drew up to 10 objects. *Home Activity:* Ask your child to find 10 objects in his or her room and draw a picture of them.

Name _____

Problem Solving:
Use Data from a Picture

Look at the picture.

1. Write how many 🦁 .

2

2. Write how many 🐘 .

0

3. Draw a ◯ for each child.

QQQQQ

4. How many did you draw?

5

Critical Thinking
Draw a bird in each tree.
How many birds are in the picture now? 6

Notes for Home Your child solved problems using pictures. *Home Activity:* Ask your child to explain how he or she found the answer for Exercise 3.

Name _____

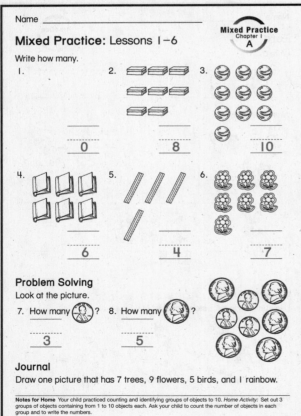

Mixed Practice: Lessons 1–6

Write how many.

1. ____0____

2. ____8____

3. ____10____

4. ____6____

5. ____4____

6. ____7____

Problem Solving
Look at the picture.

7. How many 🪙 ?   3

8. How many 🪙 ?   5

Journal
Draw one picture that has 7 trees, 9 flowers, 5 birds, and 1 rainbow.

Notes for Home Your child practiced counting and identifying groups of objects to 10. *Home Activity:* Set out 3 groups of objects containing from 1 to 10 objects each. Ask your child to count the number of objects in each group and to write the numbers.

Name _____

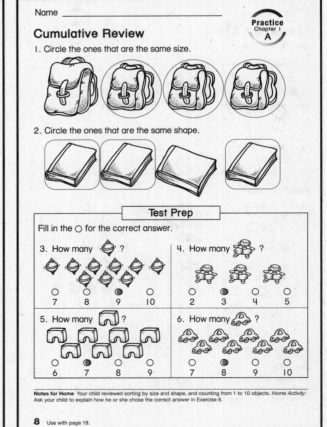

Cumulative Review

1. Circle the ones that are the same size.

2. Circle the ones that are the same shape.

Test Prep
Fill in the ◯ for the correct answer.

3. How many 🪀 ?

7   8   ●9   10

4. How many 🧸 ?

2   ●3   4   5

5. How many 🪑 ?

6   ●7   8   9

6. How many 🚗 ?

7   ●8   9   10

Notes for Home Your child reviewed sorting by size and shape, and counting from 1 to 10 objects. *Home Activity:* Ask your child to explain how he or she chose the correct answer in Exercise 6.

Name _____

Explore More and Fewer

Write how many.
Circle the group that has more.

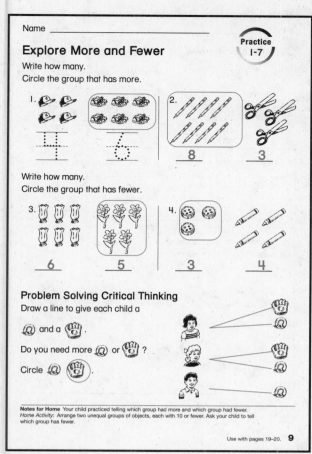

1. 4
6

2. 8
3

Write how many.
Circle the group that has fewer.

3. 6
5

4. 3
4

Problem Solving Critical Thinking

Draw a line to give each child a
⚾ and a 🧤.

Do you need more ⚾ or 🧤?

Circle ⚾ 🧤.

Notes for Home Your child practiced telling which group had more and which group had fewer. *Home Activity:* Arrange two unequal groups of objects, each with 10 or fewer. Ask your child to tell which group has fewer.

Use with pages 19–20. **9**

Name _____

Order Numbers to 10

Draw the missing towers. Write how many.

1.

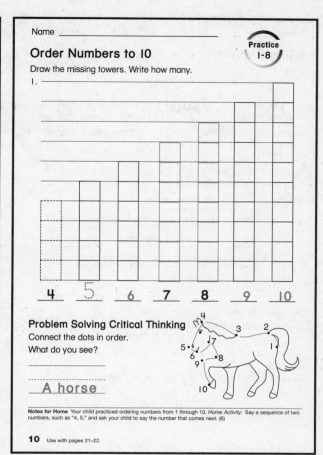

4 5 6 7 8 9 10

Problem Solving Critical Thinking

Connect the dots in order.
What do you see?

A horse

Notes for Home Your child practiced ordering numbers from 1 through 10. *Home Activity:* Say a sequence of two numbers, such as "4, 5," and ask your child to say the number that comes next. (6)

10 Use with pages 21–22.

Name _____

Understand 11 and 12

Write how many.

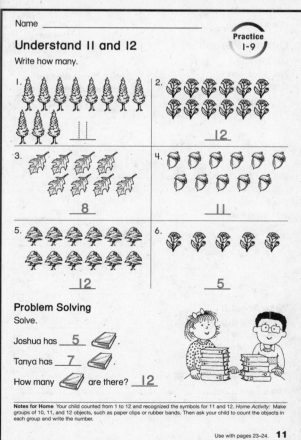

1. 11

2. 12

3. 8

4. 11

5. 12

6. 5

Problem Solving

Solve.

Joshua has 5 📕.

Tanya has 7 📗.

How many 📘 are there? 12

Notes for Home Your child counted from 1 to 12 and recognized the symbols for 11 and 12. *Home Activity:* Make groups of 10, 11, and 12 objects, such as paper clips or rubber bands. Then ask your child to count the objects in each group and write the number.

Use with pages 23–24. **11**

Name _____

Problem Solving: Look for a Pattern

Complete each pattern.
Color what comes next.

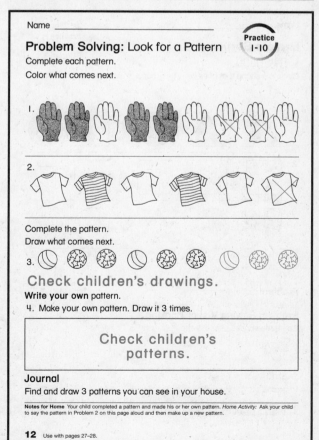

1.

2.

Complete the pattern.
Draw what comes next.

3.

Check children's drawings.

Write your own pattern.

4. Make your own pattern. Draw it 3 times.

Check children's
patterns.

Journal

Find and draw 3 patterns you can see in your house.

Notes for Home Your child completed a pattern and made his or her own pattern. *Home Activity:* Ask your child to say the pattern in Problem 2 on this page aloud and then make up a new pattern.

12 Use with pages 27–28.

Name _____

Mixed Practice: Lessons 7–10

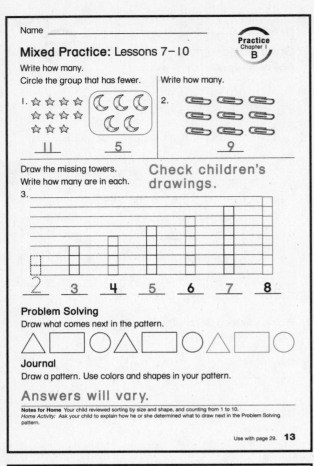

Write how many.
Circle the group that has fewer. | Write how many.

1. ☆☆☆☆☆ 🌙🌙🌙
☆☆☆☆☆ 🌙🌙
☆☆☆

__11__   __5__

2.

__9__

Draw the missing towers.
Write how many are in each.
3. _____

Check children's drawings.

__2__ __3__ __4__ __5__ __6__ __7__ __8__

Problem Solving
Draw what comes next in the pattern.

△ □ ○ △ □ ○ △ □ ○

Journal
Draw a pattern. Use colors and shapes in your pattern.

Answers will vary.

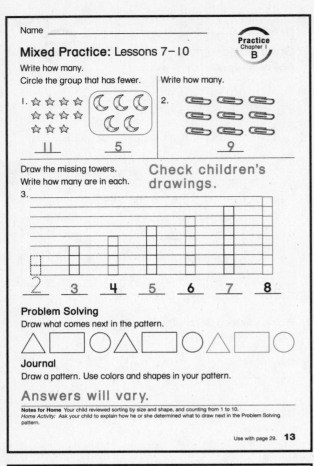

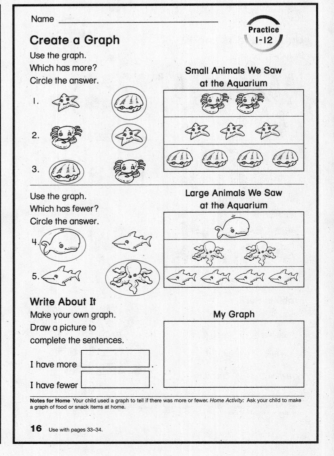

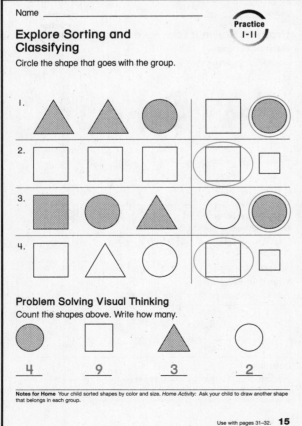

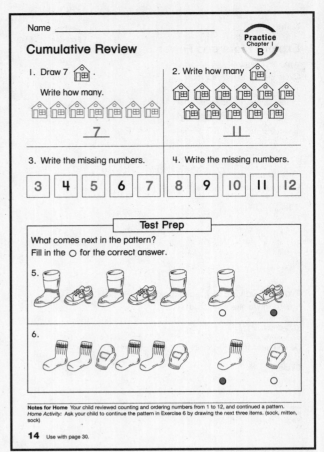

Name _____

Cumulative Review

1. Draw 7 🏠 .

Write how many.

__7__

2. Write how many.

__11__

3. Write the missing numbers.

| 3 | 4 | 5 | 6 | 7 |

4. Write the missing numbers.

| 8 | 9 | 10 | 11 | 12 |

Test Prep
What comes next in the pattern?
Fill in the ○ for the correct answer.

5.

○ ●

6.

● ○

Name _____

Explore Sorting and Classifying
Circle the shape that goes with the group.

1. △ △ ○ | □ ○
2. □ □ □ | □ □
3. □ ○ △ | ○ ○
4. □ △ ○ | □ □

Problem Solving Visual Thinking
Count the shapes above. Write how many.

○ __4__   □ __9__   △ __3__   ○ __2__

Name _____

Create a Graph
Use the graph.
Which has more?
Circle the answer.

1. ⭐ 🐚
2. 🦀 ⭐
3. 🐚 🦀

Small Animals We Saw at the Aquarium

Use the graph.
Which has fewer?
Circle the answer.

4. 🐋 🦈
5. 🦈 🐙

Large Animals We Saw at the Aquarium

Write About It
Make your own graph.
Draw a picture to
complete the sentences.

My Graph

I have more _____ .

I have fewer _____ .

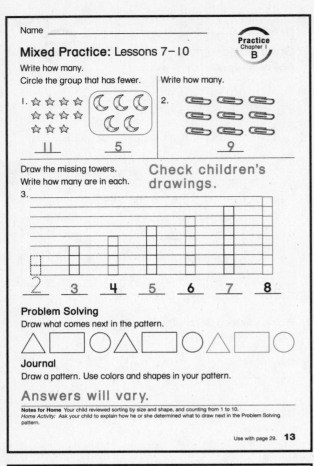

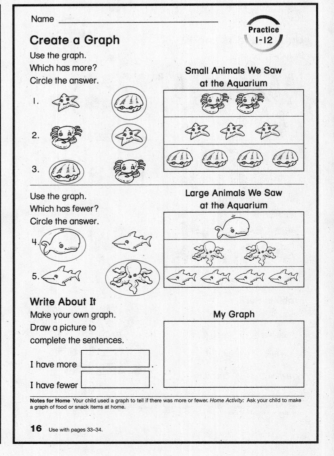

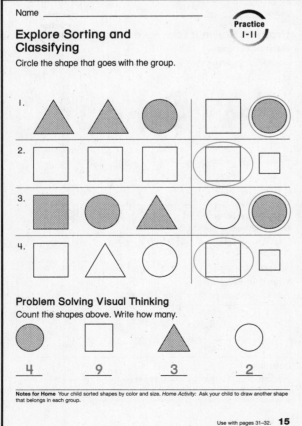

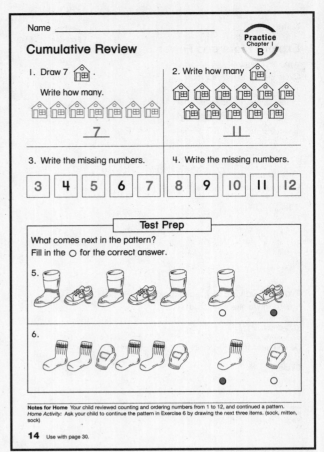

Notes for Home Your child reviewed sorting by size and shape, and counting from 1 to 10.
Home Activity: Ask your child to explain how he or she determined what to draw next in the Problem Solving pattern.

Use with page 29. **13**

Notes for Home Your child reviewed counting and ordering numbers from 1 to 12, and continued a pattern.
Home Activity: Ask your child to continue the pattern in Exercise 6 by drawing the next three items. (sock, mitten, sock)

14 Use with page 30.

Notes for Home Your child sorted shapes by color and size. *Home Activity:* Ask your child to draw another shape that belongs in each group.

Use with pages 31–32. **15**

Notes for Home Your child used a graph to tell if there was more or fewer. *Home Activity:* Ask your child to make a graph of food or snack items at home.

16 Use with pages 33–34.

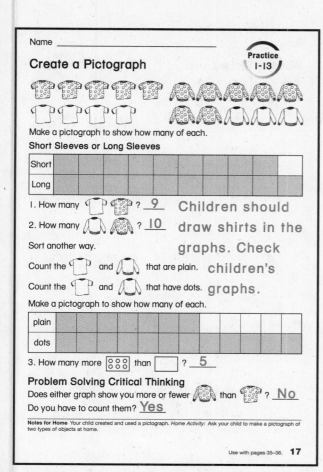

Name _____

Create a Pictograph

Make a pictograph to show how many of each.

Short Sleeves or Long Sleeves

Short									
Long									

1. How many 👕 👕 ? __9__   Children should

2. How many 👕 👕 ? __10__   draw shirts in the

Sort another way.   graphs. Check

Count the 👕 and 👕 that are plain.   children's

Count the 👕 and 👕 that have dots.   graphs.

Make a pictograph to show how many of each.

plain									
dots									

3. How many more ⚅ than ☐ ? __5__

Problem Solving Critical Thinking

Does either graph show you more or fewer 👕 than 👕 ? __No__

Do you have to count them? __Yes__

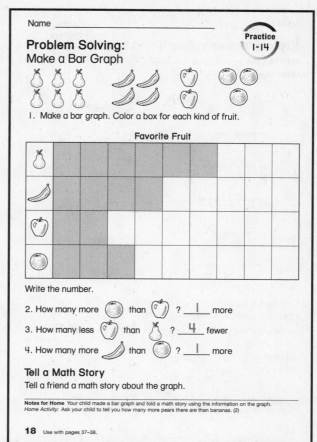

Name _____

Problem Solving:
Make a Bar Graph

1. Make a bar graph. Color a box for each kind of fruit.

Favorite Fruit

🍐							
🍌							
🍎							
🍊							

Write the number.

2. How many more 🍊 than 🍎 ? __1__ more

3. How many less 🍎 than 🍐 ? __4__ fewer

4. How many more 🍌 than 🍊 ? __1__ more

Tell a Math Story

Tell a friend a math story about the graph.

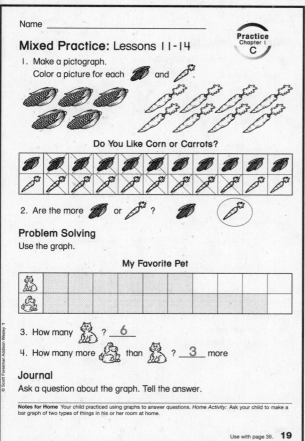

Name _____

Mixed Practice: Lessons 11-14

1. Make a pictograph.
   Color a picture for each 🌽 and 🥕

Do You Like Corn or Carrots?

2. Are the more 🌽 or 🥕 ? 🌽 (🥕)

Problem Solving
Use the graph.

My Favorite Pet

🐱							
🐶							

3. How many 🐱 ? __6__

4. How many more 🐶 than 🐱 ? __3__ more

Journal
Ask a question about the graph. Tell the answer.

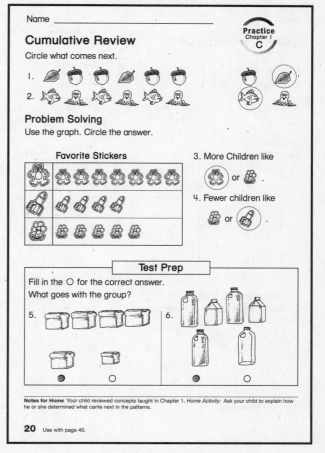

Name _____

Cumulative Review

Circle what comes next.

1. 🍂 🌰 🌰 🍂 🌰 | 🌰 🍂

2. 🐟 🐙 🐟 🐙 🐟 🐙 | 🐟 🐙

Problem Solving
Use the graph. Circle the answer.

Favorite Stickers

3. More Children like 🌸 or 🌼

4. Fewer children like 🌼 or 💄

Test Prep
Fill in the ○ for the correct answer.
What goes with the group?

5. ● ○

6. ● ○

Explore Ways to Make 4 and 5

Practice 2-1

Show ways to make 5. Color the cubes.
Write the numbers.

1. $\underline{3}$ and $\underline{2}$ is $\underline{5}$.

2. $\underline{4}$ and $\underline{1}$ is $\underline{5}$.

3. $\underline{2}$ and $\underline{3}$ is $\underline{5}$.

4. $\underline{1}$ and $\underline{4}$ is $\underline{5}$.

5. $\underline{5}$ and $\underline{0}$ is $\underline{5}$.

6. $\underline{0}$ and $\underline{5}$ is $\underline{5}$.

Problem Solving Critical Thinking

7. How can you use 🎲 to show that 4 and 1 is the same as 1 and 4?

Answers will vary.

Notes for Home Your child used snap cubes to find ways to make 5. Home Activity: Ask your child to find four different ways to make a group of 5 using household objects.

Use with pages 51–52. 21

Ways to Make 6 and 7

Practice 2-2

Show ways to make 6. Color the cubes.
Write the numbers.

1. $\underline{4}$ and $\underline{2}$ is $\underline{6}$.

2. $\underline{2}$ and $\underline{4}$ is $\underline{6}$.

3. $\underline{3}$ and $\underline{3}$ is $\underline{6}$.

4. $\underline{5}$ and $\underline{1}$ is $\underline{6}$.

5. $\underline{1}$ and $\underline{5}$ is $\underline{6}$.

6. $\underline{6}$ and $\underline{0}$ is $\underline{6}$.

Mental Math

Solve. You have 3.

7. Circle the card you need to make 6.

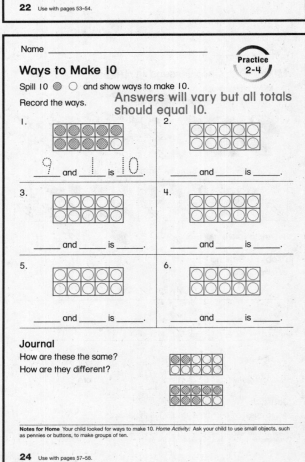

Notes for Home Your child used counters to find different ways to make 6. Home Activity: Ask your child to draw groups of 6 and 7 objects.

22 Use with pages 53–54.

Ways to Make 8 and 9

Practice 2-3

	Gray	White	In All
	3	5	8

Spill 8 ⬭ ⬬ .

Show gray and white on your ☐ .

Use the table to record.

Spill counters and show ways to make 8.
Record the ways.

	Gray	White	In All
1.	3	5	8
2.			
3.			
4.			

Answers will vary but all totals should equal 8.

Problem Solving Visual Thinking

5. Match the groups with the same number.

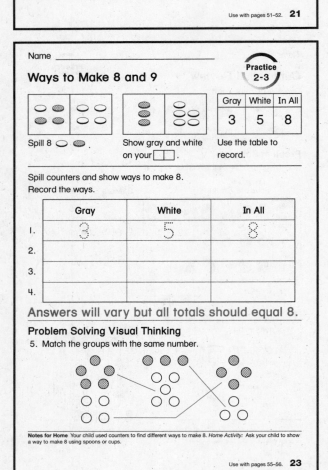

Notes for Home Your child used counters to find different ways to make 8. Home Activity: Ask your child to show a way to make 8 using spoons or cups.

Use with pages 55–56. 23

Ways to Make 10

Practice 2-4

Spill 10 ◉ ○ and show ways to make 10.
Record the ways.

Answers will vary but all totals should equal 10.

1. $\underline{9}$ and $\underline{1}$ is $\underline{10}$.

2. ___ and ___ is ___.

3. ___ and ___ is ___.

4. ___ and ___ is ___.

5. ___ and ___ is ___.

6. ___ and ___ is ___.

Journal

How are these the same?
How are they different?

Notes for Home Your child looked for ways to make 10. Home Activity: Ask your child to use small objects, such as pennies or buttons, to make groups of ten.

24 Use with pages 57–58.

Problem Solving: Make a Table

1. How many ways can you put 8 🍎 in 2 📄 ?

📄	📄	In All
0	8	8
1	7	8
2	6	8
3	5	8
4	4	8
5	3	8
6	2	8
7	1	8
8	0	8

2. How many ways can you put 10 🍪 in 2 🫙 ?

🫙	🫙	In All
0	10	10
1	9	10
2	8	10
3	7	10
4	6	10
5	5	10
6	4	10
7	3	10
8	2	10
9	1	10
10	0	10

Problem Solving Critical Thinking

3. How many ways are there to make 9? __10 ways__

4. How many ways are there to make 6? __7 ways__

How do you know? __Answers will vary.__

Notes for Home Your child made tables to find all the ways to make 8 and 10. Home Activity: Ask your child how many ways 9 pencils or pens can be placed in 2 glasses. (10 ways)

Mixed Practice: Lessons 1–5

Use 1 or 2 colors to make 7 and 8.
Color. Write the numbers.

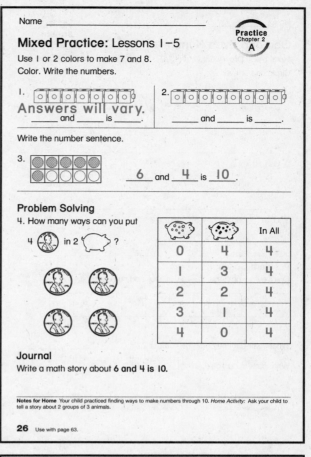

1. Answers will vary.
____ and ____ is ____.

2. ____ and ____ is ____.

Write the number sentence.

3. __6__ and __4__ is __10__.

Problem Solving

4. How many ways can you put 4 🪙 in 2 🐷 ?

🐷	🐷	In All
0	4	4
1	3	4
2	2	4
3	1	4
4	0	4

Journal

Write a math story about **6 and 4 is 10.**

Notes for Home Your child practiced finding ways to make numbers through 10. Home Activity: Ask your child to tell a story about 2 groups of 3 animals.

Cumulative Review

Write how many.

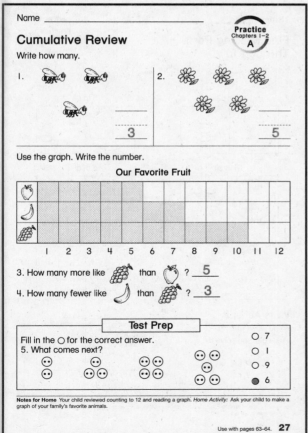

1. __3__

2. __5__

Use the graph. Write the number.

Our Favorite Fruit

	1	2	3	4	5	6	7	8	9	10	11	12

3. How many more like 🍇 than 🍎 ? __5__

4. How many fewer like 🍌 than 🍇 ? __3__

Test Prep

Fill in the ○ for the correct answer.

5. What comes next?

⚁ ⚁ ⚁ ⚁

○ 7
○ 1
○ 9
● 6

Notes for Home Your child reviewed counting to 12 and reading a graph. Home Activity: Ask your child to make a graph of your family's favorite animals.

More and Fewer

Use 🎲.

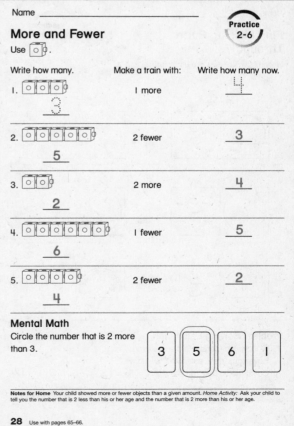

Write how many.	Make a train with:	Write how many now.
1. __3__	1 more	__4__
2. __5__	2 fewer	__3__
3. __2__	2 more	__4__
4. __6__	1 fewer	__5__
5. __4__	2 fewer	__2__

Mental Math

Circle the number that is 2 more than 3.

3	(5)	6	1

Notes for Home Your child showed more or fewer objects than a given amount. Home Activity: Ask your child to tell you the number that is 2 less than his or her age and the number that is 2 more than his or her age.

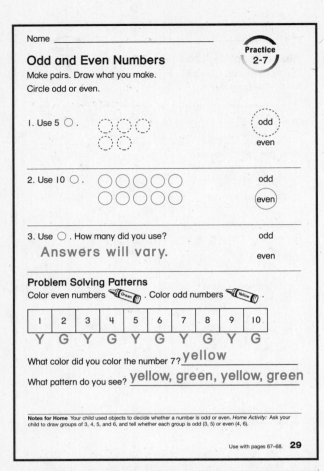

Name _____

Odd and Even Numbers

Practice 2-7

Make pairs. Draw what you make.
Circle odd or even.

1. Use 5 ○.   odd
                 even

2. Use 10 ○.   odd
                 (even)

3. Use ○. How many did you use?   odd
   Answers will vary.   even

Problem Solving Patterns

Color even numbers (Green). Color odd numbers (Yellow).

1	2	3	4	5	6	7	8	9	10
Y	G	Y	G	Y	G	Y	G	Y	G

What color did you color the number 7? yellow

What pattern do you see? yellow, green, yellow, green

Notes for Home Your child used objects to decide whether a number is odd or even. Home Activity: Ask your child to draw groups of 3, 4, 5, and 6, and tell whether each group is odd (3, 5) or even (4, 6).

Use with pages 67–68. **29**

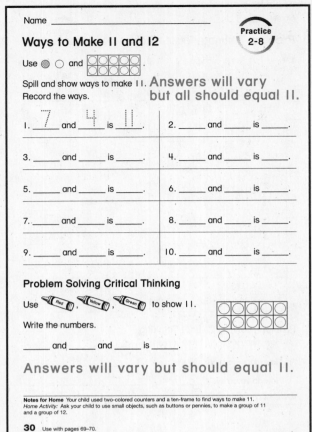

Name _____

Ways to Make 11 and 12

Practice 2-8

Use ◉ ○ and [ten-frame].

Spill and show ways to make 11.   Answers will vary
Record the ways.   but all should equal 11.

1. 7 and 4 is 11.   2. ____ and ____ is ____.

3. ____ and ____ is ____.   4. ____ and ____ is ____.

5. ____ and ____ is ____.   6. ____ and ____ is ____.

7. ____ and ____ is ____.   8. ____ and ____ is ____.

9. ____ and ____ is ____.   10. ____ and ____ is ____.

Problem Solving Critical Thinking

Use (Red), (Yellow), (Green) to show 11.

Write the numbers.

____ and ____ and ____ is ____.

Answers will vary but should equal 11.

Notes for Home Your child used two-colored counters and a ten-frame to find ways to make 11. Home Activity: Ask your child to use small objects, such as buttons or pennies, to make a group of 11 and a group of 12.

30 Use with pages 69–70.

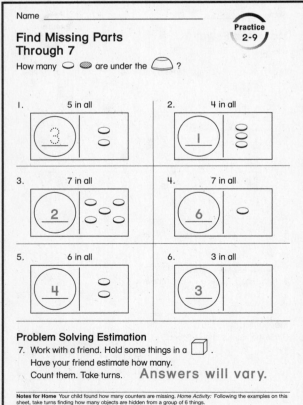

Name _____

Find Missing Parts Through 7

Practice 2-9

How many ○ ◉ are under the ⌒ ?

1. 5 in all   2. 4 in all
   3   1

3. 7 in all   4. 7 in all
   2   6

5. 6 in all   6. 3 in all
   4   3

Problem Solving Estimation

7. Work with a friend. Hold some things in a □.
   Have your friend estimate how many.
   Count them. Take turns.   Answers will vary.

Notes for Home Your child found how many counters are missing. Home Activity: Following the examples on this sheet, take turns finding how many objects are hidden from a group of 6 things.

Use with pages 71–72. **31**

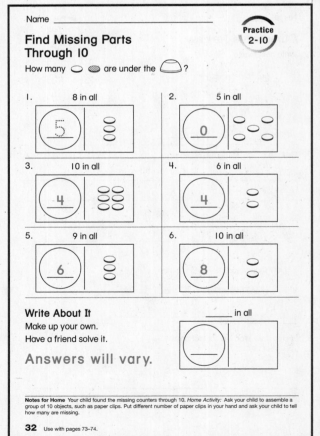

Name _____

Find Missing Parts Through 10

Practice 2-10

How many ○ ◉ are under the ⌒ ?

1. 8 in all   2. 5 in all
   5   0

3. 10 in all   4. 6 in all
   4   4

5. 9 in all   6. 10 in all
   6   8

Write About It

Make up your own.
Have a friend solve it.

____ in all

Answers will vary.

Notes for Home Your child found the missing counters through 10. Home Activity: Ask your child to assemble a group of 10 objects, such as paper clips. Put different number of paper clips in your hand and ask your child to tell how many are missing.

32 Use with pages 73–74.

Problem Solving: Draw a Picture

Practice 2-11

Draw a picture to show the problem.
Write how many in all.

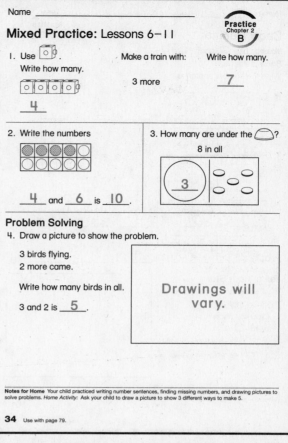

1. 2 and 3 is 5 .

2. 1 and 2 is 3 .

3. 4 and 3 is 7 .

4. 3 and 3 is 6 .

Tell a Math Story

5. Draw a picture of 3 ducks and 1 cow.
   Tell a math story about your picture.

Answers will vary.

Notes for Home Your child used the strategy Draw a Picture to solve problems. Home Activity: Ask your child to draw a picture of children playing and to tell a number story about the picture.

Use with pages 77–78. 33

Mixed Practice: Lessons 6–11

Practice Chapter 2 B

1. Use [die].   Make a train with: Write how many.
   Write how many.

   3 more   7

   4

2. Write the numbers

   4 and 6 is 10 .

3. How many are under the ⌣?
   8 in all

   3

Problem Solving

4. Draw a picture to show the problem.

   3 birds flying.
   2 more came.

   Write how many birds in all.

   3 and 2 is 5 .

   Drawings will vary.

Notes for Home Your child practiced writing number sentences, finding missing numbers, and drawing pictures to solve problems. Home Activity: Ask your child to draw a picture to show 3 different ways to make 5.

34 Use with page 79.

Cumulative Review

Practice Chapters 1–2 B

Circle the one that belongs.

1.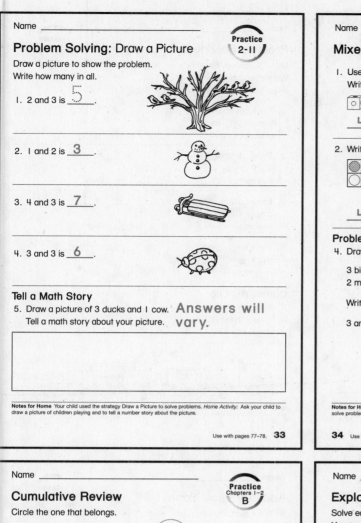

2. Draw the missing tower. Write how many in each tower.

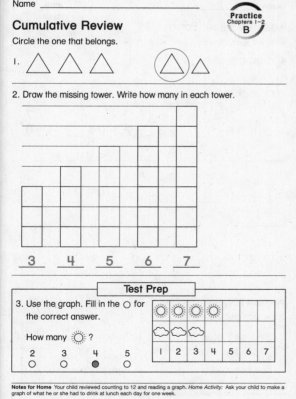

3   4   5   6   7

Test Prep

3. Use the graph. Fill in the ○ for
   the correct answer.

   How many ☀ ?

   2   3   4   5
   ○   ○   ●   ○

Notes for Home Your child reviewed counting to 12 and reading a graph. Home Activity: Ask your child to make a graph of what he or she had to drink at lunch each day for one week.

Use with page 80. 35

Explore Addition

Practice 3-1

Solve each problem.
You can use ○.

1. There are 3 🐕 .

   2 more 🐕 come.

   How many in all?

   3 and 2 is 5 .

2. There are 6 🐤 .

   2 more 🐤 come.

   How many in all?

   6 and 2 is 8 .

3. There are 5 🐈 .

   4 more 🐈 come.

   How many in all?

   5 and 4 is 9 .

4. There are 5 boys and 3 girls.

   How many children in all?

   5 and 3 is 8 .

Problem Solving Visual Thinking

5. Draw a picture. Tell a math story about the picture.

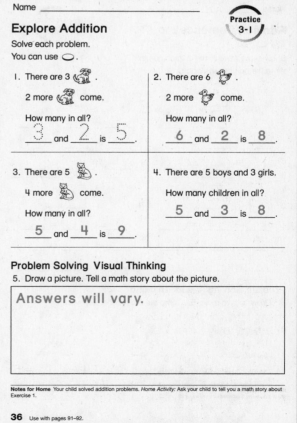

Answers will vary.

Notes for Home Your child solved addition problems. Home Activity: Ask your child to tell you a math story about Exercise 1.

36 Use with pages 91–92.

Show Addition

You can use ⬭ and ▭.
Show the parts.
Write the number sentence.

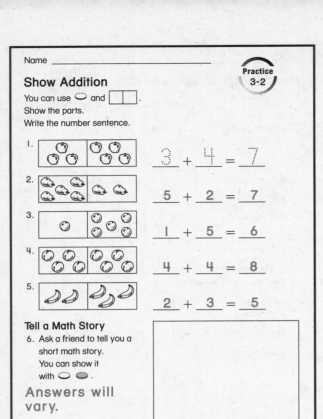

1. $3 + 4 = 7$

2. $5 + 2 = 7$

3. $1 + 5 = 6$

4. $4 + 4 = 8$

5. $2 + 3 = 5$

Tell a Math Story

6. Ask a friend to tell you a
   short math story.
   You can show it
   with ⬭ ⬬.

Answers will
vary.

Notes for Home Your child used counters and wrote number sentences to show addition. *Home Activity:* Ask your child to show 5 + 4 using common objects, such as buttons or pennies.

Problem Solving: Use Addition

Use ⬭ to show the story.
Write a number sentence.
Write how many in all.

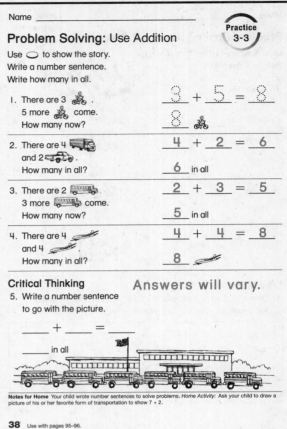

1. There are 3 🚲.
   5 more 🚲 come.
   How many now?

   $3 + 5 = 8$
   8 🚲

2. There are 4 🚚
   and 2 🚗.
   How many in all?

   $4 + 2 = 6$
   6 in all

3. There are 2 🚌.
   3 more 🚌 come.
   How many now?

   $2 + 3 = 5$
   5 in all

4. There are 4 ✈
   and 4 ✈.
   How many in all?

   $4 + 4 = 8$
   8 ✈

Critical Thinking

Answers will vary.

5. Write a number sentence
   to go with the picture.

____ + ____ = ____

____ in all

Notes for Home Your child wrote number sentences to solve problems. *Home Activity:* Ask your child to draw a picture of his or her favorite form of transportation to show 7 + 2.

Addition Sentences to 12

Use ⬭ ⬬.

Answers will
vary.

Show some ways to make each number.
Write the number sentences.

1. **8**

   $3 + 5 = 8$
   ___ + ___ = ___
   ___ + ___ = ___

2. **10**

   ___ + ___ = ___
   ___ + ___ = ___
   ___ + ___ = ___

3. **12**

   ___ + ___ = ___
   ___ + ___ = ___
   ___ + ___ = ___

4. **6**

   ___ + ___ = ___
   ___ + ___ = ___
   ___ + ___ = ___

Problem Solving Visual Thinking

5. Draw balls to make 5. Complete the number sentences.

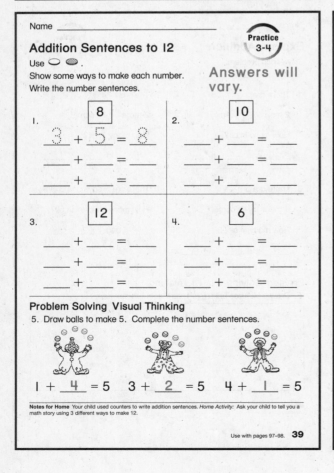

$1 + 4 = 5$ $3 + 2 = 5$ $4 + 1 = 5$

Notes for Home Your child used counters to write addition sentences. *Home Activity:* Ask your child to tell you a math story using 3 different ways to make 12.

Add in Vertical Form

Write the sums. You can use 🎲.

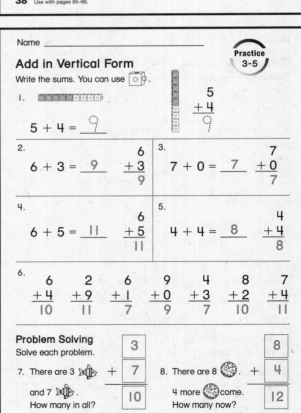

1. $5 + 4 = 9$

   $\begin{array}{r} 5 \\ +4 \\ \hline 9 \end{array}$

2. $6 + 3 = 9$ $\begin{array}{r} 6 \\ +3 \\ \hline 9 \end{array}$

3. $7 + 0 = 7$ $\begin{array}{r} 7 \\ +0 \\ \hline 7 \end{array}$

4. $6 + 5 = 11$ $\begin{array}{r} 6 \\ +5 \\ \hline 11 \end{array}$

5. $4 + 4 = 8$ $\begin{array}{r} 4 \\ +4 \\ \hline 8 \end{array}$

6. $\begin{array}{r} 6 \\ +4 \\ \hline 10 \end{array}$ $\begin{array}{r} 2 \\ +9 \\ \hline 11 \end{array}$ $\begin{array}{r} 6 \\ +1 \\ \hline 7 \end{array}$ $\begin{array}{r} 9 \\ +0 \\ \hline 9 \end{array}$ $\begin{array}{r} 4 \\ +3 \\ \hline 7 \end{array}$ $\begin{array}{r} 8 \\ +2 \\ \hline 10 \end{array}$ $\begin{array}{r} 7 \\ +4 \\ \hline 11 \end{array}$

Problem Solving

Solve each problem.

7. There are 3 🐟
   and 7 🐟.
   How many in all?

   $3 + 7 = 10$

8. There are 8 🍪.
   4 more 🍪 come.
   How many now?

   $8 + 4 = 12$

Notes for Home Your child solved addition problems that were shown both horizontally and vertically. *Home Activity:* Write 3 addition sentences horizontally. Ask your child to write them vertically and to solve them.

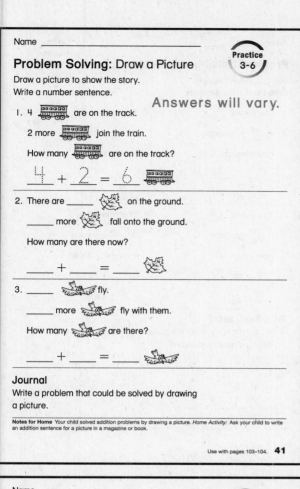

Problem Solving: Draw a Picture

Draw a picture to show the story.
Write a number sentence.

Answers will vary.

1. 4 🚃 are on the track.

   2 more 🚃 join the train.

   How many 🚃 are on the track?

   __4__ + __2__ = __6__ 🚃

2. There are _____ 🍂 on the ground.

   _____ more 🍂 fall onto the ground.

   How many are there now?

   _____ + _____ = _____ 🍂

3. _____ 🐦 fly.

   _____ more 🐦 fly with them.

   How many 🐦 are there?

   _____ + _____ = _____ 🐦

Journal

Write a problem that could be solved by drawing
a picture.

Notes for Home Your child solved addition problems by drawing a picture. *Home Activity:* Ask your child to write
an addition sentence for a picture in a magazine or book.

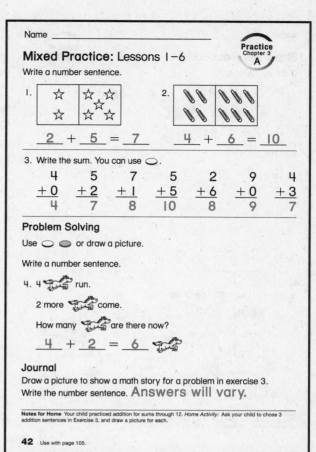

Mixed Practice: Lessons 1–6

Write a number sentence.

1. ☆ ☆☆ / ☆ ☆☆

   __2__ + __5__ = __7__

2. 🥖🥖 / 🥖🥖🥖

   __4__ + __6__ = __10__

3. Write the sum. You can use ⬭.

4	5	7	5	2	9	4
+0	+2	+1	+5	+6	+0	+3
4	7	8	10	8	9	7

Problem Solving

Use ⬭ 🍪 or draw a picture.

Write a number sentence.

4. 4 🐎 run.

   2 more 🐎 come.

   How many 🐎 are there now?

   __4__ + __2__ = __6__ 🐎

Journal

Draw a picture to show a math story for a problem in exercise 3.
Write the number sentence. **Answers will vary.**

Notes for Home Your child practiced addition for sums through 12. *Home Activity:* Ask your child to chose 3
addition sentences in Exercise 3, and draw a picture for each.

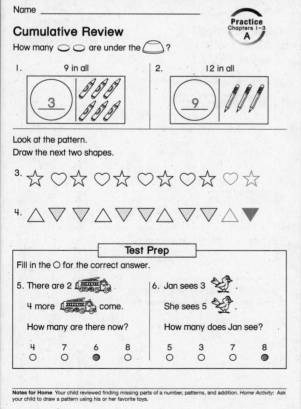

Cumulative Review

How many ⬭ ⬭ are under the ⬬ ?

1. 9 in all — ③ | 🖍️🖍️🖍️🖍️🖍️🖍️

2. 12 in all — ⑨ | ✏️✏️✏️

Look at the pattern.
Draw the next two shapes.

3. ☆ ♡ ☆ ♡ ☆ ♡ ☆ ♡ ☆ ♡ ☆

4. △ ▽ ▽ △ ▽ ▽ △ ▽ ▽ △ ▼

Test Prep

Fill in the ○ for the correct answer.

5. There are 2 🚒 .

   4 more 🚒 come.

   How many are there now?

   4 ○   7 ○   6 ●   8 ○

6. Jan sees 3 🐦 .

   She sees 5 🐦 .

   How many does Jan see?

   5 ○   3 ○   7 ○   8 ●

Notes for Home Your child reviewed finding missing parts of a number, patterns, and addition. *Home Activity:* Ask
your child to draw a pattern using his or her favorite toys.

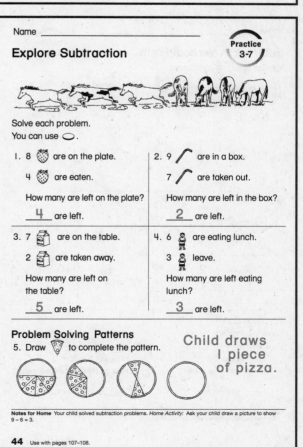

Explore Subtraction

Solve each problem.
You can use ⬭ .

1. 8 🍓 are on the plate.

   4 🍓 are eaten.

   How many are left on the plate?

   __4__ are left.

2. 9 🍬 are in a box.

   7 🍬 are taken out.

   How many are left in the box?

   __2__ are left.

3. 7 🥛 are on the table.

   2 🥛 are taken away.

   How many are left on
   the table?

   __5__ are left.

4. 6 🧍 are eating lunch.

   3 🧍 leave.

   How many are left eating
   lunch?

   __3__ are left.

Problem Solving Patterns

5. Draw 🍕 to complete the pattern.

**Child draws
1 piece
of pizza.**

Notes for Home Your child solved subtraction problems. *Home Activity:* Ask your child draw a picture to show
9 – 6 = 3.

Show Subtraction

Cross out. Subtract.

1.    2. 🐘🐘🐘

$8 - 3 =$ __5__ $5 - 2 =$ __3__

Subtract.

3. $12 - 7 =$ __5__ $7 - 6 =$ __1__ $9 - 3 =$ __6__

4. $6 - 4 =$ __2__ $5 - 2 =$ __3__ $4 - 4 =$ __0__

5. $8 - 4 =$ __4__ $10 - 2 =$ __8__ $11 - 8 =$ __3__

Mental Math

6. Use the clues. Write each number.

My number is 6 more than 3.

My number is 4 less than 11.

My number is __9__ .   My number is __7__ .

Notes for Home Your child subtracted by crossing out objects in a picture and then wrote how many were left. Home Activity: Ask your child to draw a picture of 12 objects, cross out 2, 3, and 4 of the objects, and write the subtraction sentence for each. (12 − 2 = 10, 12 − 3 = 9, 12 − 4 = 8)

Problem Solving: Use Subtraction

Use ◯. Show the story.
Write the number sentence.

1. There are 8 🐰.

6 🐰 hop away.

How many are left?

__8__ − __6__ = __2__

__2__ are left.

2. There are 6 🐍.

2 🐍 slide away.

How many now?

__6__ − __2__ = __4__

__4__ 🐍.

3. There are 7 🦌.

4 🦌 run away.

How many now?

__7__ − __4__ = __3__

__3__ 🦌.

4. There are 12 🐿.

3 🐿 run away.

How many are left?

__12__ − __3__ = __9__

__9__ are left.

Tell a Math Story

5. Tell a math story about the picture.
Write the number sentence.

There are 5 birds.
2 fly away.
3 are left.

$5 - 2 =$ __3__

Notes for Home Your child read math stories and wrote number sentences to answer the questions. Home Activity: Ask your child to draw a picture for the number sentence 10 − 9 and then have him or her solve it.

Subtract in Vertical Form

You can use 🎲 to subtract.

1. $6 - 2 =$ __4__

$$\begin{array}{r} 6 \\ -2 \\ \hline 4 \end{array}$$

2. $11 - 8 =$ __3__

$$\begin{array}{r} 11 \\ -8 \\ \hline 3 \end{array}$$

3. $7 - 7 =$ __0__

$$\begin{array}{r} 7 \\ -7 \\ \hline 0 \end{array}$$

4. $10 - 9 =$ __1__

$$\begin{array}{r} 10 \\ -9 \\ \hline 1 \end{array}$$

5. $12 - 6 =$ __6__

$$\begin{array}{r} 12 \\ -6 \\ \hline 6 \end{array}$$

6.
$$\begin{array}{r} 5 \\ -1 \\ \hline 4 \end{array} \quad \begin{array}{r} 12 \\ -1 \\ \hline 11 \end{array} \quad \begin{array}{r} 9 \\ -6 \\ \hline 3 \end{array} \quad \begin{array}{r} 8 \\ -8 \\ \hline 0 \end{array} \quad \begin{array}{r} 10 \\ -2 \\ \hline 8 \end{array} \quad \begin{array}{r} 6 \\ -4 \\ \hline 2 \end{array}$$

Problem Solving

Solve the problem.

7. There were 12 🍪.
Now there are 7.
How many were eaten?

__5__ were eaten.

8. Kara had 8 🐶.
Now she has 3.
How many did she give away?

__5__ were given away.

Notes for Home Your child subtracted in horizontal and vertical forms. Home Activity: Ask your child to write the Problem Solving problem in horizontal form and solve it.

Relate Addition and Subtraction

You can use 🎲🎲.

Complete the number sentences.

1.

$5 + 3 =$ __8__

$8 - 3 =$ __5__

2.

$7 + 2 =$ __9__

$9 - 2 =$ __7__

3.

$4 + 1 =$ __5__

$5 - 1 =$ __4__

4.

$8 + 3 =$ __11__

$11 - 3 =$ __8__

Problem Solving Critical Thinking

5. How many ways can you subtract from 2? __3__

$2 -$ __2__ $=$ __0__

$2 -$ __1__ $=$ __1__

$2 -$ __0__ $=$ __2__

Notes for Home Your child wrote related addition and subtraction sentences. Home Activity: Ask your child write how many ways he or she can subtract from 4. (There are 5 ways: 4 − 0 = 4, 4 − 1 = 3, 4 − 2 = 2, 4 − 3 = 1, 4 − 4 = 0.)

Problem Solving:
Choose an Operation

Practice
3-12

Use ⬭ ⬤ to show the story.
Circle add or subtract. Write the number sentence.

1. There are 12 🟡.   add   (subtract)

   3 🟡 are eaten.

   How many are there now?   12 ⊖ 3 = 9

2. There are 2 🥛.   (add)   subtract

   2 more 🥛 are poured.

   How many in all?   2 ⊕ 2 = 4

3. 4 🍪 are on the plate.   add   (subtract)

   3 🍪 are taken away.

   How many are on the plate?   4 ⊖ 3 = 1

4. 5 🎲 on the table.   (add)   subtract

   Children bring 4 more 🎲.

   How many are on the table now? 5 ⊕ 4 = 9

Journal

Stories will vary.

Think about 5 things that you have.

Write an addition story.

Write a subtraction story.

Notes for Home Your child read number stories, chose and wrote the addition or subtraction sign, and then solved the problems. *Home Activity:* Ask your child to write an addition and a subtraction story about people who come and go in your family.

Mixed Practice: Lessons 7–12

Practice
Chapter 3
B

Subtract.
You can use 🎲 🎲.

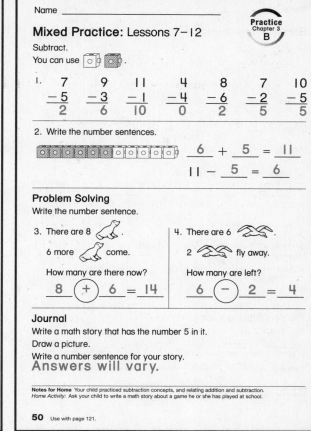

1.
$$\begin{array}{cc} 7 \\ -5 \\ \hline 2 \end{array} \quad \begin{array}{cc} 9 \\ -3 \\ \hline 6 \end{array} \quad \begin{array}{cc} 11 \\ -1 \\ \hline 10 \end{array} \quad \begin{array}{cc} 4 \\ -4 \\ \hline 0 \end{array} \quad \begin{array}{cc} 8 \\ -6 \\ \hline 2 \end{array} \quad \begin{array}{cc} 7 \\ -2 \\ \hline 5 \end{array} \quad \begin{array}{cc} 10 \\ -5 \\ \hline 5 \end{array}$$

2. Write the number sentences.

   6 + 5 = 11

   11 − 5 = 6

Problem Solving

Write the number sentence.

3. There are 8 🦭.   4. There are 6 🦅.

   6 more 🦭 come.   2 🦅 fly away.

   How many are there now?   How many are left?

   8 ⊕ 6 = 14   6 ⊖ 2 = 4

Journal

Write a math story that has the number 5 in it.

Draw a picture.

Write a number sentence for your story.

Answers will vary.

Notes for Home Your child practiced subtraction concepts, and relating addition and subtraction. *Home Activity:* Ask your child to write a math story about a game he or she has played at school.

Cumulative Review

Practice
Chapters 1–3
B

Use 1 or 2 colors.
Color to show 2 ways to make the number.
Write a number sentence.

1.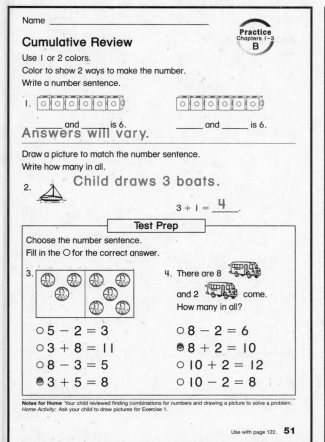

   ____ and ____ is 6.   ____ and ____ is 6.

Answers will vary.

Draw a picture to match the number sentence.
Write how many in all.

2. ⛵ *Child draws 3 boats.*

   3 + 1 = 4 .

Test Prep

Choose the number sentence.
Fill in the ⭘ for the correct answer.

3.
⭘ 5 − 2 = 3
⭘ 3 + 8 = 11
⭘ 8 − 3 = 5
⬤ 3 + 5 = 8

4. There are 8 🚌
   and 2 🚌 come.
   How many in all?

⭘ 8 − 2 = 6
⬤ 8 + 2 = 10
⭘ 10 + 2 = 12
⭘ 10 − 2 = 8

Notes for Home Your child reviewed finding combinations for numbers and drawing a picture to solve a problem. *Home Activity:* Ask your child to draw pictures for Exercise 1.

Count On 1 or 2

Practice
4-1

Count on to add.

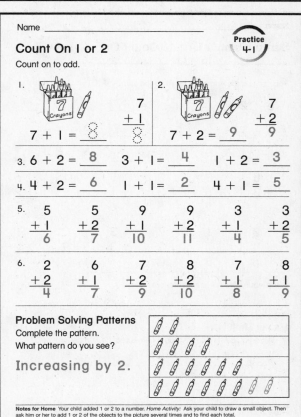

1.
   7 + 1 = 8
   $$\begin{array}{c} 7 \\ +1 \\ \hline 8 \end{array}$$

2.
   7 + 2 = 9
   $$\begin{array}{c} 7 \\ +2 \\ \hline 9 \end{array}$$

3. 6 + 2 = 8   3 + 1 = 4   1 + 2 = 3

4. 4 + 2 = 6   1 + 1 = 2   4 + 1 = 5

5.
$$\begin{array}{c} 5 \\ +1 \\ \hline 6 \end{array} \quad \begin{array}{c} 5 \\ +2 \\ \hline 7 \end{array} \quad \begin{array}{c} 9 \\ +1 \\ \hline 10 \end{array} \quad \begin{array}{c} 9 \\ +2 \\ \hline 11 \end{array} \quad \begin{array}{c} 3 \\ +1 \\ \hline 4 \end{array} \quad \begin{array}{c} 3 \\ +2 \\ \hline 5 \end{array}$$

6.
$$\begin{array}{c} 2 \\ +2 \\ \hline 4 \end{array} \quad \begin{array}{c} 6 \\ +1 \\ \hline 7 \end{array} \quad \begin{array}{c} 7 \\ +2 \\ \hline 9 \end{array} \quad \begin{array}{c} 8 \\ +2 \\ \hline 10 \end{array} \quad \begin{array}{c} 7 \\ +1 \\ \hline 8 \end{array} \quad \begin{array}{c} 8 \\ +1 \\ \hline 9 \end{array}$$

Problem Solving Patterns

Complete the pattern.
What pattern do you see?

Increasing by 2.

Notes for Home Your child added 1 or 2 to a number. *Home Activity:* Ask your child to draw a small object. Then ask him or her to add 1 or 2 of the objects to the picture several times and to find each total.

Explore Turnaround Facts

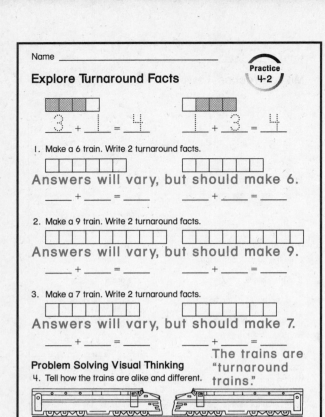

$3 + 1 = 4$ $1 + 3 = 4$

1. Make a 6 train. Write 2 turnaround facts.

Answers will vary, but should make 6.

____ + ____ = ____   ____ + ____ = ____

2. Make a 9 train. Write 2 turnaround facts.

Answers will vary, but should make 9.

____ + ____ = ____   ____ + ____ = ____

3. Make a 7 train. Write 2 turnaround facts.

Answers will vary, but should make 7.

____ + ____ = ____   ____ + ____ = ____

Problem Solving Visual Thinking

4. Tell how the trains are alike and different.

The trains are "turnaround trains."

Notes for Home Your child learned that turnaround facts like 1 + 3 and 3 + 1 always have the same sum. Home Activity: Ask your child to make an 8 train and show 2 turnaround facts.

Count On from Any Number

Think of the greater number.
Count on to add.

1. $2 + 3 = 5$ $\begin{array}{r} 2 \\ +3 \\ \hline 5 \end{array}$

2. $4 + 3 = 7$ | $8 + 1 = 9$ | $4 + 2 = 6$
   $3 + 4 = 7$ | $1 + 8 = 9$ | $2 + 4 = 6$

3. $\begin{array}{r} 4 \\ +1 \\ \hline 5 \end{array}$ $\begin{array}{r} 1 \\ +4 \\ \hline 5 \end{array}$ $\begin{array}{r} 5 \\ +2 \\ \hline 7 \end{array}$ $\begin{array}{r} 2 \\ +5 \\ \hline 7 \end{array}$ $\begin{array}{r} 3 \\ +7 \\ \hline 10 \end{array}$ $\begin{array}{r} 7 \\ +3 \\ \hline 10 \end{array}$

4. $\begin{array}{r} 6 \\ +2 \\ \hline 8 \end{array}$ $\begin{array}{r} 2 \\ +6 \\ \hline 8 \end{array}$ $\begin{array}{r} 1 \\ +9 \\ \hline 10 \end{array}$ $\begin{array}{r} 9 \\ +1 \\ \hline 10 \end{array}$ $\begin{array}{r} 1 \\ +3 \\ \hline 4 \end{array}$ $\begin{array}{r} 3 \\ +1 \\ \hline 4 \end{array}$

Tell a Math Story

5. Look at the picture.
   Think of a math story.
   Tell it to a friend.

Notes for Home Your child added 1, 2, or 3 to the greater number. Home Activity: Ask your child to choose a number sentence in Exercise 5 and to illustrate it.

Use a Number Line to Count On

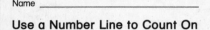

0 1 2 3 4 5 6 7 8 9 10 11 12

You can use the number line. Write the sum.

1. $5 + 2 = 7$ $4 + 3 = 7$ $3 + 1 = 4$

2. $6 + 1 = 7$ $2 + 3 = 5$ $8 + 1 = 9$

3. $4 + 1 = 5$ $2 + 7 = 9$ $3 + 5 = 8$

4. $\begin{array}{r} 8 \\ +3 \\ \hline 11 \end{array}$ $\begin{array}{r} 3 \\ +6 \\ \hline 9 \end{array}$ $\begin{array}{r} 2 \\ +3 \\ \hline 5 \end{array}$ $\begin{array}{r} 5 \\ +1 \\ \hline 6 \end{array}$ $\begin{array}{r} 1 \\ +9 \\ \hline 10 \end{array}$ $\begin{array}{r} 6 \\ +2 \\ \hline 8 \end{array}$

5. $\begin{array}{r} 2 \\ +4 \\ \hline 6 \end{array}$ $\begin{array}{r} 1 \\ +7 \\ \hline 8 \end{array}$ $\begin{array}{r} 7 \\ +3 \\ \hline 10 \end{array}$ $\begin{array}{r} 3 \\ +3 \\ \hline 6 \end{array}$ $\begin{array}{r} 2 \\ +9 \\ \hline 11 \end{array}$ $\begin{array}{r} 1 \\ +2 \\ \hline 3 \end{array}$

Write your own number sentences.
Answers will vary.

6. ____ + 1 = ____   ____ + 2 = ____

Mental Math

7. What number is 3 more than 6? How can the number line help?

9 is 3 more than 6. Possible answer: Start at 6 and count on 3.

Notes for Home Your child used a number line to add numbers. Home Activity: Write 3 addition facts such as 4 + 5, 2 + 7, and 6 + 3, and ask your child to find the sums using a number line.

Add Zero

Add.

1.  $3 + 0 = 3$ 2.  $\begin{array}{r} 5 \\ +0 \\ \hline 5 \end{array}$

3. $5 + 2 = 7$ $3 + 0 = 3$ $1 + 3 = 4$

4. $2 + 0 = 2$ $0 + 0 = 0$ $0 + 6 = 6$

5. $\begin{array}{r} 0 \\ +4 \\ \hline 4 \end{array}$ $\begin{array}{r} 1 \\ +0 \\ \hline 1 \end{array}$ $\begin{array}{r} 3 \\ +5 \\ \hline 8 \end{array}$ $\begin{array}{r} 7 \\ +0 \\ \hline 7 \end{array}$ $\begin{array}{r} 2 \\ +2 \\ \hline 4 \end{array}$ $\begin{array}{r} 9 \\ +1 \\ \hline 10 \end{array}$

6. $\begin{array}{r} 8 \\ +0 \\ \hline 8 \end{array}$ $\begin{array}{r} 9 \\ +2 \\ \hline 11 \end{array}$ $\begin{array}{r} 0 \\ +5 \\ \hline 5 \end{array}$ $\begin{array}{r} 2 \\ +1 \\ \hline 3 \end{array}$ $\begin{array}{r} 6 \\ +0 \\ \hline 6 \end{array}$ $\begin{array}{r} 0 \\ +0 \\ \hline 0 \end{array}$

Problem Solving Critical Thinking

Try this super fact.

$800 + 0 = 800$

Write your own super fact. ____ + 0 = ____
Answers will vary.

Notes for Home Your child added zero. Home Activity: Ask your child to write and solve 3 addition sentences that include adding zero.

Add with 5

Add.

1. 7 + 5 = _12_   5 + 5 = _10_   1 + 5 = _6_

2.
2	4	3	0	5	5
+5	+5	+5	+5	+4	+6
7	9	8	5	9	11

Mixed Practice

Add.

3.
9	7	8	6	5	2
+3	+0	+1	+2	+5	+3
12	7	9	8	10	5

4.
3	2	4	0	9	1
+1	+7	+1	+8	+0	+5
4	9	5	8	9	6

Problem Solving Critical Thinking

5. Circle what you can buy with 🪙 and 🪙🪙🪙🪙🪙.

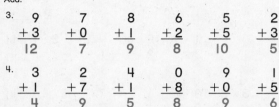

5¢   14¢   20¢

You can buy gum or pretzels.

Notes for Home Your child added 5, 0, and 1, 2, or 3. Home Activity: Ask your child to draw a picture that shows adding 0.

Problem Solving: Make a List

Choose 2 boxes. Make a list.

1. Your friend wants exactly 12 party favors.

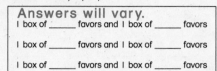

1 box of _9_ favors and 1 box of _3_ favors

1 box of _8_ favors and 1 box of _4_ favors

1 box of _7_ favors and 1 box of _5_ favors

2 boxes of _6_ favors.

2. You want exactly 9 party favors.

Answers will vary.

1 box of _____ favors and 1 box of _____ favors

1 box of _____ favors and 1 box of _____ favors

1 box of _____ favors and 1 box of _____ favors

Critical Thinking

3. Add the numbers in circles.
   Add the numbers in triangles.
   Add the numbers in squares.
   What do you find?
   Each sum is 8.

1 ⑦ ③ △2 ⑤ △6

③ + ⑤ = _8_

△2 + △6 = _8_

1 + 7 = _8_

Notes for Home Your child solved problems by choosing numbers to get a given sum. Home Activity: Ask your child to list 4 ways to get 10 party favors. (Answers will vary, but may include: 5 + 5, 6 + 4, 8 + 2, 7 + 3.)

Chapter 4

Mixed Practice: Lessons 1–7

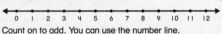

0 1 2 3 4 5 6 7 8 9 10 11 12

Count on to add. You can use the number line.

1.
6	5	8	7	2	1
+3	+2	+3	+1	+4	+9
9	7	11	8	6	10

Add.

2. 6 + 2 = _8_   0 + 3 = _3_   6 + 5 = _11_

3.
9	1	0	8	3	7
+1	+9	+8	+0	+7	+3
10	10	8	8	10	10

Problem Solving

4. Miguel wants exactly 9 apples. Make a list.

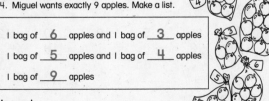

1 bag of _6_ apples and 1 bag of _3_ apples

1 bag of _5_ apples and 1 bag of _4_ apples

1 bag of _9_ apples

Journal

5. Draw pictures to show ways to make 8.

Notes for Home Your child practiced addition facts to 12. Home Activity: Ask your child to list 3 ways to make 2 groups of food items, such as eggs, that make 12. (Answers will vary, but may include: 10 + 2, 6 + 6, 4 + 8.)

Cumulative Review

Write the missing numbers.

1. 1 _2_ _3_ 4 _5_ 6 7 8 9 _10_

2. 10 9 _8_ 7 6 _5_ _4_ _3_ 2 1

Write the number sentence.

3.
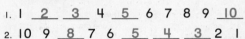

4.
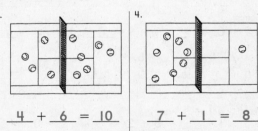

_4_ + _6_ = _10_   _7_ + _1_ = _8_

Test Prep

Fill in the ○ for the correct answer.

Solve:

5.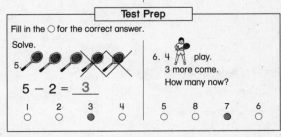

5 − 2 = _3_

1	2	3	4
○	○	●	○

6. 4 🏸 play.
   3 more come.
   How many now?

5	8	7	6
○	○	●	○

Notes for Home Your child reviewed ordering numbers, addition, and subtraction. Home Activity: Ask your child to create and solve 4 addition sentences using the fingers of each hand to show the addends.

Practice 4-8

Name _____

Use a Number Line to Count Back

0 1 2 3 4 5 6 7 8 9 10 11 12

You can use the number line.
Write the difference.

1. $6 - 1 = 5$ $5 - 1 = 4$ $7 - 2 = 5$

2. $9 - 1 = 8$ $8 - 2 = 6$ $5 - 3 = 2$

3.
5	8	10	6	7	4
−2	−1	−2	−2	−1	−1
3	7	8	4	6	3

4.
9	3	8	3	2	2
−2	−1	−2	−2	−1	−2
7	2	6	1	1	0

Write your own number sentences.

5. ___ − 1 = ___   6. ___ − 1 = ___

7. ___ − 2 = ___   8. ___ − 2 = ___

Answers will vary.

Mental Math

9. Start at 12.
Count back 2.
Write the answer. 10

12 − 2 =

Notes for Home Your child subtracted by counting back. *Home Activity:* Ask your child to use the number line to show you how to solve the Mental Math problem.

Use with pages 149–150. **61**

Practice 4-9

Name _____

Count Back 1 or 2

Count back to subtract.

1. $3 - 1 = 2$ $\begin{array}{r} 3 \\ -1 \\ \hline 2 \end{array}$

2.  $5 - 2 = 3$ $\begin{array}{r} 5 \\ -2 \\ \hline 3 \end{array}$

3. $8 - 1 = 7$ $9 - 2 = 7$ $4 - 1 = 3$

4. $6 - 2 = 4$ $9 - 1 = 8$ $11 - 2 = 9$

5.
10	4	12	9	3	11
−1	−2	−2	−1	−2	−1
9	2	10	8	1	10

6.
8	10	6	7	12	11
−2	−2	−1	−2	−1	−2
6	8	5	5	11	9

Problem Solving

Solve.

7. There are 11 in a . 2 fly off. How many are left? 9

8. There are 8 on a . 1 walks away. How many are left? 7

Notes for Home Your child counted back 1 or 2 to subtract. *Home Activity:* Ask your child to use 9 of his or her favorite toys. Have your child tell you a math story about them by counting back 1 and then 2.

62 Use with pages 151–152.

Practice 4-10

Name _____

Subtract All and Subtract Zero

Solve.

1. There are 5 . All are eaten. How many are left? $\begin{array}{r} 5 \\ -5 \\ \hline 0 \end{array}$

$5 - 5 = 0$

2. There are 8 . No one ate any. How many are left? $\begin{array}{r} 8 \\ -0 \\ \hline 8 \end{array}$

$8 - 0 = 8$

Subtract.

3. $9 - 0 = 9$ $9 - 9 = 0$ $11 - 0 = 11$

4.
7	7	5	6	12	12
−7	−0	−5	−6	−0	−12
0	7	0	0	12	0

Mixed Practice Subtract.

5. $6 - 1 = 5$ $5 - 2 = 3$ $2 - 0 = 2$

6.
1	9	10	6	8	4
−1	−2	−1	−6	−2	−3
0	7	9	0	6	1

Problem Solving Critical Thinking

7. Try this super fact. $200 - 0 = \underline{200}$

Write your own super fact. ___ − 0 = ___

Answers will vary.

Notes for Home Your child subtracted all or 0. *Home Activity:* Have your child use small objects, such as beans, to show show you 8 − 0 and 8 − 8.

Use with pages 155–156. **63**

Practice 4-11

Name _____

Subtract with 5

Subtract.

1. $8 - 5 = 3$

2. $9 - 5 = 4$

3. $6 - 5 = 1$ $10 - 5 = 5$ $7 - 5 = 2$

4.
9	11	12	8	5	10
−5	−5	−5	−5	−5	−5
4	6	7	3	0	5

Mixed Practice Subtract.

5.
10	6	12	11	8	9
−0	−3	−5	−1	−8	−2
10	3	7	10	0	7

6.
7	11	5	9	10	12
−2	−2	−0	−1	−10	−2
5	9	5	8	0	10

Problem Solving

7. There are 9 in all. How many are in the bag?

4

Notes for Home Your child subtracted with 5, counted back 1 or 2, and subtracted 0. *Home Activity:* Write 3 subtraction sentences on a piece of paper. Ask your child to solve each subtraction sentence and to draw pictures representing each sentence.

64 Use with pages 157–158.

Panel 1 (top left)

Problem Solving:
Write a Number Sentence

You can use ⬭ 🌑 and ▭▭ to show the story.
Write a number sentence.

1. 7 🍐 are on a plate.

All 7 🍐 are eaten.

How many are left?

$7 - 7 = 0$

2. 8 children put their ✏ in a box.

2 more children put their ✏ in the box.

How many are in the box?

$8 + 2 = 10$

3. Michele has 5 🚗 .

She gives 2 🚗 away.

How many are left?

$5 - 2 = 3$

4. Joshua has 3 🥧 .

He eats all 3 🥧 .

How many are left?

$3 - 3 = 0$

Write About It

Here is a number sentence. $9 - 8 = 1$

You write the story. _____

_____

Stories will vary.

_____

Notes for Home Your child wrote number sentences to solve problems. *Home Activity:* Ask your child to draw a picture to illustrate the story they told in Write About It.

Use with pages 161–162. **65**

Panel 2 (top right)

Mixed Practice: Lessons 8–12

0 1 2 3 4 5 6 7 8 9 10 11 12

Count back to subtract.

1.
$\begin{array}{r}9\\-2\\\hline7\end{array}$
$\begin{array}{r}10\\-2\\\hline8\end{array}$
$\begin{array}{r}7\\-1\\\hline6\end{array}$
$\begin{array}{r}5\\-2\\\hline3\end{array}$
$\begin{array}{r}9\\-1\\\hline8\end{array}$
$\begin{array}{r}12\\-1\\\hline11\end{array}$

Subtract.

2.
$\begin{array}{r}10\\-0\\\hline10\end{array}$
$\begin{array}{r}10\\-10\\\hline0\end{array}$
$\begin{array}{r}6\\-6\\\hline0\end{array}$
$\begin{array}{r}6\\-0\\\hline6\end{array}$
$\begin{array}{r}8\\-8\\\hline0\end{array}$
$\begin{array}{r}8\\-0\\\hline8\end{array}$

Problem Solving

You can use ▭▭ and ⬭ 🌑 to show the story.
Write the number sentence.

3. There are 2 🦐 .

5 more 🦐 join them.
How many are there?

$2 + 5 = 7$

4. There are 3 🪙 .

Tom and Paul take 3 🪙 .
How many are left?

$3 - 3 = 0$

Journal

5. Write a math story and a number sentence.

Notes for Home Your child practiced subtraction and problem solving. *Home Activity:* Ask your child to use small food items, such as raisins or crackers, to show subtraction problems by eating 1 or 2 of them.

66 Use with page 163.

Panel 3 (bottom left)

Cumulative Review

Add.

1.
$\begin{array}{r}2\\+7\\\hline9\end{array}$
$\begin{array}{r}9\\+2\\\hline11\end{array}$
$\begin{array}{r}4\\+5\\\hline9\end{array}$
$\begin{array}{r}6\\+4\\\hline10\end{array}$
$\begin{array}{r}4\\+4\\\hline8\end{array}$
$\begin{array}{r}1\\+8\\\hline9\end{array}$
$\begin{array}{r}10\\+0\\\hline10\end{array}$

Problem Solving

Use the graph. Write the number.

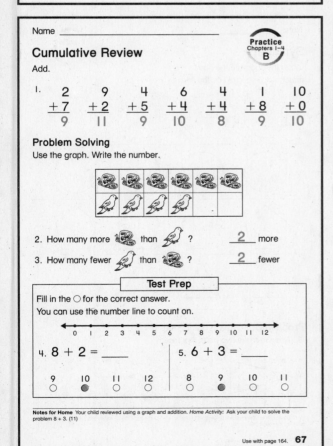

2. How many more 🐍 than 🐦 ?   __2__ more

3. How many fewer 🐦 than 🐍 ?   __2__ fewer

Test Prep

Fill in the ○ for the correct answer.
You can use the number line to count on.

0 1 2 3 4 5 6 7 8 9 10 11 12

4. $8 + 2 =$ ____

9 ○   10 ●   11 ○   12 ○

5. $6 + 3 =$ ____

8 ○   9 ●   10 ○   11 ○

Notes for Home Your child reviewed using a graph and addition. *Home Activity:* Ask your child to solve the problem 8 + 3. (11)

Use with page 164. **67**

Panel 4 (bottom right)

Explore Solids

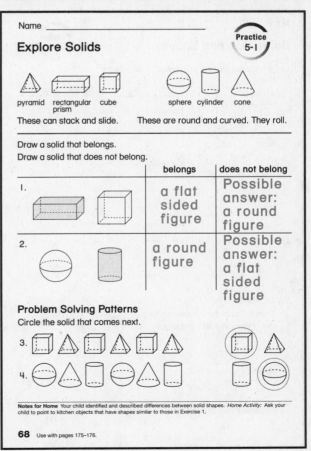

pyramid   rectangular prism   cube   sphere   cylinder   cone

These can stack and slide.   These are round and curved. They roll.

Draw a solid that belongs.
Draw a solid that does not belong.

	belongs	does not belong
1.	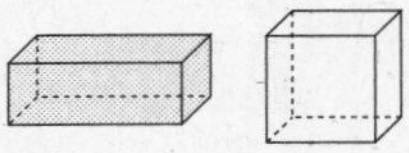 a flat sided figure	Possible answer: a round figure
2.	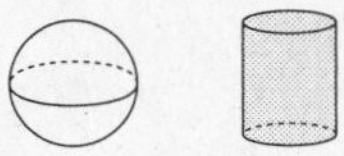 a round figure	Possible answer: a flat sided figure

Problem Solving Patterns

Circle the solid that comes next.

3. 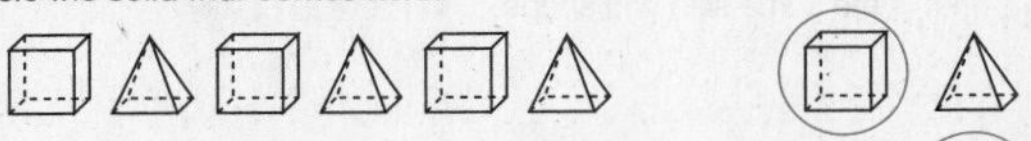 (cube, pyramid, cube, pyramid, cube, pyramid) → ⓒube ○pyramid

4.  (sphere, cone, cylinder, cone, cone, cylinder) → ○cylinder ○sphere

Notes for Home Your child identified and described differences between solid shapes. *Home Activity:* Ask your child to point to kitchen objects that have shapes similar to those in Exercise 1.

68 Use with pages 175–176.

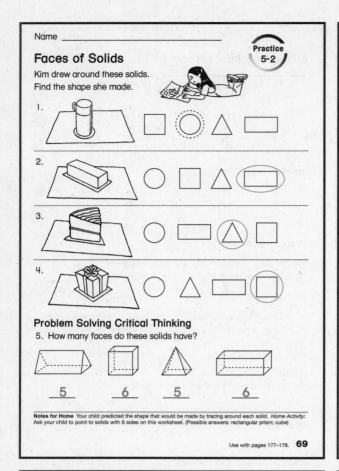

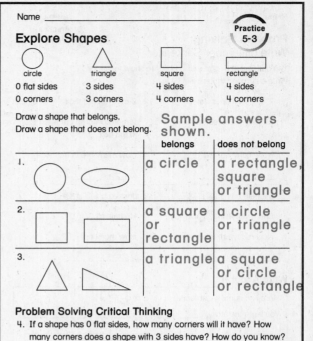

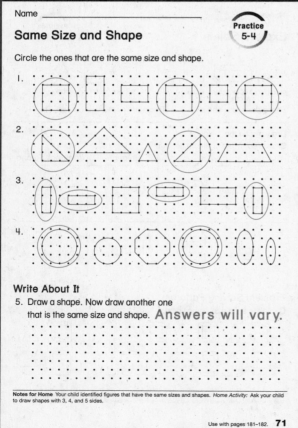

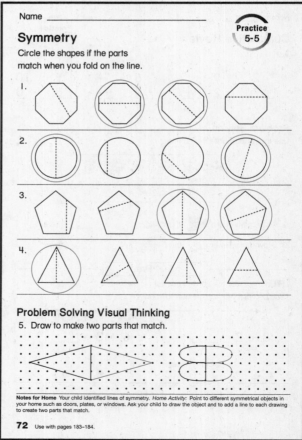

Faces of Solids

Practice 5-2

Kim drew around these solids.
Find the shape she made.

1.

2.

3.

4.

Problem Solving Critical Thinking

5. How many faces do these solids have?

    5   6   5   6

Notes for Home Your child predicted the shape that would be made by tracing around each solid. Home Activity: Ask your child to point to solids with 6 sides on this worksheet. (Possible answers: rectangular prism; cube)

Explore Shapes

Practice 5-3

circle	triangle	square	rectangle
0 flat sides	3 sides	4 sides	4 sides
0 corners	3 corners	4 corners	4 corners

Draw a shape that belongs.
Draw a shape that does not belong.

Sample answers shown.

		belongs	does not belong
1.		a circle	a rectangle, square or triangle
2.		a square or rectangle	a circle or triangle
3.		a triangle	a square or circle or rectangle

Problem Solving Critical Thinking

4. If a shape has 0 flat sides, how many corners will it have? How many corners does a shape with 3 sides have? How do you know?

    (0; 3; Possible answer: because a triangle has 3 sides and 3 corners.)

Notes for Home Your child compared shapes to find similarities and differences. Home Activity: Ask your child to point to 5 objects in a room that have a square or rectangular shape.

Same Size and Shape

Practice 5-4

Circle the ones that are the same size and shape.

1.

2.

3.

4.

Write About It

5. Draw a shape. Now draw another one that is the same size and shape. **Answers will vary.**

Notes for Home Your child identified figures that have the same sizes and shapes. Home Activity: Ask your child to draw shapes with 3, 4, and 5 sides.

Symmetry

Practice 5-5

Circle the shapes if the parts match when you fold on the line.

1.

2.

3.

4.

Problem Solving Visual Thinking

5. Draw to make two parts that match.

Notes for Home Your child identified lines of symmetry. Home Activity: Point to different symmetrical objects in your home such as doors, plates, or windows. Ask your child to draw the object and to add a line to each drawing to create two parts that match.

Problem Solving: Make a Table

Use pattern blocks.
How many ways
can you make this shape?

Record the blocks
you used.

Shapes I used	⏢	▢	△	▱
1st way	2	2	0	0
2nd way	1	2	3	0
3rd way	0	2	6	0
4th way	1	2	1	1
5th way	0	2	2	2

Patterns

Draw what comes next.

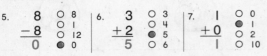

Mixed Practice: Lessons 1–6

1. Circle the things that can roll.

2. Draw one the same size and shape.

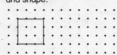

3. Circle the shape if both parts match when you fold on the line.

Problem Solving

4. How many of each shape are there?
   Record the numbers in the table.

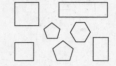

	4 sides	5 sides	6 sides
Number of Shapes	4	2	1

Journal

5. Write about the shape of a box.

Cumulative Review

Count on to add.

1. $2 + 5 = \underline{7}$ 2. $1 + 8 = \underline{9}$
   $5 + 2 = \underline{7}$ $8 + 1 = \underline{9}$

Subtract.

3.
$$\begin{array}{r} 6 \\ -2 \\ \hline 4 \end{array} \quad \begin{array}{r} 8 \\ -1 \\ \hline 7 \end{array} \quad \begin{array}{r} 9 \\ -6 \\ \hline 3 \end{array} \quad \begin{array}{r} 10 \\ -8 \\ \hline 2 \end{array} \quad \begin{array}{r} 7 \\ -2 \\ \hline 5 \end{array} \quad \begin{array}{r} 5 \\ -4 \\ \hline 1 \end{array} \quad \begin{array}{r} 4 \\ -4 \\ \hline 0 \end{array}$$

Problem Solving

4. Draw a picture to match the number sentence.
   Write how many in all.

Pictures will vary.

$2 + 7 = \underline{9}$ $9 - 7 = \underline{2}$

Test Prep

Fill in the ◯ for the correct answer.
Add or subtract.

5.
$$\begin{array}{r} 8 \\ -8 \\ \hline 0 \end{array}$$
◯ 8
◯ 1
◯ 12
● 0

6.
$$\begin{array}{r} 3 \\ +2 \\ \hline 5 \end{array}$$
◯ 3
◯ 4
● 5
◯ 6

7.
$$\begin{array}{r} 1 \\ +0 \\ \hline 1 \end{array}$$
◯ 0
● 1
◯ 2
◯ 10

Fair Shares

Draw lines to show fair shares.

1.    2.

3.    4.

5.    6.

Problem Solving

Solve.

7. Jon, Pablo, and Tania want to share some pie.
   There are 6 pieces of pie. How can they make fair shares?

   Each child gets 2 pieces.

Halves

Color to show one half.

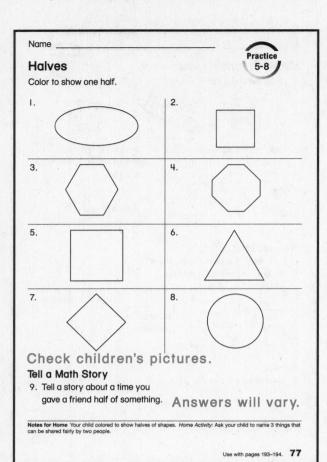

1.   2.

3.   4.

5.   6.

7.   8.

Check children's pictures.

Tell a Math Story

9. Tell a story about a time you gave a friend half of something. **Answers will vary.**

Notes for Home Your child colored to show halves of shapes. *Home Activity:* Ask your child to name 3 things that can be shared fairly by two people.

Fourths

Color to show $\frac{1}{4}$.

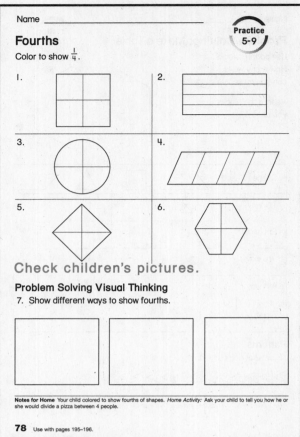

1.   2.

3.   4.

5.   6.

Check children's pictures.

Problem Solving Visual Thinking

7. Show different ways to show fourths.

Notes for Home Your child colored to show fourths of shapes. *Home Activity:* Ask your child to tell you how he or she would divide a pizza between 4 people.

Thirds

Color to show $\frac{1}{3}$.

Check children's pictures.

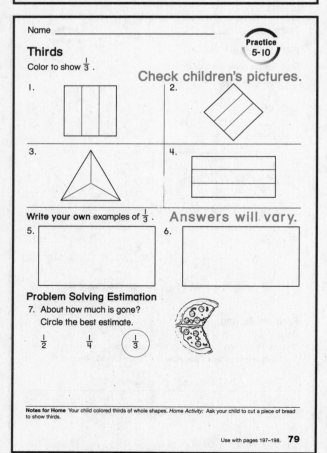

1.   2.

3.   4.

Write your own examples of $\frac{1}{3}$. **Answers will vary.**

5.   6.

Problem Solving Estimation

7. About how much is gone? Circle the best estimate.

$\frac{1}{2}$ $\frac{1}{4}$ $\left(\frac{1}{3}\right)$

Notes for Home Your child colored thirds of whole shapes. *Home Activity:* Ask your child to cut a piece of bread to show thirds.

Explore Probability

What will happen if you use the spinner? Circle the word.

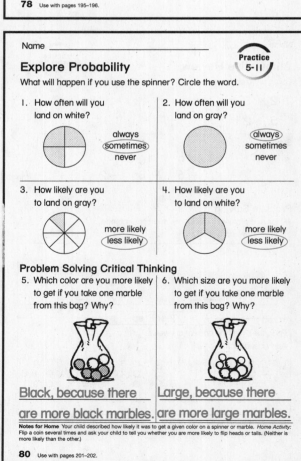

1. How often will you land on white?

always
(sometimes)
never

2. How often will you land on gray?

(always)
sometimes
never

3. How likely are you to land on gray?

more likely
(less likely)

4. How likely are you to land on white?

more likely
(less likely)

Problem Solving Critical Thinking

5. Which color are you more likely to get if you take one marble from this bag? Why?

<u>Black, because there are more black marbles.</u>

6. Which size are you more likely to get if you take one marble from this bag? Why?

<u>Large, because there are more large marbles.</u>

Notes for Home Your child described how likely it was to get a given color on a spinner or marble. *Home Activity:* Flip a coin several times and ask your child to tell you whether you are more likely to flip heads or tails. (Neither is more likely than the other.)

Fractions and Probability

1. Make your own spinner. Use 3 colors.

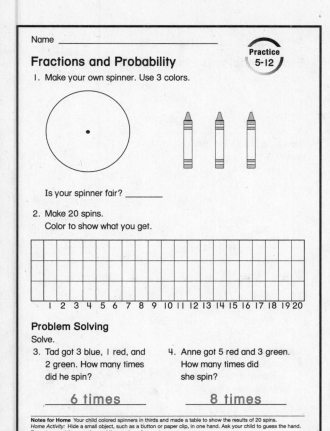

Is your spinner fair? _____

2. Make 20 spins.
Color to show what you get.

| | | | | | | | | | | | | | | | | | | | |
|1|2|3|4|5|6|7|8|9|10|11|12|13|14|15|16|17|18|19|20|

Problem Solving
Solve.

3. Tad got 3 blue, 1 red, and 2 green. How many times did he spin?

___6 times___

4. Anne got 5 red and 3 green. How many times did she spin?

___8 times___

Problem Solving:
Use Data from a Picture

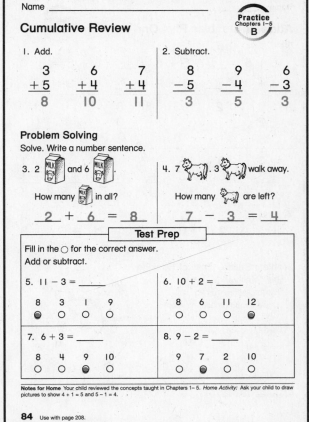

Answer the riddles.

1. I show halves. I am round. Which am I?

___B___

2. I show thirds. Which am I?

___A___

3. I show fourths. Which am I?

___C___

4. I show halves. I am a fruit. Which am I?

___D___

Mental Math

5. The girls are going to eat the 🍎.

Kendra has $\frac{1}{4}$ of the 🍎. Rhea has $\frac{1}{4}$ of the 🍎.

Is there any of the 🍎 left for Alicia? Why or why not?

Yes; Kendra and Rhea have two fourths. There are two equal parts left.

Mixed Practice: Lessons 7–13

Draw a line to show 2 fair shares.

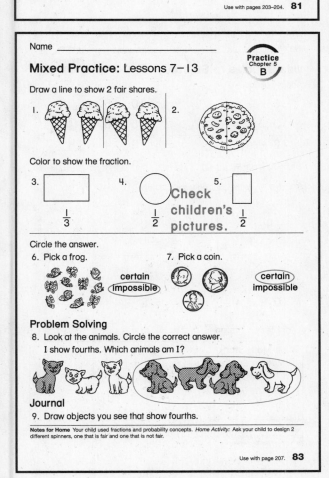

1. 2.

Color to show the fraction.

3. $\frac{1}{3}$

4. $\frac{1}{2}$ Check children's pictures.

5. $\frac{1}{2}$

Circle the answer.

6. Pick a frog.   certain (impossible)

7. Pick a coin.   (certain) impossible

Problem Solving

8. Look at the animals. Circle the correct answer.
I show fourths. Which animals am I?

Journal

9. Draw objects you see that show fourths.

Cumulative Review

1. Add.

$3 + 5 = 8$ $6 + 4 = 10$ $7 + 4 = 11$

2. Subtract.

$8 - 5 = 3$ $9 - 4 = 5$ $6 - 3 = 3$

Problem Solving
Solve. Write a number sentence.

3. 2 MILK and 6 MILK.

How many in all?

$2 + 6 = 8$

4. 7 cows. 3 walk away.

How many are left?

$7 - 3 = 4$

Test Prep

Fill in the ○ for the correct answer.
Add or subtract.

5. $11 - 3 =$ _____

8 ●   3 ○   1 ○   9 ○

6. $10 + 2 =$ _____

8 ○   6 ○   11 ○   12 ●

7. $6 + 3 =$ _____

8 ○   4 ○   9 ●   10 ○

8. $9 - 2 =$ _____

9 ○   7 ●   2 ○   10 ○

Add with Doubles

 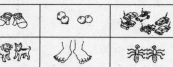

Write the sum. Use the doubles to help.

1. $6 + 6 = \underline{12}$ $2 + 2 = \underline{4}$ $0 + 0 = \underline{0}$

2.
$$\begin{array}{cccccccc} 3 & 6 & 0 & 5 & 4 & 1 & 3 \\ \underline{+3} & \underline{+6} & \underline{+0} & \underline{+5} & \underline{+4} & \underline{+1} & \underline{+3} \\ 6 & 12 & 0 & 10 & 8 & 2 & 6 \end{array}$$

Mixed Practice Write the sum. Circle the doubles.

3.
$$\begin{array}{ccccccc} \boxed{3} & 7 & 2 & \boxed{5} & 2 & 9 & \boxed{2} \\ \underline{+3} & \underline{+3} & \underline{+3} & \underline{+5} & \underline{+4} & \underline{+2} & \underline{+2} \\ 6 & 10 & 5 & 10 & 6 & 11 & 4 \end{array}$$

4.
$$\begin{array}{ccccccc} \boxed{4} & 3 & 3 & 5 & 9 & \boxed{6} & 5 \\ \underline{+4} & \underline{+1} & \underline{+4} & \underline{+2} & \underline{+1} & \underline{+6} & \underline{+6} \\ 8 & 4 & 7 & 7 & 10 & 12 & 11 \end{array}$$

Problem Solving Critical Thinking

5. Can you use doubles to make 11? Why not? **No. You need 2 different numbers to make 11.**

Notes for Home Your child solved addition facts to 12. *Home Activity:* Write these fact families on a piece of paper: 3 + 4, 4 + 4, 0 + 0, 5 + 4. Ask your child to solve the problems and to identify the doubles. (3 + 4 = 7, 4 + 4 = 8 doubles fact, 0 + 0 = 0 is a doubles fact, 5 + 4 = 9)

Explore Adding Doubles Plus One

Use a doubles fact to add other facts.

  $2 + 3 = 5$

Write the doubles fact that helps.
Add.

1.
$$\begin{array}{c} 1 \\ \underline{+2} \\ 3 \end{array} + \begin{array}{c} \boxed{1} \\ \boxed{1} \\ \boxed{2} \end{array}$$

2.
$$\begin{array}{c} 6 \\ \underline{+5} \\ 11 \end{array} + \begin{array}{c} \boxed{5} \\ \boxed{5} \\ \boxed{10} \end{array}$$

3.
$$\begin{array}{c} 3 \\ \underline{+4} \\ 7 \end{array} + \begin{array}{c} \boxed{3} \\ \boxed{3} \\ \boxed{6} \end{array}$$

Add.

4. $5 + 6 = \underline{11}$ $5 + 5 = \underline{10}$ $4 + 5 = \underline{9}$

5.
$$\begin{array}{ccccccc} 4 & 6 & 1 & 3 & 7 & 6 & 2 \\ \underline{+4} & \underline{+3} & \underline{+2} & \underline{+5} & \underline{+4} & \underline{+4} & \underline{+3} \\ 8 & 9 & 3 & 8 & 11 & 10 & 5 \end{array}$$

Tell a Math Story

6. Use doubles to make up a math story about these dogs. Retell the story using doubles plus one.

Notes for Home Your child learned that facts like 3 + 4 = 7 are 1 more than a doubles fact (3 + 3 = 6). *Home Activity:* Say a doubles fact like 5 + 5 = 10 and ask your child to name a fact that is 1 more. (5 + 6 = 11 or 6 + 5 = 11)

Add with Doubles Plus One

Add.

1. $5 + 5 = \underline{10}$ $5 + 6 = \underline{11}$ $6 + 5 = \underline{11}$

2. $3 + 3 = \underline{6}$ $3 + 4 = \underline{7}$ $4 + 3 = \underline{7}$

3.
$$\begin{array}{ccc} 2 & 2 & 3 \\ \underline{+2} & \underline{+3} & \underline{+2} \\ 4 & 5 & 5 \end{array}$$
4.
$$\begin{array}{ccc} 0 & 0 & 1 \\ \underline{+0} & \underline{+1} & \underline{+0} \\ 0 & 1 & 1 \end{array}$$

5.
$$\begin{array}{cccccc} 3 & 0 & 5 & 6 & 4 & 1 \\ \underline{+3} & \underline{+0} & \underline{+5} & \underline{+6} & \underline{+4} & \underline{+1} \\ 6 & 0 & 10 & 12 & 8 & 2 \end{array}$$

6.
$$\begin{array}{cccccc} 4 & 3 & 1 & 5 & 1 & 6 & 4 \\ \underline{+5} & \underline{+2} & \underline{+0} & \underline{+6} & \underline{+2} & \underline{+5} & \underline{+3} \\ 9 & 5 & 1 & 11 & 3 & 11 & 7 \end{array}$$

Problem Solving Critical Thinking

7. Billy Bee threw 3 darts.
   His total score was 9.
   Circle the 3 numbers he scored.

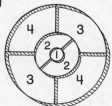

He scored with a 4, 3, and 2 or 4, 4, and 1 or 3, 3, and 3.

Notes for Home Your child used doubles plus one. *Home Activity:* Ask your child to find 5 numbers on the dart board that equal 11 when added. (3 + 3 + 2 + 2 + 1)

Use Doubles to Subtract

Add or subtract.

1. $6 - 3 = \underline{3}$
   $3 + 3 = \underline{6}$
2. $10 - 5 = \underline{5}$
   $5 + 5 = \underline{10}$

3. $12 - 6 = \underline{6}$
   $6 + 6 = \underline{12}$
4. $8 - 4 = \underline{4}$
   $4 + 4 = \underline{8}$

Subtract. Write the addition facts that help.

5.
$$\begin{array}{c} 8 \\ \underline{-4} \\ 4 \end{array} \quad \boxed{4} + \boxed{4} = \boxed{8}$$

6.
$$\begin{array}{c} 6 \\ \underline{-3} \\ 3 \end{array} \quad \boxed{3} + \boxed{3} = \boxed{6}$$

7.
$$\begin{array}{c} 12 \\ \underline{-6} \\ 6 \end{array} \quad \boxed{6} + \boxed{6} = \boxed{12}$$

8. $10 - 5 = \underline{5}$
   $\underline{5} + \underline{5} = \underline{10}$
9. $8 - 4 = \underline{4}$
   $\underline{4} + \underline{4} = \underline{8}$

Tell a Math Story

10. Make up a math story using $6 - 3$.
    Draw a picture for your story.
    Answers will vary.

Notes for Home Your child used addition and subtraction to find answers. *Home Activity:* Ask your child to say a subtraction fact for things found around your home that come in doubles, such as 4 windowpanes minus 2 windowpanes is 2 windowpanes.

Panel 1 (top-left)

Name _____

Problem Solving:
Collect and Use Data

Practice
6-5

Mrs. Shah's class went
for a walk outside.
Here is what they saw.

Critters	Tally	Total
Dogs	IIII	4
Cats	III	3
Birds	ЖHT III	8
Worms	ЖHT II	7
Insects	ЖHT ЖHT	10

Write your own questions.
Use the chart to write 3 questions.
Trade papers. Answer each other's questions.

1. Answers will vary. _____

2. Answers will vary. _____

3. Answers will vary. _____

Patterns Algebra Readiness

4. Complete the pattern.
Draw the towers.
Write the number.

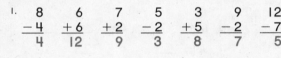

3   6   9   12   15

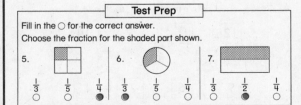

Notes for Home Your child used a tally chart to answer questions. *Home Activity:* Ask your child to show you how to make a tally chart. You may wish to count the number of forks, spoons, and knives in a drawer. Then ask *"Which do we have the fewest of?"* *"Which do we have the most of?"*

Use with pages 228–230. **89**

Panel 2 (top-right)

Name _____

Mixed Practice: Lessons 1-5

Practice
Chapter 6
A

Add. Use doubles when you can.

1.
$\begin{array}{r} 2 \\ +2 \\ \hline 4 \end{array}$
$\begin{array}{r} 2 \\ +3 \\ \hline 5 \end{array}$
$\begin{array}{r} 5 \\ +5 \\ \hline 10 \end{array}$
$\begin{array}{r} 5 \\ +6 \\ \hline 11 \end{array}$
$\begin{array}{r} 0 \\ +0 \\ \hline 0 \end{array}$
$\begin{array}{r} 0 \\ +1 \\ \hline 1 \end{array}$
$\begin{array}{r} 1 \\ +1 \\ \hline 2 \end{array}$

2. $3 + 3 = \underline{6}$ $3 + 4 = \underline{7}$ $5 + 6 = \underline{11}$

Subtract.

3.
$\begin{array}{r} 8 \\ -4 \\ \hline 4 \end{array}$
$\begin{array}{r} 0 \\ -0 \\ \hline 0 \end{array}$
$\begin{array}{r} 2 \\ -1 \\ \hline 1 \end{array}$
$\begin{array}{r} 12 \\ -6 \\ \hline 6 \end{array}$
$\begin{array}{r} 10 \\ -5 \\ \hline 5 \end{array}$
$\begin{array}{r} 6 \\ -3 \\ \hline 3 \end{array}$
$\begin{array}{r} 4 \\ -2 \\ \hline 2 \end{array}$

Problem Solving
Write the totals.
Use the chart to solve.

Favorite Colors		
Color	Tally	Total
Green	ЖHT I	6
Blue	ЖHT IIII	9
Yellow	III	3

4. How many chose green? __6__

5. Which one did the
most children choose? __blue__

Journal

6. Draw a picture to show a double for 3.
Write an addition and a subtraction sentence for the picture.

$3 + 3 = 6$ $6 - 3 = 3$

Notes for Home Your child added and subtracted through 12. *Home Activity:* Ask your child to circle all the problems on this page that use doubles to add or subtract, such as 3 + 3 and 8 – 4. Then have him or her write and solve two more different doubles problems.

90 Use with page 231.

Panel 3 (bottom-left)

Name _____

Cumulative Review

Practice
Chapters 1–6
A

Add or subtract.

1.
$\begin{array}{r} 8 \\ -4 \\ \hline 4 \end{array}$
$\begin{array}{r} 6 \\ +6 \\ \hline 12 \end{array}$
$\begin{array}{r} 7 \\ +2 \\ \hline 9 \end{array}$
$\begin{array}{r} 5 \\ -2 \\ \hline 3 \end{array}$
$\begin{array}{r} 3 \\ +5 \\ \hline 8 \end{array}$
$\begin{array}{r} 9 \\ -2 \\ \hline 7 \end{array}$
$\begin{array}{r} 12 \\ -7 \\ \hline 5 \end{array}$

2.
$\begin{array}{r} 0 \\ +1 \\ \hline 1 \end{array}$
$\begin{array}{r} 10 \\ -5 \\ \hline 5 \end{array}$
$\begin{array}{r} 6 \\ -4 \\ \hline 2 \end{array}$
$\begin{array}{r} 4 \\ +5 \\ \hline 9 \end{array}$
$\begin{array}{r} 3 \\ +3 \\ \hline 6 \end{array}$
$\begin{array}{r} 9 \\ -6 \\ \hline 3 \end{array}$
$\begin{array}{r} 10 \\ +2 \\ \hline 12 \end{array}$

Problem Solving
Write a number sentence. Solve.

3. Martin has 5 stickers.
Josh gives him 6 more.
How many stickers
does he have?

$\underline{5 + 6 = 11}$ stickers

4. Ellen has 11 marbles.
She gives 6 to her brother.
How many marbles
are left?

$\underline{11 - 6 = 5}$ marbles

Test Prep

Fill in the ○ for the correct answer.
Choose the fraction for the shaded part shown.

5. $\frac{1}{3}$ ○ $\frac{1}{5}$ ○ $\frac{1}{4}$ ●

6. $\frac{1}{3}$ ● $\frac{1}{5}$ ○ $\frac{1}{4}$ ○

7. $\frac{1}{3}$ ○ $\frac{1}{2}$ ● $\frac{1}{4}$ ○

Notes for Home Your child reviewed adding 1, 2, and 3 and subtracting 1 and 2; and identifying fractions. *Home Activity:* Ask your child to explain how he or she determined the fraction for the shaded parts shown in Exercises 5 – 7.

Use with page 232. **91**

Panel 4 (bottom-right)

Name _____

Relate Addition and Subtraction

Practice
6-6

Add or subtract. You can use ⬭ ⬯.

1.
$\begin{array}{r} 3 \\ +4 \\ \hline 4 \end{array}$
$\begin{array}{r} 7 \\ -3 \\ \hline 4 \end{array}$

2.
$\begin{array}{r} 5 \\ +6 \\ \hline 11 \end{array}$
$\begin{array}{r} 11 \\ -5 \\ \hline 6 \end{array}$

3.
$\begin{array}{r} 6 \\ +3 \\ \hline 9 \end{array}$
$\begin{array}{r} 9 \\ -3 \\ \hline 6 \end{array}$

4.
$\begin{array}{r} 7 \\ +5 \\ \hline 12 \end{array}$
$\begin{array}{r} 12 \\ -5 \\ \hline 7 \end{array}$

5.
$\begin{array}{r} 4 \\ +1 \\ \hline 5 \end{array}$
$\begin{array}{r} 5 \\ -1 \\ \hline 4 \end{array}$

6.
$\begin{array}{r} 2 \\ +5 \\ \hline 7 \end{array}$
$\begin{array}{r} 7 \\ -5 \\ \hline 2 \end{array}$

7.
$\begin{array}{r} 4 \\ +5 \\ \hline 9 \end{array}$
$\begin{array}{r} 9 \\ -5 \\ \hline 4 \end{array}$

8.
$\begin{array}{r} 6 \\ +4 \\ \hline 10 \end{array}$
$\begin{array}{r} 10 \\ -4 \\ \hline 6 \end{array}$

9. $3 + 7 = \underline{10}$ $10 - 7 = \underline{3}$

10. $6 + 1 = \underline{7}$ $7 - 1 = \underline{6}$

11. $6 + 3 = \underline{9}$ $9 - 3 = \underline{6}$

Problem Solving
Solve.

12. Mark had 5 peas on his plate.
He took 7 more. How many
peas does Mark have on his
plate?

__12__ peas

13. Mark had 12 peas on his plate.
He ate 7 peas. How many
peas does Mark have on his
plate?

__5__ peas

Notes for Home Your child used addition facts to help solve subtraction facts. *Home Activity:* Ask your child to tell you 5 ways to get 4 as an answer. (Answers may include: 4 + 0, 3 + 1, 2 + 2, 1 + 3, 0 + 4.)

92 Use with pages 233–234.

Fact Families

Name _____

Fact Families

Practice 6-7

Complete the fact family. You can use 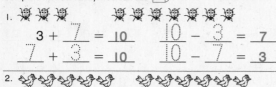.

1.
$3 + \underline{7} = \underline{10}$ $\qquad$ $\underline{10} - \underline{3} = \underline{7}$

$\underline{7} + \underline{3} = \underline{10}$ $\qquad$ $\underline{10} - \underline{7} = \underline{3}$

2.
$5 + \underline{6} = \underline{11}$ $\qquad$ $\underline{11} - \underline{6} = \underline{5}$

$\underline{6} + \underline{5} = \underline{11}$ $\qquad$ $\underline{11} - \underline{5} = \underline{6}$

Write your own fact family. Draw a picture to go with it.

3.

> Answers will vary.

___ + ___ = ___ $\qquad$ ___ − ___ = ___

___ + ___ = ___ $\qquad$ ___ − ___ = ___

Problem Solving Critical Thinking

4. There are 7 ladybugs.
   6 bees join them.
   How many ladybugs are there? $\underline{7}$

Notes for Home Your child wrote number sentences to show the number relationships in addition and subtraction. *Home Activity:* Ask your child to use objects such as 5 dry beans and 6 dry macaroni to show the four related number sentences for 5 + 6, 6 + 5, 11 − 5, and 11 − 6.

Use with pages 235–236. **93**

Name _____

Think Addition to Subtract

Practice 6-8

Use addition to help you subtract.

1.
$\begin{array}{r} 10 \\ -\ 6 \\ \hline \boxed{4} \end{array}$ $\begin{array}{r} 6 \\ +\ \boxed{4} \\ \hline 10 \end{array}$

2.
$\begin{array}{r} 9 \\ -\ 3 \\ \hline \boxed{6} \end{array}$ $\begin{array}{r} 3 \\ +\ \boxed{6} \\ \hline 9 \end{array}$

Mixed Practice Add or subtract.
Draw lines to match related facts.

3.
$\begin{array}{r} 3 \\ +8 \\ \hline 11 \end{array}$ $\begin{array}{r} 3 \\ +6 \\ \hline 9 \end{array}$ $\begin{array}{r} 7 \\ +4 \\ \hline 11 \end{array}$

$\begin{array}{r} 11 \\ -4 \\ \hline 7 \end{array}$ $\begin{array}{r} 11 \\ -3 \\ \hline 8 \end{array}$ $\begin{array}{r} 9 \\ -6 \\ \hline 3 \end{array}$

4.
$\begin{array}{r} 2 \\ +9 \\ \hline 11 \end{array}$ $\begin{array}{r} 4 \\ +3 \\ \hline 7 \end{array}$ $\begin{array}{r} 7 \\ +1 \\ \hline 8 \end{array}$

$\begin{array}{r} 7 \\ -3 \\ \hline 4 \end{array}$ $\begin{array}{r} 8 \\ -1 \\ \hline 7 \end{array}$ $\begin{array}{r} 11 \\ -9 \\ \hline 2 \end{array}$

Problem Solving Critical Thinking

Solve the riddle.

5. First double me.
   Then subtract 4.
   You will get 8.
   What number am I? $\underline{6}$

Write your own riddle.

6. Answers will vary. _____

Notes for Home Your child used addition to check subtraction. *Home Activity:* Write a subtraction sentence such as 11 − 6 = ____. Ask your child to write the answer, then write an addition fact that can help check the subtraction. (Answers may include: 5 + 6 = 11 and 6 + 5 = 11.)

94 Use with pages 237–238.

Name _____

Fact Families for 10

Practice 6-9

Complete the fact family for 10.

1.
$\underline{3} + \underline{7} = \underline{10}$ $\qquad$ $\underline{10} - \underline{7} = \underline{3}$

$\underline{7} + \underline{3} = \underline{10}$ $\qquad$ $\underline{10} - \underline{3} = \underline{7}$

Mixed Practice Add or subtract.
Draw lines to match related facts.

3.
$\begin{array}{r} 2 \\ +7 \\ \hline 9 \end{array}$ $\begin{array}{r} 4 \\ +6 \\ \hline 10 \end{array}$ $\begin{array}{r} 7 \\ +4 \\ \hline 11 \end{array}$

$\begin{array}{r} 11 \\ -4 \\ \hline 7 \end{array}$ $\begin{array}{r} 10 \\ -4 \\ \hline 6 \end{array}$ $\begin{array}{r} 9 \\ -7 \\ \hline 2 \end{array}$

4.
$\begin{array}{r} 2 \\ +10 \\ \hline 12 \end{array}$ $\begin{array}{r} 3 \\ +6 \\ \hline 9 \end{array}$ $\begin{array}{r} 6 \\ +1 \\ \hline 7 \end{array}$

$\begin{array}{r} 9 \\ -6 \\ \hline 3 \end{array}$ $\begin{array}{r} 7 \\ -1 \\ \hline 6 \end{array}$ $\begin{array}{r} 12 \\ -2 \\ \hline 10 \end{array}$

Problem Solving Visual Thinking

5. There are 7 in all.

   How many are in the water?

   $\underline{3}$

Notes for Home Your child added and subtracted with 10. *Home Activity:* Show your child 10 small objects, such as paper clips. Cover 7 of them. Have your child say an addition and a subtraction sentence to tell about the objects. (Answers may include: 7 + 3 = 10, 3 + 7 = 10, 10 − 7 = 3.)

Use with pages 241–242. **95**

Name _____

Problem Solving: Guess and Check

Practice 6-10

Use ⬭ ⬤.
Guess. Then check to find the answer.

1. Try _____ $6 + \underline{} = \underline{}$
   Try $\underline{9}$ $6 + \underline{9} = \underline{15}$
   15 in all

2. Try _____ $5 + \underline{} = \underline{}$
   Try $\underline{4}$ $5 + \underline{4} = \underline{9}$
   9 in all

3. Try _____ $9 + \underline{} = \underline{}$
   Try $\underline{2}$ $9 + \underline{2} = \underline{11}$
   11 in all

Mental Math

4. Circle numbers that are odd numbers less than 16.

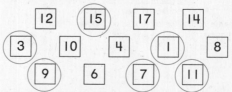

Notes for Home Your child solved addition and subtraction problems by using the Guess and Check strategy. *Home Activity:* Ask your child to find the even numbers in the Mental Math activity. (4, 6, 8, 10, 12, 14)

96 Use with pages 243–244.

222

Mixed Practice: Lessons 6–10

Use . Complete the fact family.

1.

$4 + \underline{5} = \underline{9}$ $9 - \underline{5} = \underline{4}$

$\underline{5} + \underline{4} = \underline{9}$ $9 - \underline{4} = \underline{5}$

Add or subtract.

2. $\begin{array}{r} 4 \\ +2 \\ \hline 6 \end{array}$ $\begin{array}{r} 9 \\ +3 \\ \hline 12 \end{array}$ $\begin{array}{r} 5 \\ -5 \\ \hline 0 \end{array}$ $\begin{array}{r} 12 \\ -8 \\ \hline 4 \end{array}$ $\begin{array}{r} 2 \\ +7 \\ \hline 9 \end{array}$ $\begin{array}{r} 9 \\ -8 \\ \hline 1 \end{array}$

3. $\begin{array}{r} 2 \\ +2 \\ \hline 4 \end{array}$ $\begin{array}{r} 6 \\ +2 \\ \hline 8 \end{array}$ $\begin{array}{r} 12 \\ -3 \\ \hline 9 \end{array}$ $\begin{array}{r} 5 \\ +6 \\ \hline 11 \end{array}$ $\begin{array}{r} 9 \\ -2 \\ \hline 7 \end{array}$ $\begin{array}{r} 6 \\ -5 \\ \hline 1 \end{array}$

Problem Solving

4. Guess. Then check to find the answer. You can use ⬭ ⬬.

	Guess	Check
❋❋❋❋❋❋ ❋❋❋❋❋❋	Try ____	$7 + \underline{} = \underline{}$
12 in all	Try _5_	$7 + \underline{5} = \underline{12}$

Journal

5. Take a total of 9 in two colors. Draw a picture of the cubes.
   Write the fact family.

Notes for Home Your child practiced addition and subtraction facts through 12 and problem solving.
Home Activity: Ask your child to make up one addition and one subtraction problem for you to solve.
Work together to check your answers.

Use with page 245. 97

Cumulative Review

Add or subtract.

1. $\begin{array}{r} 8 \\ +3 \\ \hline 11 \end{array}$ $\begin{array}{r} 8 \\ -5 \\ \hline 3 \end{array}$ $\begin{array}{r} 7 \\ +0 \\ \hline 7 \end{array}$ $\begin{array}{r} 4 \\ +5 \\ \hline 9 \end{array}$ $\begin{array}{r} 3 \\ +5 \\ \hline 8 \end{array}$ $\begin{array}{r} 4 \\ +4 \\ \hline 8 \end{array}$ $\begin{array}{r} 10 \\ -2 \\ \hline 8 \end{array}$

2. $\begin{array}{r} 5 \\ -1 \\ \hline 4 \end{array}$ $\begin{array}{r} 6 \\ +4 \\ \hline 10 \end{array}$ $\begin{array}{r} 6 \\ -4 \\ \hline 2 \end{array}$ $\begin{array}{r} 5 \\ +2 \\ \hline 7 \end{array}$ $\begin{array}{r} 3 \\ -0 \\ \hline 3 \end{array}$ $\begin{array}{r} 9 \\ -5 \\ \hline 4 \end{array}$ $\begin{array}{r} 3 \\ +7 \\ \hline 10 \end{array}$

3. $7 + 4 = \underline{11}$ $11 - 8 = \underline{3}$ $12 - 4 = \underline{8}$

Problem Solving

Write a number sentence.

4. Frank has 8 marbles.
   Martha gives him 4 more.
   How many does Frank have now?

   $\underline{8 + 4 = 12}$

5. Alice had 6 books.
   She gave away 2.
   How many are left?

   $\underline{6 - 2 = 4}$

Test Prep
Fill in the ○ for the correct answer.
6. Which shows a circle and a triangle?

○   ● (filled)   ○   ○

Notes for Home Your child reviewed addition and subtraction, writing number sentences, and identifying shapes.
Home Activity: Ask your child to tell you how he or she found the answer to Exercise 4.

98 Use with page 246.

Numbers to 19

Write the numbers.

1. 17 seventeen

   $\underline{10}$ and $\underline{7}$ is $\underline{17}$.

2. 13 thirteen

   $\underline{10}$ and $\underline{3}$ is $\underline{13}$.

3. 11 eleven

   $\underline{10}$ and $\underline{1}$ is $\underline{11}$.

4. 19 nineteen

   $\underline{10}$ and $\underline{9}$ is $\underline{19}$.

5. 15 fifteen

   $\underline{10}$ and $\underline{5}$ is $\underline{15}$.

6. 12 twelve

   $\underline{10}$ and $\underline{2}$ is $\underline{12}$.

7. 16 sixteen

   $\underline{10}$ and $\underline{6}$ is $\underline{16}$.

8. 14 fourteen

   $\underline{10}$ and $\underline{4}$ is $\underline{14}$.

Problem Solving

9. These are José's trucks.
   Tell how you found how many he has.

I counted to 19, or 10 large
trucks and 9 small trucks.

Notes for Home Your child wrote numbers 11–19 as 10 and ones. *Home Activity:* Ask your child to complete this
sentence for 19: ___ and ___ is ___. (10 and 9 is 19.)

Use with pages 257–258. 99

Tens

Write the number.

1. 20 and 10 is $\underline{30}$.

2. 40 and 10 is $\underline{50}$.

3. 30 and 10 is $\underline{40}$.

4. 60 and 10 is $\underline{70}$.

5. 70 and 10 is $\underline{80}$.

6. 80 and 10 is $\underline{90}$.

Each has 10 . How many in all?

7. (2 stacks) $\underline{20}$

8. (7 stacks) $\underline{70}$

9. (3 stacks) $\underline{30}$

10. (6 stacks) $\underline{60}$

Problem Solving

11. This is one page in Scott's picture book.
    How many photos are on 6 pages? $\underline{60}$ photos

Numbers to 60

Circle groups of 10. Write the numbers.

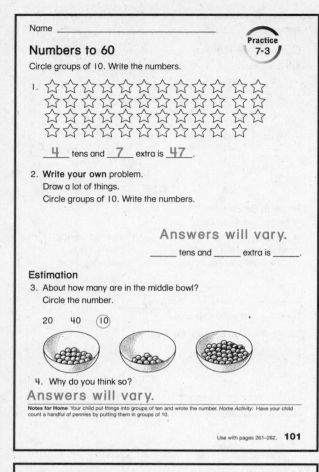

1.

__4__ tens and __7__ extra is __47__.

2. **Write your own** problem.
   Draw a lot of things.
   Circle groups of 10. Write the numbers.

Answers will vary.

_____ tens and _____ extra is _____.

Estimation

3. About how many are in the middle bowl?
   Circle the number.

   20   40   (10)

4. Why do you think so?
   Answers will vary.

Notes for Home Your child put things into groups of ten and wrote the number. *Home Activity:* Have your child count a handful of pennies by putting them in groups of 10.

Use with pages 261–262.   **101**

Explore Estimation

Take a lot of counters. Do not count yet.
Estimate how many there are.
Let your partner count how many.
Answers will vary.

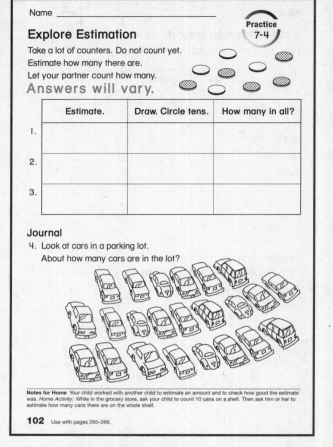

	Estimate.	Draw. Circle tens.	How many in all?
1.			
2.			
3.			

Journal

4. Look at cars in a parking lot.
   About how many cars are in the lot?

Notes for Home Your child worked with another child to estimate an amount and to check how good the estimate was. *Home Activity:* While in the grocery store, ask your child to count 10 cans on a shelf. Then ask him or her to estimate how many cans there are on the whole shelf.

102   Use with pages 265–266.

Estimation

Estimate how many. Circle the number.

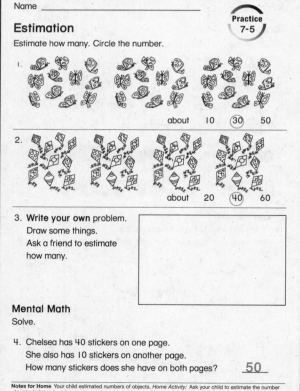

1.

   about   10   (30)   50

2.

   about   20   (40)   60

3. **Write your own** problem.
   Draw some things.
   Ask a friend to estimate
   how many.

Mental Math

Solve.

4. Chelsea has 40 stickers on one page.
   She also has 10 stickers on another page.
   How many stickers does she have on both pages?   __50__

Notes for Home Your child estimated numbers of objects. *Home Activity:* Ask your child to estimate the number of socks in his or her drawer.

Use with pages 267–268.   **103**

Problem Solving:
Use Data from a Graph

This graph shows how many paper apples the children have made.

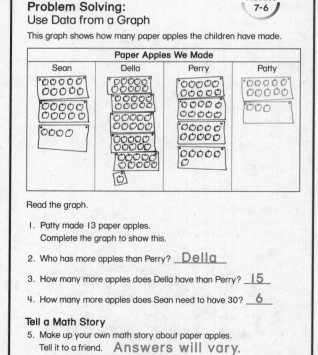

Paper Apples We Made

| Sean | Della | Perry | Patty |

Read the graph.

1. Patty made 13 paper apples.
   Complete the graph to show this.

2. Who has more apples than Perry?   __Della__

3. How many more apples does Della have than Perry?   __15__

4. How many more apples does Sean need to have 30?   __6__

Tell a Math Story

5. Make up your own math story about paper apples.
   Tell it to a friend.   Answers will vary.

Notes for Home Your child practiced using a graph to find information. *Home Activity:* Ask your child to use the graph to answer "Who has the most apples?" (Della)

104   Use with pages 269–270.

Mixed Practice: Lessons 1-6

Practice Chapter 7 **A**

Write the number.

1. 10 and 6 is __16__ .

2. 10 and 9 is __19__ .

3. 40 and 10 is __50__ .

4. 30 and 10 is __40__ .

5. Estimate how many. Circle the number.

about 10 20 (40)

Problem Solving

Read the graph.

Seashells collected	
Jennifer	🐚🐚🐚🐚🐚 🐚🐚🐚🐚🐚 🐚🐚🐚🐚🐚 🐚🐚🐚🐚🐚 🐚🐚🐚🐚🐚 🐚🐚🐚
Bart	🐚🐚🐚🐚🐚 🐚🐚🐚🐚🐚 🐚🐚🐚🐚🐚 🐚🐚🐚🐚 🐚🐚🐚

6. How many does Jennifer have? __28__

Journal

7. What are some things you might count by tens? Why?

Notes for Home Your child practiced counting groups of numbers to 60. *Home Activity:* Ask your child to tell how many toes three people have in all. (30)

Cumulative Review

Practice Chapters 1-7 **A**

1. Circle the one that comes next in this pattern.

Problem Solving

Write the number sentence.

2. I had 9 stamps.
   I got 3 more.
   How many do I have now?

   __9__ + __3__ = __12__

3. Nell had 7 cards.
   She gave away 3.
   How many are left?

   __7__ − __3__ = __4__

Test Prep

Fill in the ○ for the correct answer.

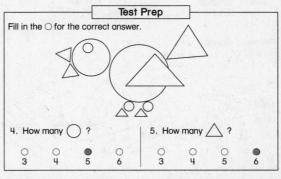

4. How many ○ ?

○ 3   ○ 4   ● 5   ○ 6

5. How many △ ?

○ 3   ○ 4   ○ 5   ● 6

Notes for Home Your child reviewed concepts taught in Chapters 1-7. *Home Activity:* Ask your child to tell you how he or she solved Exercise 3.

Count by 2s and 10s

Practice **7-7**

1. How many fingers? Count by 10s.

__10__ __20__ __30__ __40__ __50__ __60__ __70__

2. Count by 10s. You can use a 🖩.

Press	Display
	0
+ 1 0 =	10
+ 1 0 =	20
+ 1 0 =	30

Press	Display
+ 1 0 =	40
+ 1 0 =	50
+ 1 0 =	60
+ 1 0 =	70

Problem Solving Patterns

Use a 🖩. Press the buttons shown below.

3. Count by 2s.

[+ 2 = = =]

4. Count by 10s.

[+ 1 0 = = =]

5. What happens each time you press [=] ?

The number increases by 10s or 2s.

Notes for Home Your child counted by 2s and 10s. *Home Activity:* Ask your child to count how many ears there are in your family.

Count by 2s, 5s, and 10s

Practice **7-8**

Count by 5s.

1. 10, 15, 20, __25__, __30__, __35__, __40__, 45

2. 35, __40__, __45__, __50__, 55, __60__, 65, __70__

3. 55, 60, __65__, __70__, 75, 80, __85__, __90__

Count by 2s.

4. 10, 12, __14__, __16__, 18, __20__, 22, __24__

5. 46, 48, 50, __52__, __54__, __56__, __58__, 60

6. 72, 74, __76__, 78, 80, 82, __84__, __86__

Count by 10s.

7. 30, __40__, 50, __60__, __70__, __80__

Write your own counting pattern.

8. ___, ___, ___, ___, ___ Answers will vary.

Problem Solving Visual Thinking

9. Look at the picture.
   Count by 10s.
   How many muffins
   will be baked?

   __50__ muffins

Notes for Home Your child practiced counting by 10s, 5s, and 2s. *Home Activity:* Ask your child to count by 2s from 8 to 20. (8, 10, 12, 14, 16, 18, 20)

Ordinals

1. Color the shelves.

second RED
third BLUE
fourth YELLOW
fifth GREEN

2. Color the cars.

fourth RED
fifth BLUE
sixth YELLOW
seventh GREEN
eighth ORANGE

R B Y G O

Problem Solving Visual Thinking

3. How many cars are in this tunnel?

seventh
eighth
second first

Write how many. 4

Notes for Home Your child used number words from *first* through *tenth* to identify position. *Home Activity:* Ask your child to arrange 5 things in a line and show you the ones that are first, third, and fifth.

Use with pages 277–278. **109**

Problem Solving: Look for a Pattern

Color the charts to continue the pattern.

1. Start with 2. Count by 2s.

1	2	3	4	5	6	7	8	9	10
11	12	13	14	15	16	17	18	19	20
21	22	23	24	25	26	27	28	29	30

2. Start with 10. Count by 10s.

1	2	3	4	5	6	7	8	9	10
11	12	13	14	15	16	17	18	19	20
21	22	23	24	25	26	27	28	29	30
31	32	33	34	35	36	37	38	39	40
41	42	43	44	45	46	47	48	49	50
51	52	53	54	55	56	57	58	59	60
61	62	63	64	65	66	67	68	69	70
71	72	73	74	75	76	77	78	79	80

Write About It

3. Write about one of the patterns. You can use the words in the list.

Answers will vary.

_____

odd	pattern
even	diagonal
row	chart
column	count

Notes for Home Your child continued patterns on a chart. *Home Activity:* Ask your child to tell you which numbers he or she would color if each chart had another row. (32, 34, 36, 38, 40; 90)

110 Use with pages 281–282.

Mixed Practice: Lessons 7-10

1. Count by 2s.   6, 8, 10, 12, 14, 16, 18, 20

2. Count by 5s.   10, 15, 20, 25, 30, 35, 40, 45

3. Count by 10s.   20, 30, 40, 50, 60, 70

4. Color the tops.

fifth blue
sixth orange
seventh yellow

B O Y

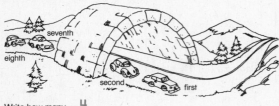

Problem Solving

5. Color to continue the pattern.

1	2	3	4	5	6	7	8	9	10
11	12	13	14	15	16	17	18	19	20
21	22	23	24	25	26	27	28	29	30
31	32	33	34	35	36	37	38	39	40
41	42	43	44	45	46	47	48	49	50
51	52	53	54	55	56	57	58	59	60

Journal

6. Write about how you count by 2s, 5s, or 10s to find how much money is in a pile of nickels and dimes.

Notes for Home Your child practiced counting by 2s, 5s, and 10s, and matching numbers to positions in line. *Home Activity:* Ask your child to count aloud by 2s from 10 to 30. (10, 12, 14, 16, 18, 20, 22, 24, 26, 28, 30)

Use with pages 283. **111**

Cumulative Review

Count on to add.

1. $8 + 2 = \underline{10}$ $4 + 8 = \underline{12}$ $6 + 3 = \underline{9}$

2.
$\begin{array}{r} 8 \\ +1 \\ \hline 9 \end{array}$
$\begin{array}{r} 3 \\ +7 \\ \hline 10 \end{array}$
$\begin{array}{r} 5 \\ +4 \\ \hline 9 \end{array}$
$\begin{array}{r} 10 \\ +2 \\ \hline 12 \end{array}$
$\begin{array}{r} 5 \\ +3 \\ \hline 8 \end{array}$
$\begin{array}{r} 4 \\ +2 \\ \hline 6 \end{array}$
$\begin{array}{r} 1 \\ +9 \\ \hline 10 \end{array}$

3. Draw 3 more. Write the sum.

$6 + 3 = \underline{9}$

4. Cross out 3. Write the difference.

$9 - 3 = \underline{6}$

Test Prep

Fill in the ○ for the correct answer. Add or subtract.

5.
$\begin{array}{r} 10 \\ +0 \end{array}$

○ 7   ○ 8   ○ 9   ● 10

6. $7 - 0 = \underline{}$

● 7   ○ 8   ○ 9   ○ 10

Notes for Home Your child reviewed basic addition and subtraction facts. *Home Activity:* Ask you child to explain how he or she used a ten frame to solve Exercise 3.

112 Use with page 284.

Name _____

Explore Tens and Ones

Use 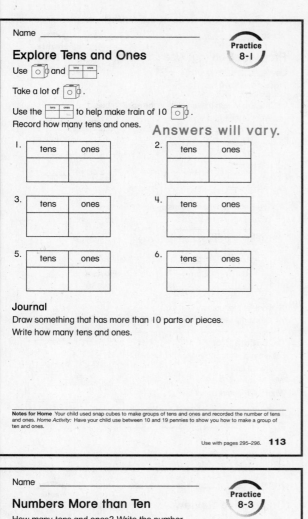 and ▭.

Take a lot of ▭.

Use the ▭ to help make train of 10 ▭.
Record how many tens and ones.

Answers will vary.

1. tens	ones

2. tens	ones

3. tens	ones

4. tens	ones

5. tens	ones

6. tens	ones

Journal

Draw something that has more than 10 parts or pieces.
Write how many tens and ones.

Notes for Home Your child used snap cubes to make groups of tens and ones and recorded the number of tens and ones. *Home Activity:* Have your child use between 10 and 19 pennies to show you how to make a group of ten and ones.

Use with pages 295–296. **113**

Name _____

Tens and Ones to 60

Use ▭ and ▭.

Count how many tens and ones. Write the number.

1.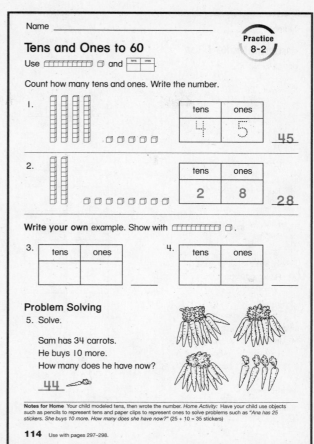

tens	ones
4	5

45

2.

tens	ones
2	8

28

Write your own example. Show with ▭.

3. tens	ones

4. tens	ones

Problem Solving

5. Solve.

Sam has 34 carrots.
He buys 10 more.
How many does he have now?

44

Notes for Home Your child modeled tens, then wrote the number. *Home Activity:* Have your child use objects such as pencils to represent tens and paper clips to represent ones to solve problems such as *"Ana has 25 stickers. She buys 10 more. How many does she have now?"* (25 + 10 = 35 stickers)

114 Use with pages 297–298.

Name _____

Numbers More than Ten

How many tens and ones? Write the number.

1.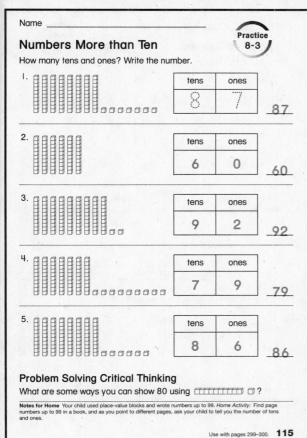

tens	ones
8	7

87

2.

tens	ones
6	0

60

3.

tens	ones
9	2

92

4.

tens	ones
7	9

79

5.

tens	ones
8	6

86

Problem Solving Critical Thinking

What are some ways you can show 80 using ▭ ?

Notes for Home Your child used place-value blocks and wrote numbers up to 99. *Home Activity:* Find page numbers up to 99 in a book, and as you point to different pages, ask your child to tell you the number of tens and ones.

Use with pages 299–300. **115**

Name _____

Estimation

Estimate.
Make groups of 10.

Count.
Write the number.

1.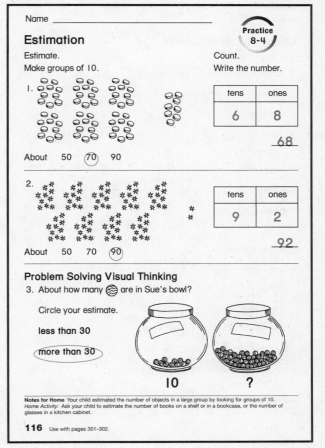

tens	ones
6	8

68

About 50 (70) 90

2.

tens	ones
9	2

92

About 50 70 (90)

Problem Solving Visual Thinking

3. About how many 🔵 are in Sue's bowl?

Circle your estimate.

less than 30

(more than 30)

10   ?

Notes for Home Your child estimated the number of objects in a large group by looking for groups of 10. *Home Activity:* Ask your child to estimate the number of books on a shelf or in a bookcase, or the number of glasses in a kitchen cabinet.

116 Use with pages 301–302.

Panel 1 (Practice 8-5)

Name _____

10 Ones Make 1 Ten

Use ▭▭▭▭▭▭▭▭▭▭ ▢

and ▦ .

Show this many.

	Add 2 more. Do you need to make a trade? Circle yes or no.	Write how many tens and ones.

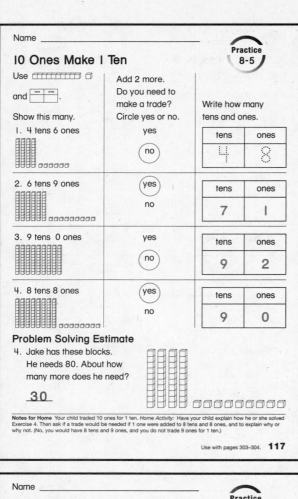

1. 4 tens 6 ones — yes / (no)

tens	ones
4	8

2. 6 tens 9 ones — (yes) / no

tens	ones
7	1

3. 9 tens 0 ones — yes / (no)

tens	ones
9	2

4. 8 tens 8 ones — (yes) / no

tens	ones
9	0

Problem Solving Estimate

4. Jake has these blocks.
He needs 80. About how many more does he need?

__30__

Notes for Home Your child traded 10 ones for 1 ten. Home Activity: Have your child explain how he or she solved Exercise 4. Then ask if a trade would be needed if 1 one were added to 8 tens and 8 ones, and to explain why or why not. (No, you would have 8 tens and 9 ones, and you do not trade 9 ones for 1 ten.)

Use with pages 303–304. **117**

Panel 2 (Practice 8-6)

Name _____

Problem Solving: Use Objects

Use ▭▭▭▭▭▭▭▭▭▭ ▢ and ▦ .
Trade if you need to.

1. The Blues won these points in the spelling bee.
What is their final score?

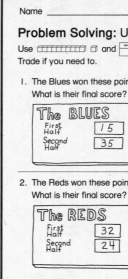

The BLUES
First Half — 15
Second Half — 35

tens	ones
5	0

Final score: __50__

2. The Reds won these points in the spelling bee.
What is their final score?

The REDS
First Half — 32
Second Half — 24

Final score: __56__

3. Look at the team's scores.
Circle the team that won the spelling bee.   The Blues   (The Reds)

Tell a Math Story

Tell a math story about this spelling bee.
How will it end?
Which team will win?
What will the final score be?

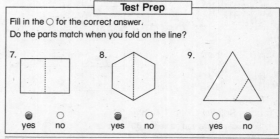

The REDS — 49
The BLUES — 47

Notes for Home Your child solved problems using place-value blocks. Home Activity: Point to the results of some game scores in a newspaper. Ask your child to tell who won each game and to explain how they know. (Possible answer: The Knicks won. They had 9 tens and 6 ones. The other team had 8 tens and 9 ones.)

118 Use with pages 307–308.

Panel 3 (Practice Chapter 8 A)

Name _____

Mixed Practice: Lessons 1–6

Write the number.

1. Estimate how many. Make groups of 10.

About   30   (50)   70   __4__ tens __8__ ones

2. Count how many.

Add 2 more. Do you need to make a trade? Circle yes or no.	Write how many tens and ones.
(yes) no	tens: 6 ones: 0

Problem Solving

Use ▭▭▭▭▭▭▭▭▭▭ ▢ and ▦ . Trade if you need to.

3. What is the Honey Bees final score?

The HONEY BEES
First Half — 31
Second Half — 19

Final Score: __50__

Journal

Draw a picture that shows 2 tens and 7 ones.
Write the number.

Notes for Home Your child practiced estimating, counting numbers to 99, and problem solving. Home Activity: Have your child look for numbers displayed on products in your home. Ask your child to explain what the numbers show. (Answer might include the dates of a month on a calendar, weights on food packaging, etc.)

Use with page 309. **119**

Panel 4 (Practice Chapters 1–8 A)

Name _____

Cumulative Review

Complete the fact family.

1. $8 + 3 = \underline{11}$
$3 + 8 = \underline{11}$
$11 - 8 = \underline{3}$
$11 - 3 = \underline{8}$

2. $6 + 7 = \underline{13}$
$7 + 6 = \underline{13}$
$13 - 6 = \underline{7}$
$13 - 7 = \underline{6}$

Write a number sentence.

3. 12 children played tag.
3 left to play ball.
How many play tag now?

$\underline{12 - 3 = 9}$

4. Maya found 7 shells.
Ellie found 5 shells.
How many shells do they have all together?

$\underline{7 + 5 = 12}$

Test Prep

Fill in the ○ for the correct answer.
Do the parts match when you fold on the line?

7.

8.

9.

7. ● yes   ○ no
8. ● yes   ○ no
9. ○ yes   ● no

Notes for Home Your child reviewed fact families and finding shapes with parts that match. Home Activity: Ask your child to use objects such as pennies to model an addition and a subtraction problem on the page.

120 Use with page 310.

Compare Numbers

Practice
8-7

Use ▭▭▭▭▭▭ ▱ and [tens|ones].
Write the tens and ones. Circle the number that is less.

1. 73 **7** tens **3** ones
   (48) **4** tens **8** ones

2. (24) **2** tens **4** ones
   49 **4** tens **9** ones

3. (56) **5** tens **6** ones
   85 **8** tens **5** ones

4. 90 **9** tens **0** ones
   (67) **6** tens **7** ones

5. (36) **3** tens **6** ones
   63 **6** tens **3** ones

6. (17) **1** tens **7** ones
   71 **7** tens **1** ones

Write your own numbers. Circle the number that is less.

Answers will vary.

7. ____ ____ tens ____ ones
   ____ ____ tens ____ ones

8. ____ ____ tens ____ ones
   ____ ____ tens ____ ones

Problem Solving Visual Thinking
Circle the one that is less.

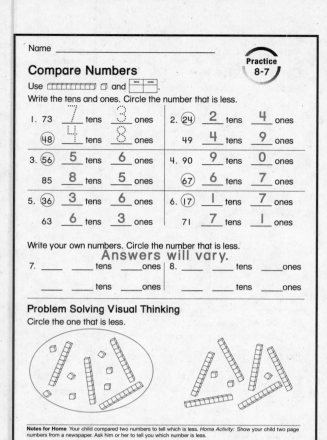

Notes for Home Your child compared two numbers to tell which is less. Home Activity: Show your child two page numbers from a newspaper. Ask him or her to tell you which number is less.

Use with pages 311–312. **121**

Order Numbers to 100

Practice
8-8

Write the number that comes after.

1. 82 **83**
2. 39 **40**
3. 71 **72**
4. 68 **69**
5. 42 **43**
6. 94 **95**

Write the numbers that come before.

7. **19** 20
8. **56** 57
9. **87** 88
10. **64** 65
11. **41** 42
12. **78** 79

Write the numbers that come between.

13. 68, **69**, **70**, 71
14. 87, **88**, **89**, 90
15. 49, **50**, **51**, 52
16. 75, 76, **77**, **78**, 79

Problem Solving Critical Thinking
17. Al picked three of these stickers.
They were odd numbers between 77 and 85.
Circle the stickers he picked.

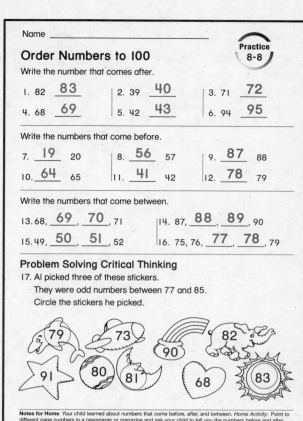

Notes for Home Your child learned about numbers that come before, after, and between. Home Activity: Point to different page numbers in a newspaper or magazine and ask your child to tell you the numbers before and after.

122 Use with pages 313–314.

Patterns on the 100 Chart

Practice
8-9

Write the missing numbers.

1. | 37 | 38 | 39 |
   |----|----|----|
   | 47 | 48 | 49 |

2. | 21 | 22 | 23 |
   |----|----|----|
   | 31 | 32 | 33 |

3. | 81 | 82 | 83 |
   |----|----|----|
   | 91 | 92 | 93 |

4. | 52 | 53 | 54 | 55 |
   |----|----|----|----|
   | 62 | 63 | 64 | 65 |

5. | 11 | 12 | 13 |
   |----|----|----|
   | 21 | 22 | 23 |

6. | 64 | 65 | 66 | 67 |
   |----|----|----|----|
   | 74 | 75 | 76 | 77 |

7. | 45 | 46 | 47 |
   |----|----|----|
   | 55 | 56 | 57 |

8. | 77 | 78 | 79 | 80 |
   |----|----|----|----|
   | 87 | 88 | 89 | 90 |

Problem Solving Patterns
9. What comes next?
Circle the next shape in the pattern.

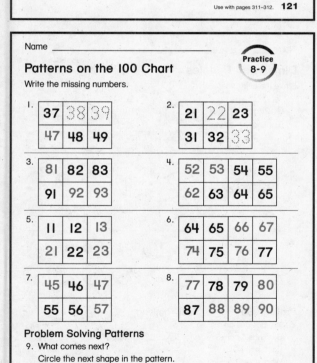

Notes for Home Your child used the patterns in a 100 chart to help find missing numbers. Home Activity: Ask your child to write 3 numbers to extend the following pattern: 5, 10, 15. (20, 25, 30)

Use with pages 315–316. **123**

Problem Solving:
Collect and Use Data

Practice
8-10

1. Put your name where it belongs. **Answers will vary.**
Ask 6 friends to put their names in the circles.

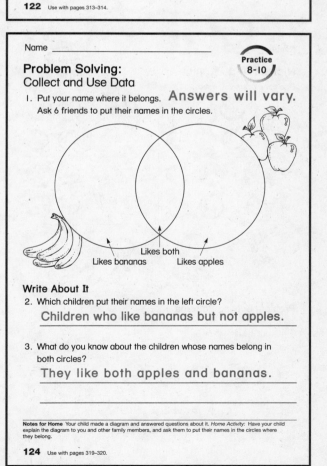

Likes bananas   Likes both   Likes apples

Write About It
2. Which children put their names in the left circle?
Children who like bananas but not apples.

3. What do you know about the children whose names belong in both circles?
They like both apples and bananas.

Notes for Home Your child made a diagram and answered questions about it. Home Activity: Have your child explain the diagram to you and other family members, and ask them to put their names in the circles where they belong.

124 Use with pages 319–320.

Mixed Practice: Lessons 7 - 10

1. Write the missing numbers.

71	72	73	74	75	76	77	78	79	80
81	82	83	84	85	86	87	88	89	90
91	92	93	94	95	96	97	98	99	100

Write the missing numbers.

2. 45, 46, __47__   3. 29, __30__, 31   4. __49__, 50, 51

5. 92, __93__, 94   6. __60__, 61, 62   7. 18, 19, __20__

Problem Solving

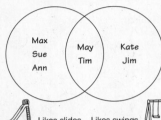

8. How many children like swings? __4__

9. Who likes both slides and swings? __May, Tim__

Likes slides   Likes swings

Journal

Which is greater, 69 or 72? How do you know?

Notes for Home Your child practiced using numbers to 99 and reading a diagram to solve problems.
Home Activity: Ask your child to tell you whether more children like swings or slides. (More children like slides.)

Use with page 321. **125**

Cumulative Review

Subtract.

1. $\begin{array}{r} 6 \\ +4 \\ \hline 10 \end{array}$ $\begin{array}{r} 10 \\ -4 \\ \hline 6 \end{array}$ 2. $\begin{array}{r} 12 \\ -5 \\ \hline 7 \end{array}$ $\begin{array}{r} 7 \\ +5 \\ \hline 12 \end{array}$ 3. $\begin{array}{r} 5 \\ +6 \\ \hline 11 \end{array}$ $\begin{array}{r} 11 \\ -6 \\ \hline 5 \end{array}$

4. $3 + 4 = \underline{7}$ 5. $1 + 11 = \underline{12}$ 6. $8 + 4 = \underline{12}$

$7 - 4 = \underline{3}$ $12 - 1 = \underline{11}$ $12 - 4 = \underline{8}$

Problem Solving

7. Circle the shape that shows $\frac{1}{3}$.

Test Prep

What number comes next?
Fill in ○ for the correct answer.

8. 3 6 9 12 _____   ● 15   9. 15 20 25 30 _____   ○ 32
                        ○ 13   ● 35

Notes for Home Your child reviewed basic addition and subtraction facts, problem solving, and skip counting.
Home Activity: Ask your child to find something in the kitchen that he or she can count by 2s.

126 Use with page 322.

Nickels and Pennies

Circle the coins you need. Answers will vary.

1. 3¢
2. 6¢
3. 7¢
4. 5¢
5. 10¢

Problem Solving Patterns

6. Is there enough money to buy the apples?
   Count the nickles by 5s.
   Circle Yes or No.

Yes

No

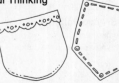

5¢ 10¢ 15¢ __20__ __25__   20¢

Notes for Home Your child practiced counting groups of nickels and pennies. Home Activity: Ask your child to
show you how to make 9¢ with pennies, and then with nickels and pennies. (9 pennies, and
1 nickel and 4 pennies)

Use with pages 333–334. **127**

Dimes and Pennies

Circle the coins you need.

1. 12¢      2. 13¢
3. 2¢   4. 30¢
5. 16¢

Problem Solving Critical Thinking

6. Mia has one coin.
   Sam has 6 coins.
   Each has 10¢.
   What coins do
   they have?
   Draw their coins.

Mia's coins   Sam's coins

Mia: 1 dime; Sam 1 nickel, 5 pennies.

Notes for Home Your child practiced counting groups of dimes and pennies. Home Activity: Using dimes and
pennies, ask your child to show you how to make 15¢. (1 dime and 5 pennies)

128 Use with pages 335–336.

Dimes, Nickels, and Pennies

Count. Write the amount.

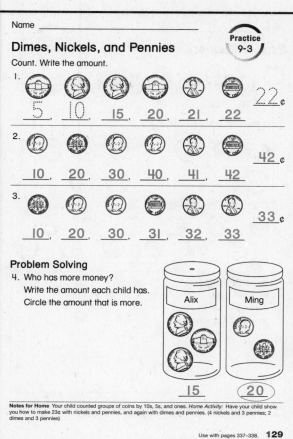

1. 5, 10, 15, 20, 21, 22   22¢

2. 10, 20, 30, 40, 41, 42   42¢

3. 10, 20, 30, 31, 32, 33   33¢

Problem Solving

4. Who has more money?
   Write the amount each child has.
   Circle the amount that is more.

   Alix   Ming

   15   (20)

Notes for Home Your child counted groups of coins by 10s, 5s, and ones. Home Activity: Have your child show you how to make 23¢ with nickels and pennies, and again with dimes and pennies. (4 nickels and 3 pennies; 2 dimes and 3 pennies)

Use with pages 337–338. 129

Count Mixed Coins

Circle the coins you need.

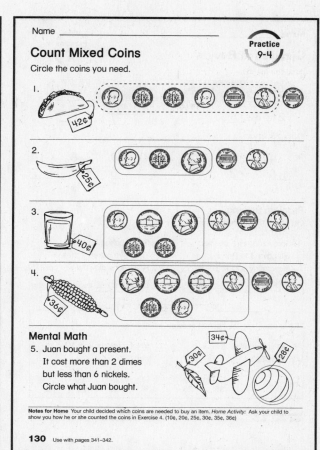

1. 42¢

2. 25¢

3. 40¢

4. 36¢

Mental Math

5. Juan bought a present.
   It cost more than 2 dimes
   but less than 6 nickels.
   Circle what Juan bought.

   30¢   34¢   28¢

Notes for Home Your child decided which coins are needed to buy an item. Home Activity: Ask your child to show you how he or she counted the coins in Exercise 4. (10¢, 20¢, 25¢, 30¢, 35¢, 36¢)

130 Use with pages 341–342.

Problem Solving:
Use Data from a Picture

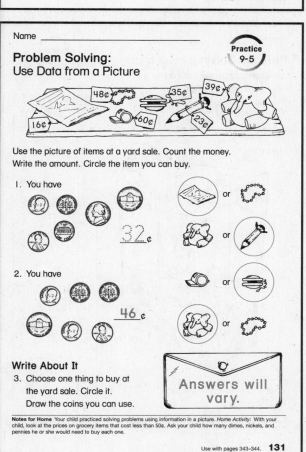

48¢ 35¢ 39¢
16¢ 60¢ 23¢

Use the picture of items at a yard sale. Count the money.
Write the amount. Circle the item you can buy.

1. You have   32¢   or

2. You have   46¢   or

Write About It

3. Choose one thing to buy at
   the yard sale. Circle it.
   Draw the coins you can use.

   Answers will vary.

Notes for Home Your child practiced solving problems using information in a picture. Home Activity: With your child, look at the prices on grocery items that cost less than 50¢. Ask your child how many dimes, nickels, and pennies he or she would need to buy each one.

Use with pages 343–344. 131

Mixed Practice: Lessons 1–5

Count the money. Write the amount.

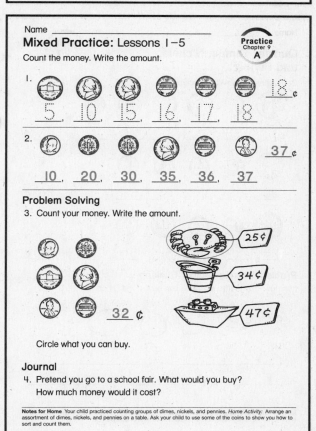

1. 5, 10, 15, 16, 17, 18   18¢

2. 10, 20, 30, 35, 36, 37   37¢

Problem Solving

3. Count your money. Write the amount.

   32¢   25¢   34¢   47¢

   Circle what you can buy.

Journal

4. Pretend you go to a school fair. What would you buy?
   How much money would it cost?

Notes for Home Your child practiced counting groups of dimes, nickels, and pennies. Home Activity: Arrange an assortment of dimes, nickels, and pennies on a table. Ask your child to use some of the coins to show you how to sort and count them.

132 Use with page 345.

Top Left Panel

Name _____

Cumulative Review

Write the number.

1.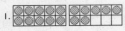
   17

2.
   27

Add or Subtract.

3.
$$\begin{array}{c} 4 \\ +6 \\ \hline 10 \end{array} \quad \begin{array}{c} 3 \\ -2 \\ \hline 5 \end{array} \quad \begin{array}{c} 12 \\ -9 \\ \hline 3 \end{array} \quad \begin{array}{c} 5 \\ +7 \\ \hline 12 \end{array} \quad \begin{array}{c} 9 \\ -6 \\ \hline 3 \end{array} \quad \begin{array}{c} 8 \\ +0 \\ \hline 8 \end{array} \quad \begin{array}{c} 10 \\ -7 \\ \hline 3 \end{array}$$

Problem Solving

Complete the number sentence.

4. Jamie made 12 snacks.
   He gave 3 to Ben.
   How many snacks are left?

   $12 - \underline{3} = \underline{9}$

5. Sarah baked four pies.
   Then she baked 7 pies.
   How many pies did she bake?

   $4 + \underline{7} = \underline{11}$

Test Prep

Fill in the ○ for the correct answer.

6. Which number is less than 32?

   ○ 38 ○ 63 ○ 35 ● 23

7. Which number is greater than 89?

   ○ 39 ○ 88 ● 94 ○ 72

Notes for Home Your child reviewed counting to 50, using addition and subtraction, and comparing numbers. Home Activity: Ask your child to name another number that is less than 32 and another that is greater than 89.

Top Right Panel

Name _____

Explore Quarters

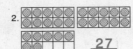   **25¢**

10, 20, 21, 22, 23, 24, 25

Circle the coins that show 25¢.

1.

2.

3.

Problem Solving

4. You have 25¢ to spend.
   You have 4 coins.
   Draw the coins you have.

   (5¢) (5¢)
   (5¢) (10¢)

Notes for Home Your child practiced counting groups of coins that equal 25¢. Home Activity: Give your child 2 dimes, 5 nickels, and 5 pennies. Ask him or her to show you different ways to make 25¢.

Bottom Left Panel

Name _____

Quarter, Dimes, Nickels, and Pennies

Count the money. Write the amount.

1.
   25, 35, 40, 45, 46, 47   **47** ¢

2.
   25, 35, 45, 55, 56   **56** ¢

3.
   25, 35, 45, 50, 51   **51** ¢

Problem Solving Critical Thinking

Answers will vary.

You have 30¢. Write what you can buy.

cherries 20¢   banana 5¢   apple 15¢   pear 10¢   watermelon 25¢

4. _____ and _____.

5. _____ and _____ and _____.

Notes for Home Your child counted mixed groups of coins. Home Activity: Ask your child to name 2 fruits he or she could buy and spend exactly one quarter. (grapes and banana, or apple and pear)

Bottom Right Panel

Name _____

Problem Solving: Make a List

Susie gets 25¢ to spend at the zoo.
What coins might Susie get?

Use to find all the ways to make 25¢.

Make a list.

2	1	0
2	0	5
1	3	0
1	2	5
1	1	10
1	0	15
0	5	0
0	4	5
0	3	10
0	2	15
0	1	20
0	0	25

Journal

What would you buy at the zoo for 20¢ or 25¢?

Notes for Home Your child made a list of all the ways to make 25¢ with dimes, nickels, and pennies. Home Activity: Ask your child to solve this riddle: What coins do I use to make the same amount with 25 coins or 1 coin? (25 pennies and 1 quarter)

Mixed Practice: Lessons 6–8

Practice
Chapter 9
B

1. Circle the coins that show 30¢.

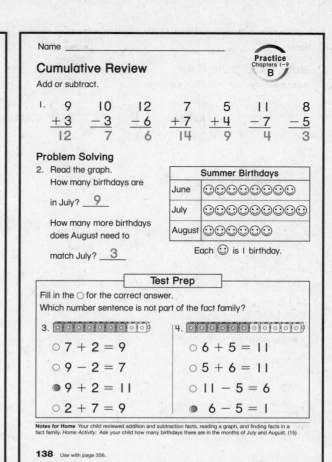

2. Count the money. Write the amount.

52 ¢

Problem Solving

3. Amy buys a toy for 25¢.
   She has no pennies.
   Find the ways she can pay 25¢.
   Make a list.

25¢

1	0	0
0	2	1
0	1	3
0	0	5

Journal

4. Do you think it is easier to pay for a toy
   with 25 pennies or 5 nickels? Why?

Notes for Home Your child practiced counting groups of coins and solving a problem by making a list. Home Activity: Ask your child what is the fewest number of coins needed to buy something for 30¢. (1 quarter and 1 nickel)

Cumulative Review

Practice
Chapters 1–9
B

Add or subtract.

1.
$$\begin{array}{r} 9 \\ +3 \\ \hline 12 \end{array} \quad \begin{array}{r} 10 \\ -3 \\ \hline 7 \end{array} \quad \begin{array}{r} 12 \\ -6 \\ \hline 6 \end{array} \quad \begin{array}{r} 7 \\ +7 \\ \hline 14 \end{array} \quad \begin{array}{r} 5 \\ +4 \\ \hline 9 \end{array} \quad \begin{array}{r} 11 \\ -7 \\ \hline 4 \end{array} \quad \begin{array}{r} 8 \\ -5 \\ \hline 3 \end{array}$$

Problem Solving

2. Read the graph.
   How many birthdays are
   in July? __9__

   How many more birthdays
   does August need to
   match July? __3__

Summer Birthdays	
June	☺☺☺☺☺☺☺
July	☺☺☺☺☺☺☺☺☺
August	☺☺☺☺☺☺

Each ☺ is 1 birthday.

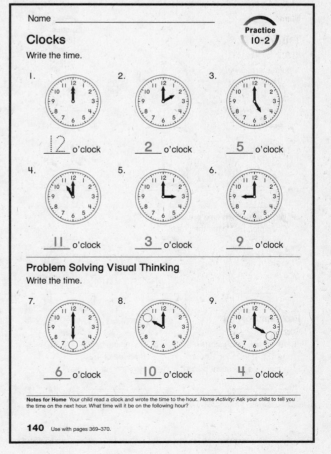

Test Prep

Fill in the ○ for the correct answer.
Which number sentence is not part of the fact family?

3.
○ 7 + 2 = 9
○ 9 − 2 = 7
◉ 9 + 2 = 11
○ 2 + 7 = 9

4.
○ 6 + 5 = 11
○ 5 + 6 = 11
○ 11 − 5 = 6
◉ 6 − 5 = 1

Notes for Home Your child reviewed addition and subtraction facts, reading a graph, and finding facts in a fact family. Home Activity: Ask your child how many birthdays there are in the months of July and August. (15)

Explore Time

Practice
10-1

A clock shows time. Where can you see a clock?
Here are places you could see a clock.
Draw a clock you could see in each place.

in the kitchen		outside
in a bedroom	at home	in another room

Talk About It

Name three places you think a clock would be useful.
Explain your choices. **Answers will vary.**

Notes for Home Your child talked about and drew pictures of clocks. Home Activity: Ask your child to point out clocks inside or outside the home.

Clocks

Practice
10-2

Write the time.

1. __12__ o'clock

2. __2__ o'clock

3. __5__ o'clock

4. __11__ o'clock

5. __3__ o'clock

6. __9__ o'clock

Problem Solving Visual Thinking

Write the time.

7. __6__ o'clock

8. __10__ o'clock

9. __4__ o'clock

Notes for Home Your child read a clock and wrote the time to the hour. Home Activity: Ask your child to tell you the time on the next hour. What time will it be on the following hour?

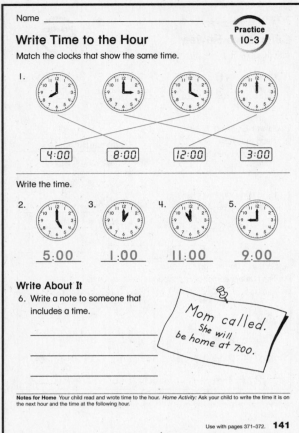

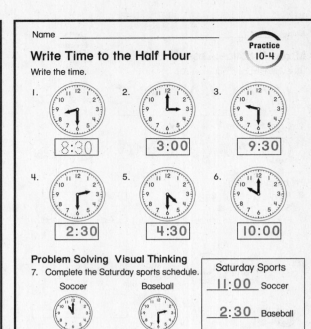

Top Left Quadrant

Name _____

Write Time to the Hour

Practice
10-3

Match the clocks that show the same time.

1.

| 4:00 | 8:00 | 12:00 | 3:00 |

Write the time.

2. **5**:00   3. **1**:00   4. **11**:00   5. **9**:00

Write About It

6. Write a note to someone that includes a time.

_____

_____

_____

Mom called. She will be home at 7:00.

Notes for Home Your child read and wrote time to the hour. *Home Activity:* Ask your child to write the time it is on the next hour and the time at the following hour.

Use with pages 371–372. **141**

Top Right Quadrant

Name _____

Write Time to the Half Hour

Practice
10-4

Write the time.

1. 8:30   2. 3:00   3. 9:30

4. 2:30   5. 4:30   6. 10:00

Problem Solving Visual Thinking

7. Complete the Saturday sports schedule.

Soccer   Baseball

Basketball   Hockey

Saturday Sports	
11:00	Soccer
2:30	Baseball
5:00	Basketball
7:30	Hockey

Notes for Home Your child read and wrote time to the half hour. *Home Activity:* Help your child write a schedule for a Saturday or Sunday afternoon. For example: clean room 1:30, pull weeds 3:00, shopping 3:30, visit family 4:00.

142 Use with pages 373–374.

Bottom Left Quadrant

Name _____

Tell Time

Practice
10-5

1. 4:30   5:00   5:30

2. 7:00   7:30   8:00

3. **Write your own** time problem. Draw pictures. Write the times.

| : | : | : |

Drawings and times will vary.

Problem Solving

Solve.

4. At school, lunch starts at 12:00. It lasts for 1 hour. What time does lunch end?
1:00

5. Swimming began at 3:30. It ended at 4:30. How long did it take?
1 hour

Notes for Home Your child wrote time to the hour and half hour. *Home Activity:* Ask your child: *Choir practice began at 1:30. It ended at 2:30. How long did it last?* (1 hour)

Use with pages 375–376. **143**

Bottom Right Quadrant

Name _____

Problem Solving: Logical Reasoning

Practice
10-6

Solve.

1. Sean is first in line.
Jim is behind Sean.
Tasha is in front of Jim.
Who is last in line?
___Jim___

2. Kisha eats breakfast at 8:30.
Jane eats breakfast at 7:00.
Monroe eats breakfast at 7:30.
Who eats breakfast last?
___Kisha___

3. Shawna gets home from school at 3:30.
She begins her homework after she eats her snack. She eats a snack at 4:00.
After what time does she begin her homework? ___after 4:00___

Critical Thinking

4. Choose and write the time that goes with each picture.

4:30   4:00   3:30

3:30   4:00   4:30

Notes for Home Your child solved problems. *Home Activity:* Ask your child to explain his or her reasoning in solving Problem 1.

144 Use with pages 379–380.

Panel 1 (top left)

Mixed Practice: Lessons 1-6

Write the time.

1. __3__ o'clock

2. __12__ o'clock

3. __9__ o'clock

4. [11:30]

5. [7:30]

6. [6:00]

7. [7:00]

8. [2:00]

9. [4:30]

Problem Solving

10. Solve.

Anya has a flute lesson at 4:30. Her sister
Laryssa has a lesson at 5:30. Joseph has a
lesson before Anya. Who has the last lesson?

Laryssa

Journal

11. Draw something you do at 12:00. Add a clock to your picture.

Panel 2 (top right)

Cumulative Review

1. Add or subtract.

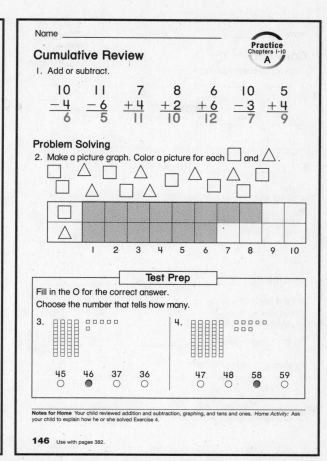

$$\begin{array}{cccccc} 10 & 11 & 7 & 8 & 6 & 10 & 5 \\ -4 & -6 & +4 & +2 & +6 & -3 & +4 \\ \hline 6 & 5 & 11 & 10 & 12 & 7 & 9 \end{array}$$

Problem Solving

2. Make a picture graph. Color a picture for each ☐ and △.

	1	2	3	4	5	6	7	8	9	10
☐	■	■	■	■	■	■	■	■		
△	■	■	■	■	■	■				

Test Prep

Fill in the O for the correct answer.
Choose the number that tells how many.

3. 45 46 37 36
    ○   ●   ○   ○

4. 47 48 58 59
    ○   ○   ●   ○

Panel 3 (bottom left)

Order Events

Write 1st, 2nd, 3rd to put the pictures in order.

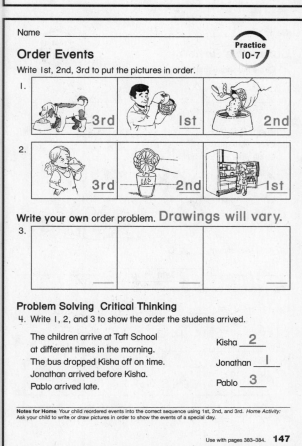

1. __3rd__   __1st__   __2nd__

2. __3rd__   __2nd__   __1st__

Write your own order problem. **Drawings will vary.**

3. _____ _____ _____

Problem Solving Critical Thinking

4. Write 1, 2, and 3 to show the order the students arrived.

The children arrive at Taft School
at different times in the morning.
The bus dropped Kisha off on time.
Jonathan arrived before Kisha.
Pablo arrived late.

Kisha __2__

Jonathan __1__

Pablo __3__

Panel 4 (bottom right)

Estimate Time

Circle the time it takes.

1. about 1 minute (about 1 hour)

2. about 1 minute (about 1 hour)

3. (about 1 minute) about 1 hour

4. about 1 minute (about 1 hour)

5. **Draw your own** time problem.

Tell a Math Story

6. Tell about something you did yesterday.
Tell what time you started and what time you stopped.
Answers will vary.

Calendar

1. Make a calendar for this month.

Calendars will vary.

Month: _____

Sunday	Monday	Tuesday	Wednesday	Thursday	Friday	Saturday

Use your calendar.   **Responses will vary.**

2. Today is _____

3. The day before yesterday was _____

4. In five more days it will be _____

5. The day after tomorrow is _____

Problem Solving Patterns

6. What is the number date of the Monday of next week? _____

Notes for Home Your child completed a calendar for the current month. *Home Activity:* Mark your family calendar with special days of family members and friends. Ask your child to tell you the month, date, and day of the week for each event.

Use with pages 387–388. **149**

Problem Solving:
Too Much Information

Cross out what you do not need. Solve.

1. Stacy bought 9 stickers on Monday.
   ~~She likes those with animals.~~
   Stacy gave away 3 stickers on Tuesday.
   How many stickers does Stacy have now?   **6**

2. Mark collected 11 soup can labels.
   Debbie collected 5 labels. ~~The school will buy a new computer with the labels.~~
   How many labels do they have in all?   **16**

3. There are 14 children in Peggy's
   music class. ~~There are 5 boys and 9 girls.~~
   6 of the children also take a dance class.
   How many children in the music class
   do not take a dance class?   **8**

Problem Solving Visual Thinking
What does each clock show? Write the time.

4.   **9:00**

5.   **6:30**

6.   **2:00**

Notes for Home Your child solved problems that give too much information. *Home Activity:* Ask your child to tell you about a time when he or she had more information than was needed to solve a problem or perform an activity.

150 Use with pages 392–393.

Mixed Practice: Lessons 7-10

Write 1st, 2nd, and 3rd to put the pictures in order.

1.

Use the calendar to answer the question.

2.
July

Thursday	Friday	Saturday
4	5	6
11	12	13
18	19	20

Circle the correct day.

July 20	(Saturday)	Sunday
July 4	Wednesday	(Thursday)
July 19	(Friday)	Saturday
July 13	Friday	(Saturday)

Problem Solving
Cross out what you do not need.
Solve.

3. ~~Jack went to the store at 3:30 with his brother.~~
   They bought 4 apples.
   Jack bought 6 bananas.
   His brother bought 5 oranges.
   How many pieces of fruit did they buy?   **15**

Journal
Write about something you do that takes less time
than it takes to brush your teeth.

Notes for Home Your child practiced ordering events, reading a calendar, and solving problems. *Home Activity:* Ask your child to look at the calendar on this page and tell you the date of the first Sunday. (7)

Use with page 393. **151**

Cumulative Review

1. Circle the shape that belongs.

Problem Solving

2. Count your money.
   Circle what you can buy.

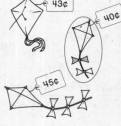

Write the amount.   **42** ¢

Test Prep

Fill in the ○ for the correct answer. Add.

3. $6 + 4 =$ ___
   ○ ● ○ ○
   9 10 11 12

4. $4 + 6 =$ ___
   ○ ○ ● ○
   12 11 10 9

5. $5 + 7 =$ ___
   ○ ○ ○ ●
   9 10 11 12

6. $7 + 5 =$ ___
   ● ○ ○ ○
   12 11 10 9

Notes for Home Your child reviewed sorting, using money, and addition. *Home Activity:* Ask your child how much more money is needed to buy the 45¢ kite in exercise 2. (3¢)

152 Use with page 394.

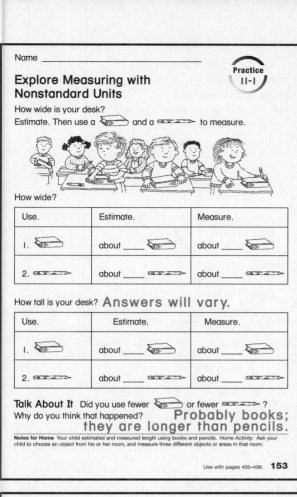

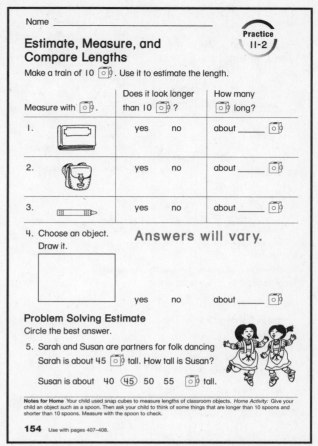

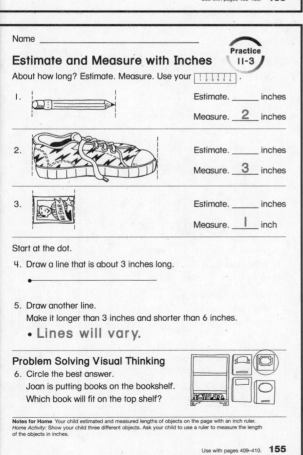

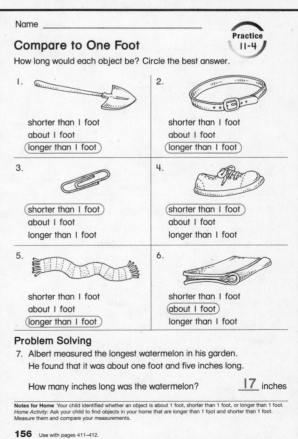

Explore Measuring with Nonstandard Units

Name _____

How wide is your desk?
Estimate. Then use a 📕 and a ✏️ to measure.

How wide?

Use.	Estimate.	Measure.
1. 📕	about _____ 📕	about _____ 📕
2. ✏️	about _____ ✏️	about _____ ✏️

How tall is your desk? Answers will vary.

Use.	Estimate.	Measure.
1. 📕	about _____ 📕	about _____ 📕
2. ✏️	about _____ ✏️	about _____ ✏️

Talk About It Did you use fewer 📕 or fewer ✏️?
Why do you think that happened? Probably books;
they are longer than pencils.

Notes for Home Your child estimated and measured length using books and pencils. Home Activity: Ask your child to choose an object from his or her room, and measure three different objects or areas in that room.

Use with pages 405–406. **153**

Estimate, Measure, and Compare Lengths

Name _____

Make a train of 10 🎲. Use it to estimate the length.

Measure with 🎲.	Does it look longer than 10 🎲?	How many 🎲 long?
1. 📖	yes no	about _____ 🎲
2. 👜	yes no	about _____ 🎲
3. ✏️	yes no	about _____ 🎲

4. Choose an object.   Answers will vary.
   Draw it.

   [ ]   yes   no   about _____ 🎲

Problem Solving Estimate
Circle the best answer.

5. Sarah and Susan are partners for folk dancing
   Sarah is about 45 🎲 tall. How tall is Susan?

   Susan is about   40 (45) 50 55   🎲 tall.

Notes for Home Your child used snap cubes to measure lengths of classroom objects. Home Activity: Give your child an object such as a spoon. Then ask your child to think of some things that are longer than 10 spoons and shorter than 10 spoons. Measure with the spoon to check.

154 Use with pages 407–408.

Estimate and Measure with Inches

Name _____

About how long? Estimate. Measure. Use your [ruler].

1. Estimate. _____ inches
   Measure. __2__ inches

2. Estimate. _____ inches
   Measure. __3__ inches

3. Estimate. _____ inches
   Measure. __1__ inch

Start at the dot.

4. Draw a line that is about 3 inches long.

   •_____

5. Draw another line.
   Make it longer than 3 inches and shorter than 6 inches.

   • Lines will vary.

Problem Solving Visual Thinking
6. Circle the best answer.
   Joan is putting books on the bookshelf.
   Which book will fit on the top shelf?

Notes for Home Your child estimated and measured lengths of objects on the page with an inch ruler. Home Activity: Show your child three different objects. Ask your child to use a ruler to measure the length of the objects in inches.

Use with pages 409–410. **155**

Compare to One Foot

Name _____

How long would each object be? Circle the best answer.

1. shorter than 1 foot
   about 1 foot
   (longer than 1 foot)

2. shorter than 1 foot
   about 1 foot
   (longer than 1 foot)

3. (shorter than 1 foot)
   about 1 foot
   longer than 1 foot

4. (shorter than 1 foot)
   about 1 foot
   longer than 1 foot

5. shorter than 1 foot
   about 1 foot
   (longer than 1 foot)

6. shorter than 1 foot
   (about 1 foot)
   longer than 1 foot

Problem Solving
7. Albert measured the longest watermelon in his garden.
   He found that it was about one foot and five inches long.

   How many inches long was the watermelon? __17__ inches

Notes for Home Your child identified whether an object is about 1 foot, shorter than 1 foot, or longer than 1 foot. Home Activity: Ask your child to find objects in your home that are longer than 1 foot and shorter than 1 foot. Measure them and compare your measurements.

156 Use with pages 411–412.

Top Left

Name _____

Estimate and Measure with Centimeters

About how long? Estimate. Measure. Use your ▭.

1. Estimate. _____ centimeters

   Measure. __9__ centimeters

2. Estimate. _____ centimeters

   Measure. __8__ centimeters

3. Estimate. _____ centimeters

   Measure. __7__ centimeters

Start at the dot.

4. Draw a line. Make it longer than 10 centimeters and shorter than 15 centimeters.

   • Lines will vary.

Problem Solving Critical Thinking

5. Solve.
   Rover is taller than Rex.
   Princess is taller than Rover.
   Spot is shorter than Rex.

   Who is the shortest? __Spot__

Notes for Home Your child estimated and measured lengths of objects with a centimeter ruler. Home Activity: Have your child select 4 small kitchen utensils. Ask your child to guess and then measure the length of these objects in centimeters.

Use with pages 415–416. **157**

Top Right

Name _____

Problem Solving:
Group Decision Making

Work with your group. Choose an object in the classroom to measure. Write the answers.

1. Your group has only paper clips and a centimeter ruler. Talk about how you can used these to measure your object. Draw what you will do.

   Answers will vary.

2. Estimate. How big around does the group think your object is?

   Answers will vary.

3. Measure. How big around is it?

   Answers will vary.

4. Talk it over. Were paper clips a good thing to use? Why or why not?

   Probably not. It is difficult to measure around an object without using a flexible measuring tool.

Journal

Write about your group. How did you work together? Would you do something differently the next time? Why or why not? If you would change something, what would it be?

Notes for Home Your child worked with a group to choose tools and carry out a measurement project. Home Activity: Work with your child to measure around some large things in your home, such as the refrigerator, a bookcase, or a television set.

158 Use with pages 417–418.

Bottom Left

Name _____

Mixed Practice: Lessons 1–6

Use the rulers to measure length. Write the answer.

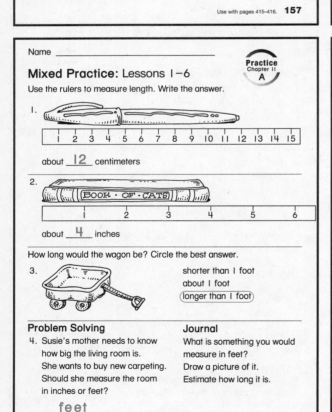

1.
   | 1 2 3 4 5 6 7 8 9 10 11 12 13 14 15 |

   about __12__ centimeters

2. BOOK · OF · CATS
   | 1 2 3 4 5 6 |

   about __4__ inches

How long would the wagon be? Circle the best answer.

3. shorter than 1 foot
   about 1 foot
   (longer than 1 foot)

Problem Solving

4. Susie's mother needs to know how big the living room is. She wants to buy new carpeting. Should she measure the room in inches or feet?

   __feet__

Journal

What is something you would measure in feet? Draw a picture of it. Estimate how long it is.

Notes for Home Your child worked with centimeters, inches and feet. Home Activity: Ask your child to find something in your home that you would measure in inches. Measure it together.

Use with page 419. **159**

Bottom Right

Name _____

Cumulative Review

1. Add or subtract.

$$\begin{array}{ccccccc} 5 & 9 & 7 & 8 & 12 & 3 & 11 \\ +6 & -5 & +3 & +4 & -9 & +3 & -9 \\ \hline 11 & 4 & 10 & 12 & 3 & 6 & 2 \end{array}$$

2. Circle the correct estimate.

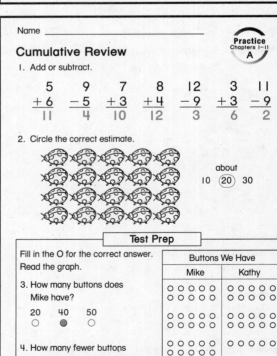

   about 10 (20) 30

Test Prep

Fill in the O for the correct answer. Read the graph.

3. How many buttons does Mike have?

   20   40   50
   ○   ●   ○

4. How many fewer buttons does Kathy have than Mike?

   5   10   15
   ○   ○   ●

Buttons We Have	
Mike	Kathy
○ ○ ○ ○ ○	○ ○ ○ ○ ○
○ ○ ○ ○ ○	○ ○ ○ ○ ○
○ ○ ○ ○ ○	○ ○ ○ ○ ○
○ ○ ○ ○ ○	○ ○ ○ ○ ○
○ ○ ○ ○ ○	
○ ○ ○ ○ ○	

Notes for Home Your child reviewed addition and subtraction, estimation, and graphing. Home Activity: Ask your child to solve 7 + 2 = (9) and 12 – 5 = (7).

160 Use with page 420.

Explore Weight

Compare these weights. Write **more**, **less**, or **same**.

1. more   less   2. less   more

3. less   more   4. same   same

Talk About It What are some other ways
you compare how heavy two things are? **Answers will vary.**

Notes for Home Your child compared the weights of objects. *Home Activity:* Have your child select two objects
and hold one in each hand. Ask him or her to tell which one weighs more and which one weighs less.

Use with pages 421–422. **161**

Compare to One Pound

How heavy would each be?
Circle the best answer.

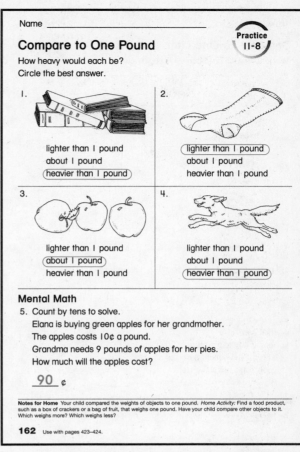

1. lighter than 1 pound
   about 1 pound
   (heavier than 1 pound)

2. (lighter than 1 pound)
   about 1 pound
   heavier than 1 pound

3. lighter than 1 pound
   (about 1 pound)
   heavier than 1 pound

4. lighter than 1 pound
   about 1 pound
   (heavier than 1 pound)

Mental Math

5. Count by tens to solve.
   Elana is buying green apples for her grandmother.
   The apples costs 10¢ a pound.
   Grandma needs 9 pounds of apples for her pies.
   How much will the apples cost?

   __90__ ¢

Notes for Home Your child compared the weights of objects to one pound. *Home Activity:* Find a food product,
such as a box of crackers or a bag of fruit, that weighs one pound. Have your child compare other objects to it.
Which weighs more? Which weighs less?

162 Use with pages 423–424.

Compare to One Kilogram

How heavy would each object be?
Circle the best answer.

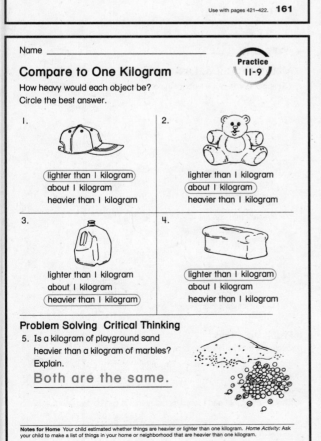

1. (lighter than 1 kilogram)
   about 1 kilogram
   heavier than 1 kilogram

2. lighter than 1 kilogram
   (about 1 kilogram)
   heavier than 1 kilogram

3. lighter than 1 kilogram
   about 1 kilogram
   (heavier than 1 kilogram)

4. (lighter than 1 kilogram)
   about 1 kilogram
   heavier than 1 kilogram

Problem Solving Critical Thinking

5. Is a kilogram of playground sand
   heavier than a kilogram of marbles?
   Explain.
   Both are the same.

Notes for Home Your child estimated whether things are heavier or lighter than one kilogram. *Home Activity:* Ask
your child to make a list of things in your home or neighborhood that are heavier than one kilogram.

Use with pages 425–426. **163**

Compare Cups, Pints, and Quarts

Circle the things that could hold less than 1 cup.
Mark an X on the things that hold more than 1 cup.

1.
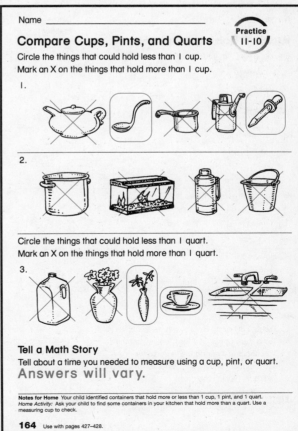

2.

Circle the things that could hold less than 1 quart.
Mark an X on the things that hold more than 1 quart.

3.

Tell a Math Story

Tell about a time you needed to measure using a cup, pint, or quart.
Answers will vary.

Notes for Home Your child identified containers that hold more or less than 1 cup, 1 pint, and 1 quart.
Home Activity: Ask your child to find some containers in your kitchen that hold more than a quart. Use a
measuring cup to check.

164 Use with pages 427–428.

Compare to One Liter

Check how much each container could hold.

	Container	Less than 1 liter	About 1 liter	More than 1 liter
1.			✓	
2.		✓		
3.				✓
4.			✓	
5.			✓	

Mental Math

6. Tanya went to the store to buy juice for a party. She bought 6 bottles of juice. Each bottle holds two liters. How many liters of juice did she buy? __12__

I can count by 2s.

Use a Thermometer

Look at the ▯.
Draw a picture to show how it looks outside.

1.
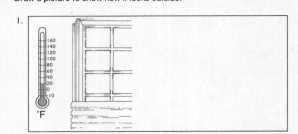

2.
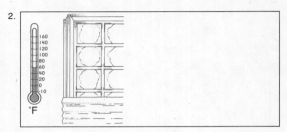

Journal

Write about some things you like to do outside when it is warm.
Write about some things you like to do outside when it is cool.

Problem Solving: Logical Reasoning

Circle the tool that you need to answer each question.

1. How heavy is it?
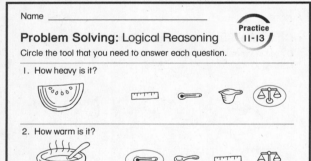

2. How warm is it?

3. How much water does it hold?

4. How long is it?
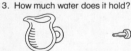

Tell a Math Story

5. Richard is baking a cake with his father.
   Tell a story about how they follow the recipe.
   Talk about measuring the ingredients.
   Tell about choosing a container for mixing and baking.
   Tell about baking the cake.

Mixed Practice: Lessons 7–13

Circle the words that tell about the object.

1. The kitten weighs

   (less than 1 kilogram.)
   about 1 kilogram.
   more than 1 kilogram.

2. The bananas weigh

   less than 1 pound.
   (about 1 pound.)
   more than 1 pound.

3. The watering can holds

   less than 1 liter.
   about 1 liter.
   (more than 1 liter.)

4. The glass holds

   less than 1 cup.
   (about 1 cup.)
   more than 1 cup.

Problem Solving

Circle the tool you need to answer the question.

5. Is your dog heavier than your cat?

Journal

Choose an object and record as many things as you can about it.

Top Left Quadrant

Name _____

Cumulative Review

Practice
Chapters 1–11
B

Add.

1. $3 + 3 = \underline{6}$ $3 + 4 = \underline{7}$ $4 + 3 = \underline{7}$

2. $2 + 2 = \underline{4}$ $2 + 3 = \underline{5}$ $3 + 2 = \underline{5}$

Problem Solving

Write a number sentence.

3. Jonathan had 11 sports cards. He gave 3 to Tom. How many are left?

$11 - 3 = 8$

4. Ellen had 6 pennies. Her mother gave her 5 more. How many pennies does Ellen have?

$6 + 5 = 11$

Test Prep

Fill in the O for the correct answer.
What time does the clock show?

5. ○ 3:30 ● 4:30 ○ 5:30

6. ● 10:00 ○ 11:00 ○ 12:00

7. ○ 6:00 ○ 7:00 ● 8:00

8. ○ 11:30 ○ 12:30 ● 1:30

Notes for Home Your child reviewed addition, writing a number sentence, and telling time. *Home Activity:* Ask your child to tell you what time it will be on the next half hour and the next hour.

Use with page 438. **169**

Top Right Quadrant

Name _____

Add Doubles to 18

Practice
12-1

Write the sum.

1. $4 + 4 = \underline{8}$ $6 + 6 = \underline{12}$ $8 + 8 = \underline{16}$

2. $5 + 5 = \underline{10}$ $7 + 7 = \underline{14}$ $9 + 9 = \underline{18}$

Mixed Practice Write the sum. Circle the doubles.

3.
$\begin{array}{r}2\\+8\\\hline10\end{array}$ $\begin{array}{r}4\\+4\\\hline8\end{array}$ $\begin{array}{r}7\\+7\\\hline14\end{array}$ $\begin{array}{r}3\\+8\\\hline11\end{array}$ $\begin{array}{r}5\\+5\\\hline10\end{array}$ $\begin{array}{r}1\\+6\\\hline7\end{array}$ $\begin{array}{r}8\\+7\\\hline15\end{array}$

4.
$\begin{array}{r}6\\+6\\\hline12\end{array}$ $\begin{array}{r}9\\+3\\\hline12\end{array}$ $\begin{array}{r}4\\+8\\\hline12\end{array}$ $\begin{array}{r}9\\+9\\\hline18\end{array}$ $\begin{array}{r}5\\+7\\\hline12\end{array}$ $\begin{array}{r}8\\+8\\\hline16\end{array}$ $\begin{array}{r}7\\+3\\\hline10\end{array}$

Problem Solving Visual Thinking

5. Jacob sets the table for dinner.
One plate goes on each mat.
One bowl goes on each mat, too.
How many dishes will Jacob use?

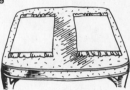

$\underline{4}$ dishes

Notes for Home Your child added doubles facts such as 6 + 6, 7 + 7, 8 + 8, and 9 + 9. **Home Activity:** Set out two equal groups of kitchen utensils and ask how many in all. (Possible answer: 6 forks + 6 forks = 12 forks.)

170 Use with pages 449–450.

Bottom Left Quadrant

Name _____

Add Doubles Plus One

Practice
12-2

Write the sum.

1.
$\begin{array}{r}4\\+4\\\hline8\end{array}$ $\begin{array}{r}4\\+5\\\hline9\end{array}$ $\begin{array}{r}5\\+4\\\hline9\end{array}$ | 2. $\begin{array}{r}5\\+5\\\hline10\end{array}$ $\begin{array}{r}5\\+6\\\hline11\end{array}$ $\begin{array}{r}6\\+5\\\hline11\end{array}$

3.
$\begin{array}{r}9\\+9\\\hline18\end{array}$ $\begin{array}{r}9\\+10\\\hline19\end{array}$ $\begin{array}{r}10\\+9\\\hline19\end{array}$ | 4. $\begin{array}{r}8\\+8\\\hline16\end{array}$ $\begin{array}{r}8\\+9\\\hline17\end{array}$ $\begin{array}{r}9\\+8\\\hline17\end{array}$

5. $6 + 6 = \underline{12}$ $1 + 2 = \underline{3}$ $8 + 9 = \underline{17}$

6. $6 + 5 = \underline{11}$ $8 + 8 = \underline{16}$ $7 + 8 = \underline{15}$

7. $7 + 6 = \underline{13}$ $4 + 3 = \underline{7}$ $7 + 7 = \underline{14}$

Problem Solving

Solve. Write the number sentence.

8. Meg made an ant farm.
She put in 8 red ants.
She put in 9 black ants.
How many ants did Meg put in?

$\underline{8} + \underline{9} = \underline{17}$
$\underline{17}$ ants

9. A fish had 6 teeth on the top.
It had 5 teeth on the bottom.
How many teeth did the fish have?

$\underline{6} + \underline{5} = \underline{11}$
$\underline{11}$ teeth

Notes for Home Your child added using a doubles fact, such as 6 + 6 = 12, to solve other facts. *Home Activity:* Have your child line up shoes to show a doubles plus one fact.

Use with pages 451–452. **171**

Bottom Right Quadrant

Name _____

Add 3 Numbers

Practice
12-3

Use a paper clip and pencil. Spin.
Write the number in the box. Add.

1.
$\begin{array}{r}4\\5\\+\Box\end{array}$ $\begin{array}{r}3\\\Box\\+2\end{array}$ $\begin{array}{r}\\6\\+0\end{array}$

Answers will vary.

2.
$\begin{array}{r}3\\7\\+\end{array}$ $\begin{array}{r}6\\\Box\\+7\end{array}$ $\begin{array}{r}\\2\\+4\end{array}$ $\begin{array}{r}1\\5\\+\Box\end{array}$

Answers will vary.

3.
$\begin{array}{r}\Box\\4\\+6\end{array}$ $\begin{array}{r}1\\8\\+\Box\end{array}$ $\begin{array}{r}5\\5\\+\Box\end{array}$ $\begin{array}{r}6\\\Box\\+3\end{array}$ $\begin{array}{r}2\\\Box\\+1\end{array}$

Answers will vary.

Mental Math

4. Coach had 3 bags of soccer balls.
He had 16 balls in all.
Color the 3 bags Coach had.

Notes for Home Your child added three numbers. *Home Activity:* Ask your child to separate a pile of 18 rocks into 3 groups. Have them write a number sentence to show how they would add the groups. (Possible answer: 5 + 5 + 8 = 18. I would add the doubles first and then add on 8 more.)

172 Use with pages 453–454.

Top Left Panel

Explore Making 10 to Add 7, 8, or 9

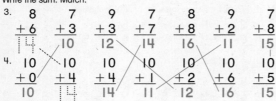

$7 + 5 = \underline{12}$ $10 + 2 = \underline{12}$

Use  and ⊞ .

Write the sum. Match.

3.
8	7	7	8	9	7
+6	+3	+3	+7	+2	+8
14	10	12	14	16	11	15

4.
10	10	10	10	10	10	10
+0	+4	+4	+1	+2	+6	+5
10	14	14	11	12	16	15

Problem Solving

3. Pedro has 9 rocks.
   He found 5 more.
   How many rocks does
   he have now?

   $\underline{14}$ rocks

   How many rocks will not fit in the box?

   $\underline{4}$ rocks

Notes for Home Your child matched facts such as 7 + 5 = 12 and 10 + 2 = 12. Home Activity: Ask your child to tell you a story problem for 8 + 8. Help him or her draw a ten frame to solve the problem.

Use with pages 457–458. **173**

Top Right Panel

Make 10 When Adding 7, 8, or 9

Draw ⬭ ◯ to show the number sentence. Add.

1.

$8 + 7 = \underline{15}$

$10 + \underline{5} = \underline{15}$

2.

$9 + 3 = \underline{12}$

$10 + \underline{2} = \underline{12}$

Add. You can use ⬭ ◯ and ⊞ .

3.
7	8	9	5	8	4	7
+4	+6	+3	+9	+5	+8	+6
11	14	12	14	13	12	13

4.
9	8	7	5	7	4	4
+5	+3	+5	+7	+7	+9	+9
14	11	12	12	14	13	13

Problem Solving Visual Thinking

5. Each hive can hold 10 bees.
   How many more bees will fit in each hive?

   $\underline{3}$ more bees $\underline{1}$ more bees $\underline{2}$ more bees

Notes for Home Your child added 7, 8, or 9 to another number by making a 10 first. Home Activity: Ask your child to write a number sentence for each bee hive problem. (7 + 3 = 10, 9 + 1 = 10, 8 + 2 = 10)

174 Use with pages 459–460.

Bottom Left Panel

Problem Solving:
Choose a Strategy

Solve. Use ⬭ ◯ and ⊞ or draw a picture.

1. A hen has 4 yellow chicks.
   She has 9 tan chicks, too.
   How many chicks does the hen have?

   $\underline{13}$ chicks

2. 19 seals go fishing.
   13 seals catch fish.
   How many seals do not catch fish?

   $\underline{6}$ seals

3. A zoo has 6 lions.
   It has 4 tigers.
   6 leopards live there, too.
   How many big cats are at the zoo?

   $\underline{16}$ big cats

Tell a Math Story

4. Tell a math story about the picture.

   Answers will vary.

Notes for Home Your child solved problems by drawing a picture or using objects. Home Activity: Ask your child to use pennies or other objects to retell the math story.

Use with pages 461–462. **175**

Bottom Right Panel

Mixed Practice: Lessons 1–6

Write the sum. Circle the doubles.

1.
5	4	6	7	9	8	4
+6	+4	+7	+5	+9	+9	+5
11	8	13	12	18	17	9

2.
7	9	5	4	6	7	3
+8	+4	+5	+7	+9	+7	+3
15	13	10	11	15	14	6

Add.

3.
2	4	3	1	6	5	4
1	3	5	4	2	3	2
+6	+5	+3	+7	+8	+6	+9
9	12	11	12	16	14	15

Problem Solving

Solve. Use ⬭ ◯ and ⊞ or draw a picture.

4. Marcy found 14 paper clips in her desk.
   She gave 9 to Martha.
   How many paper clips does
   Marcy have now?

   $\underline{5}$ paper clips

Journal   Answers may vary.

5. Draw a picture to show a doubles fact. Write the fact.

Notes for Home Your child practiced adding two and three numbers and solving problems by drawing a picture or using objects. Home Activity: Ask your child how she or he could use 6 + 6 = 12 to help find the answer for 6 + 7. (13)

176 Use with pages 463.

Cumulative Review

Add or subtract.

1. $6 + 3 = \underline{9}$ | $4 + 9 = \underline{13}$ | $5 + 6 = \underline{11}$

   $9 - 6 = \underline{3}$ | $13 - 9 = \underline{4}$ | $11 - 5 = \underline{6}$

Problem Solving

Count these coins. Record the coins in the table.

2.

	Pennies	Nickels	Dimes
How many coins?	1	2	4

Test Prep

Fill in the ○ for the correct answer.

Count the money.

3.

   39¢   31¢   41¢   45¢
   ○   ●   ○   ○

4.

   74¢   40¢   27¢   47¢
   ○   ○   ○   ●

Notes for Home Your child reviewed addition and subtraction, making a table, and counting money. *Home Activity:* Ask your child to make a table to show the number of shapes he or she can find in the kitchen.

Relate Addition and Subtraction

Add. Use the addition fact to help you subtract.

You can use .

1. 5   11   2. 7   11   3. 9   11
   +6   −5   +4   −4   +2   −9
   11   6   11   7   11   2

4. 11   11   5. 7   12   6. 9   12
   +0   −11   +5   −7   +3   −9
   11   0   12   5   12   3

Add or subtract.

Draw a line to match an addition with a subtraction fact.

7. $8 + 4 = \underline{12}$ ———— $12 - 8 = \underline{4}$

8. $3 + 9 = \underline{12}$ ⟍ $11 - 7 = \underline{4}$

9. $7 + 4 = \underline{11}$ ⟋ $12 - 3 = \underline{9}$

Write About It

10. Complete the number sentences.
    Draw or write a story to go with them.

    $3 + 8 = \underline{11}$

    $11 - 3 = \underline{8}$

Stories or pictures should reflect number sentences.

Notes for Home Your child used an addition fact such as 8 + 4 = 12 to solve a related subtraction fact such as 12 − 8 = 4. *Home Activity:* Ask your child to name a subtraction fact that uses the same numbers as 6 + 5 = 11. (11 − 5 = 6 or 11 − 6 = 5)

Use Doubles to Subtract

Add or subtract.

1. $6 + 6 = \underline{12}$ $5 + 5 = \underline{10}$ $8 + 8 = \underline{16}$

   $12 - 6 = \underline{6}$ $10 - 5 = \underline{5}$ $16 - 8 = \underline{8}$

2. $4 + 4 = \underline{8}$ $9 + 9 = \underline{18}$ $7 + 7 = \underline{14}$

   $8 - 4 = \underline{4}$ $18 - 9 = \underline{9}$ $14 - 7 = \underline{7}$

Subtract. Write the addition fact that helps.

3. 6   4. 18   5. 12
   −3   −9   −6
   3   9   6
   +3   +9   +6
   6   18   12

Problem Solving Patterns

6. Draw the missing dots
   on the last domino.
   Tell how you solved
   the puzzle.

   _____

   _____

   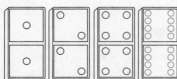

Notes for Home Your child used an addition double such as 5 + 5 to solve a related subtraction fact such as 10 − 5. *Home Activity:* Ask your child to write an addition fact and a subtraction fact for the last domino. (8 + 8 = 16, 16 − 8 = 8)

Subtraction Facts for 13 and 14

Subtract. Write the addition fact that helps.

1. 13   8   2. 14   5
   −8   +5   −5   +9
   5   13   9   14

3. 14   8   14   2   13   6
   −8   +6   −2   +12   −6   +7
   6   14   12   14   7   13

Subtract.

4. $13 - 5 = \underline{8}$ $13 - 7 = \underline{6}$ $13 - 9 = \underline{4}$

5. $14 - 4 = \underline{10}$ $14 - 9 = \underline{5}$ $14 - 1 = \underline{13}$

Tell a Math Story

6. Use these numbers: 8, 6, 14.
   Write an addition and subtraction fact.

   Possible answers given.

   $\underline{8} + \underline{6} = \underline{14}$ $\underline{14} - \underline{6} = \underline{8}$

7. Use each fact to tell a math story.

   Stories will vary.

Notes for Home Your child subtracted facts from 13 and 14. *Home Activity:* Ask your child to tell how the math stories in Exercise 7 are alike and different.

Subtraction Facts for 15 to 18

Complete the addition fact.
Write the subtraction facts.

You can use .

1. $7 + 9 = 16$ $16 - 7 = 9$
                   $16 - 9 = 7$

Mixed Practice

Subtract.

2.
12	13	14	15	17	17	18
-3	-5	-7	-9	-9	-8	-9
9	8	7	6	8	9	9

3.
13	16	16	15	14	16	18
-7	-7	-8	-6	-5	-9	-0
6	9	8	9	9	7	18

Problem Solving Critical Thinking

5. Mark the coins to buy 2 bags of elephant food.

How much money will you have left? __2__ ¢

Notes for Home Your child subtracted facts such as 15 − 7 = 8 and 15 − 8 = 7. *Home Activity:* Ask your child to use real money to show how much they would have left if they bought only one bag of food in Exercise 4. (11¢)

Fact Families

Complete the fact family. You can use  .

1. $9 + 3 = 12$ $12 - 3 = 9$
   $3 + 9 = 12$ $12 - 9 = 3$

2. $8 + 7 = 15$ $15 - 8 = 7$
   $7 + 8 = 15$ $15 - 7 = 8$

3. $6 + 8 = 14$ $14 - 6 = 8$
   $8 + 6 = 14$ $14 - 8 = 6$

4. Write your own fact family.   **Answers will vary.**

___ + ___ = ___   ___ − ___ = ___

___ + ___ = ___   ___ − ___ = ___

Problem Solving Critical Thinking

5. Most fact families have four facts.
   This fact family has only two facts. Why?

   $6 + 6 = 12$ $12 - 6 = 6$ **6+6 is a doubles.**

   Which other fact families have only two facts?

   doubles

Notes for Home Your child added and subtracted using fact families. *Home Activity:* Ask your child to draw a picture to illustrate the fact family in Exercise 3.

Problem Solving:
Choose an Operation

Circle add or subtract.
Complete the number sentence. Solve.

1. 12 penguins are on a hill.   add (subtract)
   4 slide down the hill.
   How many are left?

   There are __8__ penguins left. $12 ⊖ 4 = 8$

2. 6 brown cows come into the barn.   (add) subtract
   7 tan cows came in too.
   How many cows are in the barn?

   There are __13__ cows in the barn. $6 ⊕ 7 = 13$

3. 8 bats are in a cave.   (add) subtract
   8 more bats fly in.
   How many bats are there all together?

   There are __16__ bats. $8 ⊕ 8 = 16$

Tell a Math Story

4. Use the picture to tell a math story.
   Write a number sentence to go with your story.

   Answers will vary.

Notes for Home Your child solved problems by deciding whether to add or subtract. *Home Activity:* Ask your child to name words used in math stories that help them to know to add. (The list should include in all and all together.)

Mixed Practice: Lessons 7–12

Add or subtract.

1.	8	15	2.	14	14	3.	6	13
	$+7$	-7		-5	-9		$+7$	-6
	15	8		9	5		13	7

Subtract.

4.
18	15	16	13	14	17	14
-9	-8	-8	-5	-8	-8	-7
9	7	8	8	6	9	7

Problem Solving

Circle add or subtract.
Complete the number sentence. Solve.

5. Mother bear picked 15 berries.   add (subtract)
   She gave her cub 6 berries.
   How many are left for Mother?

   Mother bear has __9__ berries. $15 ⊖ 6 = 9$

Journal

6. Write or draw a math story about 15 penguins.
   Write a number sentence for your story.

   Stories and number sentences will vary.

Notes for Home Your child practiced addition and subtraction facts to 18, and choosing addition or subtraction to solve a problem. *Home Activity:* Ask your child how he or she could use 6 + 5 = 11 to help answer 11 − 5 and 11 − 6.

Top-left worksheet

Name _____

Cumulative Review

1.
3	6	2	1	4	5	3
2	1	3	3	0	5	3
+3	+1	+5	+7	+8	+1	+3
8	8	10	11	12	11	9

Problem Solving

2. Count the money. **32¢**

3. Circle what you can buy.

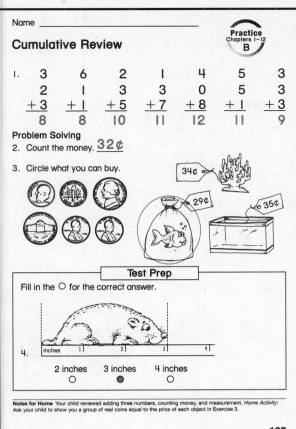

34¢   29¢   35¢

Test Prep

Fill in the ○ for the correct answer.

4.

2 inches	3 inches	4 inches
○	●	○

Notes for Home Your child reviewed adding three numbers, counting money, and measurement. *Home Activity:* Ask your child to show you a group of real coins equal to the price of each object in Exercise 3.

Use with page 480.   **185**

Top-right worksheet

Name _____

Explore Adding Tens

46 and 3 tens more is 76.
Use a ▦ to add tens to these numbers.

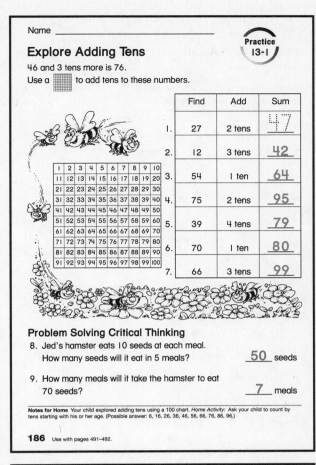

	Find	Add	Sum
1.	27	2 tens	47
2.	12	3 tens	42
3.	54	1 ten	64
4.	75	2 tens	95
5.	39	4 tens	79
6.	70	1 ten	80
7.	66	3 tens	99

Problem Solving Critical Thinking

8. Jed's hamster eats 10 seeds at each meal.
   How many seeds will it eat in 5 meals?   **50** seeds

9. How many meals will it take the hamster to eat
   70 seeds?   **7** meals

Notes for Home Your child explored adding tens using a 100 chart. *Home Activity:* Ask your child to count by tens starting with his or her age. (Possible answer: 6, 16, 26, 36, 46, 56, 66, 76, 86, 96.)

186   Use with pages 491–492.

Bottom-left worksheet

Name _____

Add Tens

Add. Use [tens|ones] and ▯.

	tens ones		tens ones		tens ones		tens ones
1.	2 0	2.	4 5	3.	1 0	4.	5 1
	+3 4		+4 0		+5 2		+3 0
	5 4		8 5		6 2		8 1

5.
26	44	16	30	40	60
+10	+40	+50	+22	+57	+17
36	84	66	52	97	77

6.
80	60	49	23	50	12
+14	+26	+10	+20	+31	+20
94	86	59	43	81	32

7.
50	14	17	30	40	55
+23	+20	+40	+62	+28	+10
73	34	57	92	68	65

Problem Solving Patterns

8. Brian uses a 🖩 to find the
total for these packets of seeds.
He presses these keys once:

[2][5] [+] [1][0]

He presses [=] 4 times.
He sees 35, 45, 55, 65.
What pattern did Brian use to add? **+10**

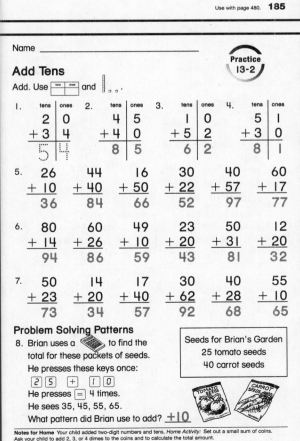

Seeds for Brian's Garden
25 tomato seeds
40 carrot seeds

Notes for Home Your child added two-digit numbers and tens. *Home Activity:* Set out a small sum of coins. Ask your child to add 2, 3, or 4 dimes to the coins and to calculate the total amount.

Use with pages 493–494.   **187**

Bottom-right worksheet

Name _____

Add Tens and Ones

Add. Use [tens|ones] and ▯.

	tens ones	tens ones	tens ones	tens ones
1.	2 4	5 1	1 6	6 3
	+1 5	+2 6	+5 2	+3 2
	3 9	7 7	6 8	9 5

2.
41	36	50	61	22	18
+21	+11	+5	+28	+23	+31
62	47	55	89	45	49

3.
81	28	13	15	34	32
+4	+41	+33	+53	+43	+22
85	69	46	68	77	54

4.
94	27	38	40	25	15
+4	+51	+50	+8	+52	+40
98	78	88	48	77	55

Problem Solving Critical Thinking

5. Use [tens|ones] and ▯ to find 4 ways to get the sum of 56.

tens ones	tens ones	tens ones	tens ones
1 2	2 1	0 4	3 3
+4 4	+3 5	+5 2	+2 3
5 6	5 6	5 6	5 6

Notes for Home Your child added numbers like 36 + 12. *Home Activity:* Look at a calendar. Ask your child to add the number of days in his two favorite months.

188   Use with pages 495–496.

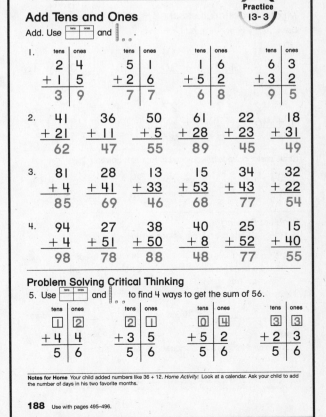

245

Regroup with Addition

Use and |..

	Show this many.	Add this many.	Do you need to regroup?	Solve.
1.	24	3	yes (no)	24 + 3 = 27
2.	56	7	(yes) no	56 + 7 = 63
3.	44	5	yes (no)	44 + 5 = 49
4.	19	4	(yes) no	19 + 4 = 23
5.	67	8	(yes) no	67 + 8 = 75
6.	35	6	(yes) no	35 + 6 = 41

Mental Math

What's My Rule? What number does each robot add?

7. $32 + \underline{4} = 36$ 8. $21 + \underline{6} = 27$

$14 + \underline{4} = 18$ $60 + \underline{6} = 66$

$55 + \underline{4} = 59$ $43 + \underline{6} = 49$

This robot adds $\underline{4}$.   This robot adds $\underline{6}$.

Notes for Home Your child combed materials to find sums for number sentences like 28 + 6.
Home Activity: Ask your child to explain how they know when to regroup ones when adding. (Regroup when there are ten or more ones.)

Problem Solving: Use Objects

Use 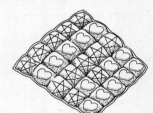 and |.. .
Write the number sentence. Solve.

1. 26 sparklers lit the sky.
   3 firecrackers made a BOOM!
   How many fireworks did Jimmy see? $26 + 3 = 29$ fireworks

2. 40 flags are on top of a float.
   Then 14 more flags are put around it.
   How many flags are there now? $40 + 14 = 54$ flags

3. One band has 17 drums.
   Another band has 30 drums.
   How many drums are there in all? $17 + 30 = 47$ drums

4. 31 children ate tomato soup at lunch.
   6 children ate chicken soup.
   How many children ate soup? $31 + 6 = 37$ children

Visual Thinking

Solve.

5. 25 stars are on this quilt.
   How many are on the back?

   $\underline{13}$ stars

Notes for Home Your child solved problems involving addition. *Home Activity:* Ask your child to use beans, rocks or other small objects to check their answer to Exercise 4. (31 children + 6 children = 37 children)

Mixed Practice: Lessons 1–5

Use and |.. . Add.

1.
50	40	14	47	85	60
+16	+41	+30	+20	+10	+16
66	81	44	67	95	76

42	35	27	24	51	73
+46	+24	+42	+13	+22	+12
88	59	69	37	73	85

Circle yes or no to tell if you need to regroup. Solve.

2. $37 + 2 = \underline{39}$ yes (no)   3. $24 + 7 = \underline{31}$ (yes) no

4. $15 + 6 = \underline{21}$ (yes) no   5. $74 + 3 = \underline{77}$ yes (no)

Problem Solving

Use |.. . Write the number sentence. Solve.

6. 26 frogs jump in a pond.
   13 more frogs jump in.
   How many frogs are in
   the pond now? $\underline{39}$

   $26 + 13 = 39$ frogs

7. 44 girls go to camp.
   27 boys go to camp.
   How many children go
   to camp? $\underline{71}$

   $44 + 27 = 71$ children

Journal

8. Write an addition math story using 10 and 17.

Notes for Home Your child practiced the concepts, skills, and problem solving taught in lessons 1-5.
Home Activity: Ask your child to use dimes and pennies to solve Exercise 3. Remind them to regroup 10 pennies as 1 dime when possible. (2 dimes and 4 pennies + 7 pennies = 3 dimes and 1 penny, or 31¢.)

Cumulative Review

How many tens and ones?

1. 51 $\underline{5}$ tens $\underline{1}$ one   2. 60 $\underline{6}$ tens $\underline{0}$ ones

3. 97 $\underline{9}$ tens $\underline{7}$ ones   4. 34 $\underline{3}$ tens $\underline{4}$ ones

5. 46 $\underline{4}$ tens $\underline{6}$ ones   6. 23 $\underline{2}$ tens $\underline{3}$ ones

7. 15 $\underline{1}$ ten $\underline{5}$ ones   8. 78 $\underline{7}$ tens $\underline{8}$ ones

Problem Solving

Write a number sentence.

9. The boys flew 13 kites.
   5 kites got caught in trees.
   How many kites are left?

   $13 - 5 = 8$

10. One kite had 7 tails.
    Kim added 7 more.
    How many tails are are left?

    $7 + 7 = 14$

Test Prep

Fill in the O for the correct answer.
Add.

11.
5	○ 9
3	● 10
+2	○ 11

12.
3	● 13
4	○ 14
+6	○ 15

13.
2	○ 13
5	○ 14
+8	● 15

14.
9	● 16
6	○ 17
+1	○ 18

Notes for Home Your child reviewed place value concepts, problem solving, and addition skills.
Home Activity: Ask your child to name 5 numbers that have no ones. (Possible answers include: 10, 20, 30, 40, 50.)

Name _____

Subtract Tens

Subtract.
Use [tens|ones] and [|..] .

1.

tens	ones
4	7
−2	0
2	7

tens	ones
2	5
−1	0
1	5

tens	ones
6	3
−4	0
2	3

tens	ones
8	1
−3	0
5	1

2.
25	37	43	56	68	72
−10	−20	−10	−20	−30	−10
15	17	33	36	38	62

Problem Solving

3. **Write your own** problem.

Write a problem about the carrots and rabbits in the picture.

Tell if you add or subtract. Write a number sentence. Solve.

_____

_____

_____

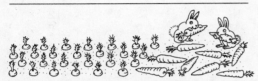

Notes for Home Your child subtracted tens from a two-digit number. Home Activity: Ask your child to count backwards by tens starting with any number between 50 and 100. How is this like subtracting tens?

Name _____

Subtract Tens and Ones

Use [tens|ones] and [|..] . Subtract.

1.

tens	ones
4	5
−2	1
2	4

tens	ones
8	3
−1	2
7	1

tens	ones
9	2
−3	2
6	0

tens	ones
5	6
−	5
5	1

2.
24	36	52	47	85	74
−11	−14	−31	−22	−54	−42
13	22	21	25	31	32

Mixed Practice Add or subtract.

3.
23	37	47	58	62	75
−10	− 6	−31	−20	−51	−14
13	31	16	38	11	61

4.
23	37	47	58	62	75
+16	+42	+50	+21	+22	+13
39	79	97	79	84	88

Problem Solving

Solve.

5. Nicki has this many fireflies.
She lets 23 go.
How many does she have left?

__7__ fireflies

Notes for Home Your child subtracted number sentences like 34 – 22. Home Activity: Ask your child to tell a subtraction math story about something that recently happened to him or her.

Name _____

Regroup with Subtraction

Use [tens|ones] and [|..] .

	Show this many.	Subtract this many.	Do you need to regroup?	Solve.
1.	24	3	yes (no)	24 − 3 = 21
2.	56	7	(yes) no	56 − 7 = 49
3.	44	5	(yes) no	44 − 5 = 39
4.	19	4	yes (no)	19 − 4 = 15
5.	62	6	(yes) no	62 − 6 = 56
6.	35	7	(yes) no	35 − 7 = 28
7.	71	8	(yes) no	71 − 8 = 63

Problem Solving

Write a number sentence. Solve.

8. Mark's soccer team has 21 players.
5 are sick on game day.
How many players can play?

__21 − 5 = 16__ players

Notes for Home Your child worked with tens and ones to find differences for number sentences like 23 – 7. Home Activity: Ask your child to explain when they need to regroup in subtraction. (You must regroup tens and ones when there are not enough ones to subtract from.)

Name _____

Problem Solving:
Choose an Operation

Circle add or subtract.
Write a number sentence.

1. Brett picked up 46 shells at the beach.
He found 12 more.
How many shells did he find in all?

(add) subtract __46 + 12 = 58__ shells

2. 38 crabs dug in the sand.
22 turtles were digging, too.
How many more crabs than
turtles are in the sand?

add (subtract) __38 − 22 = 16__ crabs

3. We made 68 muffins.
We sold 40 at the bake sale.
How many muffins are left?

add (subtract) __68 − 40 = 28__ muffins

Estimation

4. Circle the best estimate.
Fish jump 31 big waves
and 58 little waves.
About how many waves were jumped?

70   80   (90)

Notes for Home Your child continued solving problems involving addition and subtraction. Home Activity: Ask your child to name words that are used in subtraction math stories. (Answers may include: how many more, left, away, and take away.)

Mixed Practice: Lessons 6–9

Subtract. Use ▦ and ❘ .

1.
38	55	92	17	47	29
−20	−30	−40	−10	−30	−10
18	25	52	7	17	19

2.
97	84	26	34	75	28
−61	−44	−13	−22	−53	−14
36	40	13	12	22	14

Circle yes or no to tell if you need to regroup. Solve.

3. $37 − 5 = \underline{32}$ yes (no)

4. $21 − 7 = \underline{14}$ (yes) no

5. $14 − 6 = \underline{8}$ (yes) no

6. $50 − 2 = \underline{48}$ (yes) no

7. $45 − 4 = \underline{41}$ yes (no)

8. $33 − 3 = \underline{30}$ yes (no)

Problem Solving

Circle add or subtract. Write a number sentence.

9. K.T. has 32¢.
Pizza costs 75¢.
How much more does K.T.
need to buy pizza?

add   (subtract)

$75¢ − 32¢ = 43¢$

Journal

10. Write a number story for 25¢ − 10¢.

Answers will vary.

Cumulative Review

Use the ruler to measure. Write the length.

1.
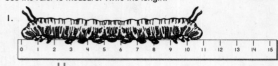

about __11__ centimeters

Add.

2. $30 + 10 = \underline{40}$ $20 + 40 = \underline{60}$ $30 + 50 = \underline{80}$

Problem Solving

Solve.

3. Liz sees 13 caterpillars.
5 turn into cocoons. How
many caterpillars are left?

__8__ caterpillars

4. 17 butterflies are blue.
3 are red. How many
more are blue than red?

__14__ butterflies

Test Prep

Fill in the ○ for the correct answer.
Subtract.

5.
14	● 7
−7	○ 8
	○ 9
	○ 10

6.
15	○ 4
−9	○ 5
	● 6
	○ 7

7.
12	● 4
−8	○ 5
	○ 6
	○ 7